Praise for the first edition of *Understanding Adult Education and Training*

'A welcome addition to the adult education literature and a useful introduction for students. Foley is in my view an outstanding writer and editor.'

Peter Willis, Centre for Research in Education and Work, University of South Australia

. . . raises thought-provoking issues without attempting to suggest simplistic responses.'

Professor Philip Candy, Queensland University of Technology

About the editor

GRIFF FOLEY is Associate Professor in Adult Education at the University of Technology, Sydney. He is author of *Learning in Social Action* (Zed Books, 1999).

Understanding Adult Education and Training

Second edition

Edited by Griff Foley

ALLEN & UNWIN

For Keith Foster
who encouraged so many of us

First published in 2000 by
Allen & Unwin
9 Atchison Street,
St Leonards NSW 1590 Australia
Phone: (61 2) 8425 0100
Fax: (61 2) 9906 2218
E-mail: frontdesk@allen-unwin.com.au
Web: http: //www.allen-unwin.com.au

National Library of Australia
Cataloguing-in-Publication entry:

Understanding adult education and training.

2nd ed.
Bibliography.
Includes index.
ISBN 1 86508 147 7.

1. Adult education—Australia. 2. Continuing education—Australia. I. Foley, Griff. II. Title. III. Title: Adult education and training.

374.994

Set in 10/11pt Garamond by DOCUPRO, Sydney
Printed by South Wind Productions, Singapore

10 9 8 7 6 5 4 3

Contents

Preface

The title of this book straightforwardly represents its purpose: to help thoughtful practitioners to better understand the contexts and dynamics of their work.

The first edition of this book was published in 1995 and was intended for and well-received by an Australian audience. At the suggestion of a number of people, this second edition has been revised for a wider international audience. In writing the new edition we have taken particular account of two developments, which, while they were in play four years ago, have become more pronounced:

1. global economic restructuring and its educational effects. The political economy of this development is addressed in the first part of chapter 7, and the ways in which these economic and political changes are being worked out in adult education and training are discussed in Parts II and III of the book;
2. the emergence of more critical analyses of adult education and training, and in particular analyses informed by political economy, critical theory and poststructuralist and postmodernist theory. These theoretical frameworks are introduced in chapter 1, and their potential contribution to understanding adult education and training is discussed in the Conclusion (chapter 18). While these perspectives inform discussion in most chapters, extended examples of their application in adult education can be found in chapters 1, 7 and 17 (political economy and critical theory) and chapters 8 and 9 (poststructuralist/ postmodernist theory).

I would like to thank my fellow contributors for taking the time to revise their chapters or to write new chapters.

As always, this book would not have happened without the love and support of my wife Lori.

Griff Foley
Sydney, March 1999

Contributors

DR LEE ANDRESEN has played a pivotal role in the development of experience-based learning in Australia and is a freelance consultant in higher education and academic development.

JIM ATHANASOU is an associate professor in adult and vocational education at UTS, where he is currently director of open learning in the Faculty of Education. He specialises in the field of assessment and research in vocational education and has worked in both private industry and the public sector.

DAVID BOUD is a professor of adult education at UTS, where he is currently associate dean of research in the Faculty of Education. He has an international reputation for his extensive writings on experience-based learning and developing student autonomy in learning.

DAPHNE BROSNAN was formerly a researcher and the coordinator of Training Programs for Centre for Workplace Communication and Culture at the University of Technology, Sydney. Her specialties include cross-cultural communication, management skills, English for speakers of other languages, and curriculum and materials development.

CLIVE CHAPPELL is a senior lecturer in the School of Adult Education at UTS. He has extensive experience in technical and vocational education, and has been heavily involved in research and consultancy related to the development of competency standards in Australia.

RUTH COHEN is a part-time lecturer in the Faculty of Education at UTS. She has an international reputation as a scholar and organiser in the field of experience-based learning.

DR ALISTAIR CROMBIE is the former executive director of the Australian Association of Adult and Community Education. He has been centrally involved in recent policy developments in adult education at state and federal level.

RICHARD EDWARDS is a senior lecturer in education at the Open University in Britain. He has published extensively on flexible learning and postmodernism in education. He is the author of *Changing Places? Flexibility, Lifelong Learning and a Learning Society* (London: Routledge, 1997).

LAURIE FIELD is a training consultant who also lectures in human resource development at UTS. He has extensive experience in consultancy and research related to workplace change, and is the author of two books about learning and workplace reform: *Skilling Australia* (Longman, 1990) and, with Bill Ford, *Managing Organisational Learning* (Longman, 1995).

RICK FLOWERS is a senior lecturer in adult education and acting director of the Centre for Popular Education at UTS. He has extensive experience as a researcher, lecturer and consultant in community and Aboriginal adult education.

GRIFF FOLEY is an associate professor in adult education at UTS. His research and publications include work on adult teaching and learning, informal learning, the political economy of adult education, learning in social action, and indigenous adult education. His book *Learning in Social Action* will be published by Zed Books, London, in early 1999.

ANDREW GONCZI is dean of education at UTS. He has published widely in technical and vocational education, and has been heavily involved in research and consultancy related to the development of competency standards in Australia.

PAUL HAGER is an associate professor in adult and vocational education at UTS. He has published widely in technical and vocational education, and in the philosophy of education, and has been heavily involved in research and consultancy related to the development of competency standards in Australia.

GEOF HAWKE is a senior research fellow in the Vocational Education Research Centre at UTS. He has extensive experience in vocational education research and is currently researching the formation of vocational education policy.

SUE KNIGHTS is a senior lecturer in the Faculty of Education at UTS, where she coordinates the Master of Education in Adult Education and teaches courses on women and adult learning. She has published on women's education and experience-based learning.

ALISON LEE is a senior lecturer in the Faculty of Education at UTS, where she coordinates the professional Doctorate in Education. She has researched and published in the fields of literacy and curriculum in the school and post-school sectors. She has a particular interest in questions of language and gender.

MICHAEL McDANIEL formerly coordinated the Aboriginal adult educator training program and taught Aboriginal studies at UTS. He is currently a commissioner on the Native Land Rights Tribunal.

JOHN McINTYRE is a senior research fellow in the Vocational Education Research Centre at UTS. He has extensive research experience in adult and vocational education, and teaches courses on adult education research at undergraduate and postgraduate levels.

ROGER MORRIS is an associate professor in adult education at UTS. His teaching and research interests include the history of adult education, trade union education and professional education.

MIKE NEWMAN is a senior lecturer in adult education at UTS. He has published widely in the fields of adult education and trade union training, and has twice won the Cyril Houle award for literature in adult education. His latest book is *Maeler's Regard: Images of Adult Learning*.

KATHERINE NICOLL is a senior lecturer in adult education at UTS. She has extensive practical experience of flexible learning course development in Australia and England and is currently researching flexibility in education.

PHILIP POGSON is the human resources manager for SAS. He has previously managed labour market programs and staff development. His research interests include non-academic intelligences, quality and organisational learning.

HERMINE SCHEERES is a senior lecturer in language and literacy education at UTS. She works across the fields of adult basic education and TESOL, and is particularly interested in changing workplace language and literacy demands arising out of industry restructuring.

DIANA SLADE is an associate professor in language and literacy education and associate dean of teaching and learning in the Faculty of Education at UTS. She has published extensively in the area of discourse analysis of English, the TESOL curriculum, and spoken and written communication in workplace contexts.

MARK TENNANT is a professor in adult education at UTS. He has written extensively on psychology and adult education, and won the Cyril Houle award for literature in adult education in 1990.

ROSIE WICKERT is a senior lecturer in language and literacy education at UTS and is currently manager of organisational development in the Faculty of Education. She has an international reputation in the literacy field, and in 1989 wrote the ground-breaking study of literacy in Australia, *No Single Measure*.

Introduction

We begin by briefly defining the scope and nature of adult education and learning. Then the purpose, integrating principle and content of the book are outlined. Finally, a suggestion is made about how to read the book, and the issues of the book's diversity and relevance to an international audience are discussed.

DEFINING ADULT EDUCATION AND LEARNING

The received definition of adult education and training is a fairly restrictive one, identifying adult learning with 'education for adults other than initial preparation for a career, with primary emphasis on non-award education' (NSW Ministry of Education 1986: 1). Even by this definition, in most countries since World War II, and particularly over the past 20 years, the field of adult education has expanded and diversified. Adult education now comprises a number of specialist fields, including human resource development in the public and private sectors (often referred to as workplace training), vocational education, community adult education, health education, the teaching of English to speakers of other languages, adult basic education, and indigenous adult education. Adult education is a vast activity, and one can readily see why governments are becoming increasingly aware of its economic and social importance.

But the significance of adult learning is even more apparent if a broader definition of the field is adopted. This expanded definition starts with the recognition that all human activity has a learning dimension. People learn, continually, informally and formally, in many different settings: in workplaces, in families, through leisure activities, through community activities, and in political action. Seen in this way, adult education and learning can take any one of the following four forms.

FORMAL EDUCATION

This is the form of adult learning with which we are most familiar. Its distinguishing characteristics are that it is organised by professional educators, there is a defined curriculum, and it often leads to a qualification. It includes study in educational institutions like universities and technical and further education colleges, and sequenced training sessions in workplaces.

NON-FORMAL EDUCATION

This sort of learning occurs when people see a need for some sort of systematic instruction, but in a one-off or sporadic way. Examples include workers being trained to operate a new machine, or environmental activists undertaking non-violent direct-action training in the midst of a campaign to save a rainforest.

INFORMAL LEARNING

This sort of learning occurs when people consciously try to learn from their experiences. It involves individual or group reflection on experience, but does not involve formal instruction. Examples include the management committee of a community centre reviewing the operations of its organisation, or workers redesigning their jobs in consultation with management.

INCIDENTAL LEARNING

This type of learning occurs while people perform other activities. So, for example, an experienced mechanic has learned a lot about cars, and elderly gardeners carry a great deal of knowledge of their craft. But such learning is incidental to the activity in which the person is involved, is often tacit and is not seen as learning—at least not at the time of its occurrence.

This broader definition enables us to place adult learning and education in its rightful place as a central feature of human life—as essential as, say, work. As the American experiential learning theorist David Kolb has noted, learning is human beings' primary mode of adaptation: if we do not learn we may not survive, and we certainly will not prosper.

That said, the limitations of the above typology need to be recognised. The boundaries between non-formal education and informal learning on the one hand, and incidental learning and informal learning on the other, are blurred. Further, a fuller exposition would point out that what distinguishes different forms of education and learning is their degree of *formalisation*—that is, the degree to which learning activities are socially organised and controlled. In its current form the typology does, however, have at least two uses: first, it helps us to move beyond limited and limiting understandings of the scope of adult education and learning; second, it directs us to the importance of informal and incidental learning. As Stephen Brookfield (1986: 150) has noted, most adult learning is not acquired in formal courses but is gained through experience or through participation in an aspect of social life such as work, community action or family activities. To date, this dimension of social life and learning has been neglected in adult education writing (see Marsick & Watkins 1991; Foley 1999). It will be dealt with in various ways in this book.

PURPOSE AND INTEGRATING PRINCIPLE

This book is an introduction to issues, debates and literatures related to a number of central areas of practice in adult education and training. The emphasis is on helping readers to understand the dynamic, complex and diverse nature of adult education practice, and to develop systematic ways of analysing adult learning and education. It is intended to take readers the next step beyond a 'how-to-do-it' text, attempting to define the field of adult education in a theoretical rather than a practical sense. Its intended audience is all those who have an interest in understanding and facilitating adult learning and education. This includes adult educators and trainers in the diversity of fields referred to above, as well as the many people (e.g. managers, nurses, community workers, trade unionists) whose work is in some way concerned with adult education and learning.

The book focuses on the development of practitioner understanding in the field as a whole, in relation to adult educators' multiple roles. It aims to be foundational, in the sense of delineating adult education as a field of study and setting out some of the key theoretical issues and debates, but it aims to be theoretical in a practical way. Its intention is to deepen readers' understanding of adult learning and education so that they can act on those processes more effectively. In this it bears some resemblence to earlier books, such as Stephen Brookfield (1986) and Usher and Bryant (1989), but is more broadly theoretical than the former and more immediately practical than the latter.

The book's integrating principle, explained in Chapter 1 and elaborated on throughout the book, is the concept of informal or practical theory. Adult educators, like other professionals, develop informal theories—understandings that emerge from and guide their practice. As practitioners, adult educators are interested in formal theory (i.e. organised and codified bodies of knowledge) only to the extent that it illuminates their practice and helps them to act more effectively. Moreover, because adult education is such a diverse field, and because adult educators and adult learners have varied experiences and understandings, there is no single body of knowledge which is appropriate to all adult educators. This book will introduce readers to a wide range of formal theory from adult education and associated fields, and it will do so in ways that enable readers to relate the theory to their own situations. Throughout the book the authors are continually— sometimes explicitly, sometimes implicitly—saying to the reader: 'You have often highly developed, informal theories about adult education and learning, developed in your work and life experience. Here is a smorgasbord of formal theory about adult education and learning. Dip into it and take what you can use. Be aware, as you do so, of your own, and the literature's, theoretical and value assumptions'. The approach adopted here is fundamentally liberal and pluralist. It is assumed that different readers will find different aspects of the book useful, and that individuals will read it in a variety of ways.

SCOPE AND CONTENT

The book is divided into four parts. Part I is foundational, in the sense that it discusses knowledge fundamental to adult education practice. The theoretical framework of the book is discussed in chapter 1. (As this chapter is fairly abstract and covers a lot of ground, some readers may prefer to come to it after having read some of the other, more concrete chapters.) The characteristics of adult learners and their developmental phases are discussed in chapter 2. Chapters 3, 4 and 5 examine issues and literature related to three core areas of adult education practice: teaching, program development and evaluation.

A central theme of this book is that adult learning and education are contextual, complex and contested activities. We argue that to understand a particular adult education policy or practice it is necessary to examine both its relationship to broad political, economic and cultural influences as well as the microprocesses of policy construction or adult education practice in particular places—how people act and how they explain and justify their actions. Each of the four chapters in Part II illustrates this theme. A variety of theoretical perpectives is employed to analyse differing perceptions of adult education research (chapter 6), directions in adult education policy (chapter 7), flexible delivery of courses (chapter 8), and the discourses of adult literacy teaching (chapter 9).

Part III is devoted to a central current issue in adult education, the relationship of workplace change, adult learning and training. Chapter 10 surveys recent trends in workplace learning and education, paying particular attention to the concept of the 'learning organisation'. Chapter 11 focuses on the 'how' of change—on how adult educators and trainers can better understand and more effectively implement change, wherever they happen to be working. Chapter 12 explores debates surrounding 'competence', a concept central to workplace reform and education, and argues for integrative and humanistic approaches to competency-based learning. Chapter 13 analyses the historical background of, and different approaches to, cross-cultural education and training, paying particular attention to workplace settings.

Part IV explores a number of other important contemporary developments in adult education. Chapter 14 discusses experience-based learning, a set of approaches of growing practical and theoretical significance in adult education. Chapter 15 examines various issues related to women's learning and education: access and participation, informal learning in community settings, workplace learning and education, the emergence of women-centred curricula and pedagogy. Chapter 16 discusses issues related to the education of indigenous peoples, in this case Aboriginal Australians: precolonial forms of learning and education, control and resistance in colonial adult education, debates around contemporary adult education policy, and contemporary attempts to construct Aboriginal-controlled adult education. Chapter 17 explores the relationship of social action, social movements and struggles for social justice on the one hand, and adult learning and education on the other.

As noted in the Preface, in recent years there has been a flourishing of critical scholarship in adult education. Our conclusion (chapter 18) reviews three varieties of critical theory that have been employed elsewhere in the book—Frankfurt School critical theory, historical materialism, and poststructuralism/postmodernism.

READING THE BOOK

Each of the four parts of the book begins with an introduction summarising the content. It is wise to begin by reading these summaries, then to read the chapters in order of their importance to you. As each chapter stands on its own, it is possible to read the chapters out of sequence.

Each chapter ends with a short list of recommended readings. There is also an extensive cumulative bibliography at the end of the book.

DIVERSITY

The chapters are inevitably diverse. This diversity has a number of dimensions. Most obviously, the book covers many different facets of adult education. Second, the authors write from a variety of different theoretical positions. Third, the book encompasses a diversity of writing styles. Some chapters are written in a textbook style, aiming to give a condensed yet comprehensive coverage of issues and literature. Other chapters are more conversational in approach, attempting to link their subject to the experience of readers. Still others are more conventionally academic in style: the writing is impersonal and claims carefully documented.

The relationship of theory to practice is also treated in a variety of ways in the book. Some chapters (e.g. chapters 10, 11 and 13) immediately yield ideas for practice. Others (e.g. chapters 2, 3, 4, 5, 12 and 14–17) are more concerned with developing readers' long-term capacity to analyse various aspects of adult education. Still others are more deeply theoretical, inviting close reading and discussion (e.g. chapters 1, 6, 7, 8 and 9).

HOW 'INTERNATIONAL' IS THE BOOK?

The question of how 'international' or distinctively 'Australian' this book is is an interesting one. All but two of the 27 contributors to the book live and work in Australia. Understandably, then, Australian contexts and examples are discussed throughout. But all the chapters draw on the international (largely English and US) literature and discuss issues relevant to an international audience.

The international focus of many chapters is in part due to the experience and education of the authors but is also a function of the accelerating 'globalisation' of economics, politics and culture that has characterised the past three decades.

PART I
THE FOUNDATIONS

Introduction to Part I

Part I provides readers with an overview of issues and theory related to adult learners and the core areas of adult education practice: teaching, program development, and the evaluation of learning. It also offers readers an approach to understanding the complex and multifaceted nature of adult education and training. It is argued that it is fruitless to search for formulas, as there are no techniques or theories that provide foolproof results. Rather, understanding adult education and training is a never-ending process of coming to grips with complexity.

Chapter 1 provides a framework both for understanding the work of adult educators and for reading this book. All adult educators and trainers have cognitive frameworks which help them to make sense of their experience. Their frameworks are made up of ideas and theories which arise partly from their work experience (these we call 'practical' or 'informal' theories) and partly from their professional education and reading (these we call 'formal' theories). This chapter discusses the relationship of practical and formal theory in adult education and training. It also looks briefly at different schools of thought in adult education and training, and discusses the notion of the 'paradigm'. This latter concept is an important means of understanding different theoretical and value positions in education, and is used on a number of occasions in the book.

Chapter 2 discusses ways of understanding the 'raw material' of adult education and training—the adult learner. Theorists have focused on two dimensions of adults' capacities as learners—the intellectual and the personality/social. For many years studies in intellectual development were wedded to the construct of IQ, to

3

dichotomies such as 'fluid' and 'crystallised' intelligence, and to cognitive stage theories. There has been a growing recognition of the narrowness of these ways of conceptualising intellectual development. There is now a developing body of data on such varied aspects of cognitive functioning as insight, practical intelligence, wisdom, creativity, tacit knowledge and expertise. Similarly, research on adult personality and social development has progressively moved away from theories that see adults moving through life stages towards a single-end point of 'maturity' or 'psychological health'. Increasingly, adult psychological life is seen as diverse, complex and contextual.

Chapter 3 discusses writing about teaching. In this huge body of literature, we can detect three broad ways of understanding teaching: instrumental, interpretive, and critical. (For explanation of these terms, which are of central importance in reading the book, see chapters 1 and 18.) If we see teaching as instrumental activity, we are concerned with effectiveness: we want to know the most effective ways in which teachers can transmit knowledge, skills and values to students. We turn, then, to studies of what teachers and learners actually do in classrooms, and to practical teaching handbooks that suggest ways in which teachers might improve and expand their repertoire of teaching strategies. On the other hand, if we understand teaching as interpretive activity, we recognise that each person understands the world differently and has their own learning style and strategies. The interest, then, is in writing that can help us to understand these different interpretations and teach to them. Here we turn to cognitive and humanistic psychologies and what they tell us about such phenomena as learning styles and learning strategies, meaningful learning, the dynamics of learning groups, self-directed learning, adult learning principles and facilitating learning. But if we see teaching as critical activity, our focus is on teaching as an activity which takes place in a particular society at a particular time in history, in accordance with particular social interests and human values. Here we turn to the literatures of critical and feminist pedagogies and the poststructuralist critiques of these pedagogies; to critical thinking and popular education; to ethnographic studies of classroom relationships; to research which locates teaching and learning in their economic, political and cultural contexts; to accounts of teaching and learning in emancipatory social movements; to accounts of attempts to build democratic teacher–learner relationships; and to the rich tradition of adult education discussion groups.

Chapter 4 examines theory and literature related to program

4

development, the deliberate production of learning experiences. It begins by discussing the diversity of adult education programs and of models of program development. Programs vary in their origins (e.g. in ideas, people, issues, fads, political and economic changes), the interests which drive them and the contexts in which they occur. In the vast literature of program development, four streams can be identified: a liberal focus on the importance of programs transmitting knowledge to learners; a behaviourist emphasis on learner performance and learning outcomes; a humanistic focus on the development of the learner as a whole person; and a radical emphasis on the contribution that education can make to developing learners' ability to critique oppressive social practices and act in socially just ways. This chapter surveys the literatures associated with each of these traditions, paying particular attention to a number of theorists (Tyler, Houle, Knowles, Brookfield, Boone, Field, Rogers, Freire) and issues (needs analysis, program design, an 'institutional' model of program development, workplace training models, competency-based curriculum, experiential learning programs, and programs for critical thinking and social action).

Chapter 5 begins by pointing out that evaluation of learning processes and outcomes is an integral part of adult education and training. The origins of educational evaluation are then discussed and some major evaluation approaches surveyed: an objectives model, judgmental models, decision-making approaches, and outcomes models. The second part of the chapter outlines a comprehensive approach to evaluation which provides information about the objectives of a program, its effects or outcomes, the stakeholders or interest groups involved, ethical issues raised by the program, the coverage or reach of the program, and cost issues.

1

A framework for understanding adult learning and education

Griff Foley

This chapter provides a framework for understanding the work of adult educators and for reading the book. It begins by distinguishing between a model of professional education which assumes that practitioners need to be introduced to a body of 'necessary knowledge', and a model which assumes that practitioners are 'practical theorists' (i.e. that they continually construct their own understandings and explanations of what happens in their work). The concepts of practice, theory and theoretical frameworks are then examined. A distinction is made between adult educators' informal and practical theories about their work and more formal theories of adult education. It is argued that adult educators and trainers need both sorts of theory. The chapter concludes by looking at three different ways of understanding adult education and training: as instrumental activity, as interpretive activity, and as critical activity.

TWO MODELS OF PROFESSIONAL EDUCATION

For many years professional education in most fields, including education, was based on a 'front-end loading' model. In this approach, professionals were taught the knowledge, skills and attitudes they were thought to need before they began to practise. The competent among these new professionals, it was argued, would then apply in practical situations the theory they had been taught.

Experienced practitioners know that the actual world of practice does not work in this way. Real work situations are complex and fluid: they do not sit and wait for theories to be applied to them. As Donald Schon (1983), an American adult educator, pointed out in the early 1980s, we need a different model of professional education, one that focuses on the ways in which practitioners think and act in actual work situations. This 'practitioner-centred' model puts the practitioner and the complex contexts in which she works at the centre of analysis. It is this view of professional education which has been adopted in this book. The book will introduce readers to a lot of new knowledge about adult education and training. They will be invited to test this new knowledge against their existing understanding. For each reader, some of the new knowledge will be illuminating while other aspects of the book will be less helpful. Overall, however, the book is intended to help adult educators working in a diversity of settings to develop their understanding of their work.

This practitioner-centred model of professional education assumes that adult educators and other practitioners are active thinkers, or 'practical theorists', who are continually trying to make sense of their work. The model also assumes that adult educators and trainers—and others with an interest in adult education and training—are active readers. It is assumed that they will read critically, taking in what is of interest to them and discarding what is not. Underpinning these assumptions about how practitioners think and read is a particular view of practice and its relationship with theory. The rest of this chapter will elaborate on this perspective, because it provides both a framework for understanding the work of adult educators and a way of reading the book.

CONCEPTUAL FRAMEWORK OF THE BOOK

As already noted, this is a book about *understanding* adult learning and education. Because it treats such a diverse and complex field of human activity, it needs an organising principle, a coherent conceptual framework. The rest of this chapter outlines this framework, whose core concepts are: theory, practice, reflection, formal and informal theory, and paradigms.

PRACTICE AND THEORY

Adult educators do things, and they think about them. When they do things they are engaged in practice; when they are thinking about their practice they are reflecting and theorising.

Theory (systematic thought) and practice (systematic action) are tied together. One cannot exist without the other. But practitioners do not always act and think systematically. They often act and think rigidly and dogmatically. It is common, for example, for adult educators to have set value positions on teaching and favourite bundles of techniques, often acquired early in their careers and never subjected to rigorous evaluation. An important goal of this book is to encourage adult educators and trainers to critically examine their practice and theory and to develop frameworks for understanding and acting on their work. Readers will be encouraged to reflect on practice situations, and to theorise.

To theorise is to attempt to make connections between variables, to explain outcomes and to predict what will happen if particular courses of action are taken in the future. Theorising can involve any or all of: solitary reflection, discussion with others, reading and writing. Theorising involves the application of concepts (i.e. systematic ideas) to experience. We can theorise well or badly: in ways which illuminate our experience and help us to act more effectively, or in ways which obscure connections and outcomes and lock us into ineffective action. In sum, theorising is something we inevitably do, and it is inevitably selective. In theorising we should endeavour to be as rigorous and comprehensive as possible, within the limitations of our competence and resources.

FRAMEWORKS

Each of us has a cognitive framework through which we understand the world. In our everyday lives we are bombarded with sense impressions. Our frameworks are filters, which allow us to make sense of what we experience. Our frameworks develop over the years—they change, or should change, as we have new experiences.

Frameworks are made up of analytical constructs that help us to summarise and systematise experience. Some examples of frequently used constructs are set out in Table 1.1.

Developing your framework

To become more effective adult educators and trainers, we need to become more aware of and systematically develop our theoretical frameworks—the ways in which we understand and explain our work. We are usually so busy getting on with the job that we don't have time to look at our theories. We need to give ourselves time to do this—to think creatively. We need to seek out and use concepts and theories that strengthen our practice.

9

Table 1.1   Examples of analytical constructs

Construct	Definition	Examples
Idea	Notion conceived in the mind, way of thinking, pattern, plan.	'I have an idea. Let's get Jack to administer the program next year.'
Concept	General notion, class of objects.	Social class, the adult learner
Theory	A supposition explaining something, based on evidence.	Adult learning principles, Kolb's experiential learning theory
Stereotype	Fixed mental impression not based on empirical evidence.	Dole bludger
Prejudice	Preconceived, opinion, bias, against or in favour or a person or thing.	'Students have to be led.' 'Aborigines are drunks and welfare bludgers.'

We also need to identify and allow for our stereotypes and prejudices.

Building a framework is a lifetime job. Because the world is so complex, no-one is ever able to say she/he understands it all. But some frameworks are more useful—and ethical—than others.

A framework for analysing adult education
To be useful, a framework should be comprehensive and rigorous.

Our work is complex. In any situation or context that we work in we are operating at a number of levels at once. First, there are our own feelings and thoughts. Then there are our most intense and immediate interpersonal relations: how we get on with those with whom we live and work. There is also the structure and culture of the institution and/or community in which we work. Then there is the social dimension, the broader economic, political and cultural context of our work. Finally, there is the question of how things got to be the way they are. Here we are talking about the historical dimension (see Figure 1.1).

If we are going to act effectively, we need to be aware of each of these levels or dimensions. But there is another issue: Why are we acting? According to what values? An important assumption of this framework, and of this book, is that anything educators do should be grounded in their values and based on the deepest possible understanding of the context of their work.

We should act strategically. We should think of the whole campaign and the long-term goals, and ways of attaining them.

We should be technically proficient, too. Technique is important. We need to be sure of our proficiency, particularly in the core adult educator skills of teaching and group work, and program development.

This framework can be represented diagrammatically (see

10

Figure 1.1   A framework for analysing adult education and training

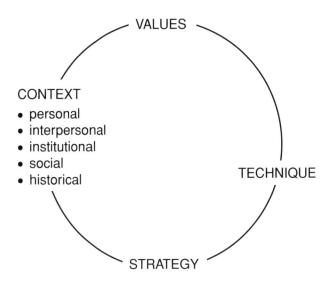

Figure 1.1). I find this framework useful. It may or may not be of use to you. The reason for presenting it here is to get you thinking about your own framework.

Your framework is, in part, intellectual. It involves you in analysing your practice in commonsense, direct ways. It may involve you in applying insight drawn from academic disciplines to analysis of your work situation. But your framework is not just intellectual. It also has its emotional, intuitive and ethical dimensions.

FORMAL AND INFORMAL THEORY

Usher (1987, 1989) and Usher and Bryant (1989) make a distinction between formal and informal theory. *Formal theory* is 'organised (and) codified bodies of knowledge—embodied in disciplines and expressed in academic discourse'. *Informal theory* is the understanding that emerges from and guides practice (1987: 28–9). Formal and informal theory can be seen as both 'framework' and 'product'. Usher distinguishes between 'theory in the sense of the general *framework* of understandings, values and assumptions which underlie theoretical activities and the particular theories which result from these activities and which can . . . be seen as the . . . *products* of the framework' (1987: 28).

11

Table 1.2 Theory as framework and product

	Framework	Product
Informal	Principles and assumptions underlying practice, e.g. an approach to teaching	Theory-in-action in a particular situation
Formal	Behaviourism Critical theory	Motivation theory Ideology critique

Usher's argument is summarised in Table 1.2. As Usher (1989: 72) points out,

> theory cannot tell us how to practice . . . Most skilled activity does not involve the conscious application of principles . . . [it involves] such things as attending and being sensitive to the situation, anticipating [and] making ad hoc decisions, none of which would be possible if we had to stop and find the appropriate theory before we acted.

'The question for the practitioner is not "what rules should I apply" but "how ought I to act in this particular situation"' (Usher & Bryant 1989: 82). Theorising about adult education should therefore be grounded in an understanding of practice and of how adult educators think about their practice (i.e. their informal theories). These informal theories should be tested and reviewed through formal theory. In this way formal theory can challenge and deepen the commonsense understandings we draw from our everyday work experience.

REFLECTION

The formal/informal theory distinction can be augmented by the notions of *tacit knowledge* and *reflection*. Polanyi argues that some things we 'just know': we have knowledge, which we use, but we do not know it as knowledge; it is buried, unarticulated, implicit. Polanyi and others maintain that it is both possible and useful to make tacit knowledge explicit (Grundy 1987: 28–9). Through reflection, we can become aware of our implicit knowledge, our informal theories (Schon 1983; Boud et al. 1985). We can then analyse these understandings and theories and modify and expand on them through reading, discussion and further reflection.

As Usher and Bryant (1989: 80–1) acknowledge, their notion of informal theory is analogous to Schon's concept of 'reflection-in-action':

Figure 1.2   The action–reflection spiral

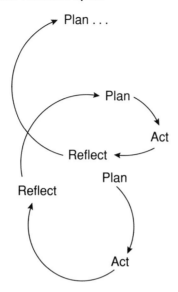

Schon problematises practice by seeing it as a world of ill-defined problems where ends are often not known in advance. Practice situations are confused and tricky and the practitioner has to 'feel' his way through them. This is done through reflection-in-action, which involves turning thinking back onto action. Through reflection, the practitioner brings to the surface the implicit and tacit knowledge in the action . . .

Seen in this way, professional work is a cycle, or a spiral, of action and reflection. The practitioner acts, reflects on the action and, learning from the reflection, plans new action (Figure 1.2).[1] This, at least, is the theory. Contextual factors, and the rigid mindsets of many practitioners, mean the plan–act–reflect cycle is often interrupted. Nevertheless, a conception of theory and practice that emphasises their mutual dependence is more useful than one that sees theory as being before practice.

Schools of thought in adult education and training
It is common in 'front-end loading' professional education courses to introduce students to typologies of theories or 'schools of thought'. Table 1.3, below, is one example. Such typologies can be useful: they can introduce us to a range of theorists and help us to locate our own theoretical and value positions. But, taking Usher's and Schon's point, they are of limited practical use,

13

Table 1.3 Schools of thought in adult education and training

School of thought	Aims of adult education	Major writers	Focus	Acceptable content	Role of teacher and learner	Teaching methods
(A) Cultivation of the intellect (traditional school)	Fill learners with politically neutral and traditionally worthwhile knowledge to discipline the mind and develop rational people	Paterson and Lawson	Individual	Intellectual knowledge in the 'classic' disciplines, e.g. history, maths, morals, philosophy. Less attention to attitudes and practical skills	Teacher in full control—decides all content and activities. Students are passive and education is teacher not student centred	Mainly lecture
(B) Individual self-actualisation	Personal development of individuals towards full happiness and 'self-actualisation'. The aim is self-direction and self-fulfilment	Carl Rogers, Malcolm Knowles	Individual	No *one* body of knowledge. Content is affective (attitudes and feelings) rather than cognitive. Main source of content is personal experience, not books.	Equals—teacher is a facilitator of learning. Teaching is student centred and personal. Assumes students are capable of deciding what to learn	Content is secondary to process. Experiential methods, including discussion and simulation
(C) Progressives (Reformist)	Main aim: Growth of the individual *and* promotion/ maintenance of a 'good' democratic society. An independent individual is seen as promoting a healthy democracy	John Dewey, Eduard Lindemann	Individual within a social context. Individual freedom is important	Curriculum focus is the immediate problems and needs of the student. Emphasis on reflection and action. Students are involved at all stages in deciding what is relevant	Partnership. Teacher is not passive. Organises, stimulates and suggests. Teacher and student learn from each other. Teacher's role similar to **B** but more *active*	Problem solving/scientific method/learning projects and contracts

Table 1.3 cont.

(D) Social transformation (Revolutionary)	Use education to help create a new social order	Paulo Freire, Myles Horton, Mao Tse-tung	Emancipatory, social transformation	The collective experience of participants, codified by educators	Teacher is an equal participant—works with the group to create the 'curriculum'	Problem posing, action and reflection on action. Dialogue is a central way of doing this
(E) Organisational Effectiveness	Development of desired skills and attitudes to help an organisation more effectively achieve its goals	Chris Argyris, Donald Schon	Organisational needs, goals and effectiveness	Organisational concerns constitute the curriculum	Trainers transmit organisational curriculum to learners	A variety of techniques are used; outcomes are assessed in terms of objectives achieved

Source: Slightly adapted from Scott 1985, in turn adapted from Darkenwald & Merriam 1982: 35–69

because in their work practitioners do not apply principles but try to find their way through complex and ambiguous situations. This said, there is still a definite place for formal theory in adult education. Formal theory can help us develop a deeper and more critical understanding of the complex dynamics and contexts of our work. Adult educators can use insights drawn from many disciplines (see Figure 1.3) and cross-disciplinary theoretical perspectives (see Figure 1.4) to illuminate their practice and enrich their theory. So, for example, Schon's concept of reflection derives from phenomenology, while the influential critical adult education theorist Paulo Freire (see chapters 3 and 4) draws on both phenomenology and Marxism. The work of adult educators also generates new ideas, for humanities and social science disciplines, and for various theoretical perspectives. For example, Kolb's (1984) work on learning styles opens up new areas of investigation for cognitive psychology. (For more on formal theory in adult education, see Usher & Bryant 1989: 169–98; Usher 1989: 66–9; Welton 1987.)

Conceptualising the relationship of practice, informal theory and formal theory in this way helps us to see that theorising is not just an abstract, impractical activity engaged in by intellectuals in academies removed from the 'real world', but is something we are doing all the time. This insight enables us to make the process of theorising more explicit. We can come to understand more clearly how we theorise, how we develop understandings of our practice. Formal theory then ceases to be seen as something external to us that we have to master and apply, and becomes something we can take into our existing understanding, and which can illuminate both our implicit, informal knowledge and our practice.

Education as a science
Behind different schools of thought in education there are radically different views of how knowledge is discovered and used. One view is that knowledge is constructed scientifically. According to this approach, educational knowledge can and should be developed in the same way that knowledge is built in the natural sciences. In this framework, knowledge is said to be objective, capable of being discovered empirically, in accordance with the following procedure:

1. State problem.
2. Formulate hypothesis.
3. Select research methods.
4. Collect data.

16

Figure 1.3 **The relationship of adult education practice to various disciplines**

Figure 1.4 **The relationship of adult education practice to various theoretical perspectives**

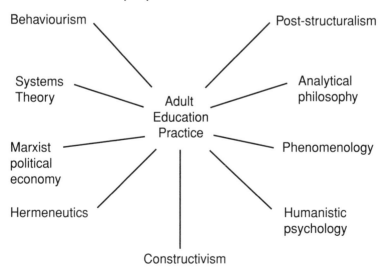

5. Analyse data.
6. Interpret data.
7. Reformulate hypothesis.

This approach aims to gradually discover the 'truth' about the world (i.e. to discover the way the world 'really' is, to uncover universal laws). An application of this approach in education is to attempt to uncover the 'rules' of classroom behaviour through systematic observation and experiment (see chapter 3). It is claimed that this 'scientific' approach is both rigorous and practical. It is said to be rigorous because the experimental method enables systematic and controlled research, which in turn allows knowledge claims to be continually modified and refuted. It is said to be practical because by discovering, for example, what 'actually' goes on in classrooms, teachers will be better able to control classroom behaviour.

The scientific, instrumental, technical, or positivist (as it is variously known) approach to education as a field of practice and study was dominant during the first half of this century. But since the 1930s this framework (see Carr & Kemmis 1986: 61) has been increasingly under challenge on intellectual, ethical and political grounds (see Usher & Bryant 1989: 10–13; Carr & Kemmis 1986: 51–70).

PARADIGMS

In his 1970 book, *The Structure of Scientific Revolutions*, Thomas Kuhn argued that, in science in any era, a particular conceptual framework or paradigm is dominant. This paradigm defines the boundaries of 'normal science': that is, it defines how knowledge is constructed and how scientists think about scientific problems. In this view there is no pure or objective knowledge: knowledge can be talked about only in relation to a particular social context and particular values (see Carr & Kemmis 1986: 71–5; Usher & Bryant 1989: 14–23).

Kuhn's notion of paradigms was quickly adopted by social scientists, who argued that in the social sciences a number of competing paradigms can exist at the same time. These paradigms are incompatible: they have such different assumptions about the nature of what they are explaining 'that no rational communication, and hence no rational resolution of disagreements, is possible across paradigms' (Usher & Bryant 1989: 20). Furthermore, although mutually incompatible paradigms can exist side by side, at any time one particular paradigm is likely to be dominant and others to be subordinate.

The interpretive paradigm

It is now generally agreed that in education, in addition to the positivist framework, there are two other paradigms: the *interpretive* (sometimes called communicative, practical, humanist, reformist, liberal or progressive or a mixture of these terms); and the *critical* (variously named emancipatory, transformative, strategic, socially critical, liberatory, radical or revolutionary). The interpretive paradigm sees knowledge as both subjective and socially constructed: its fundamental assumption is that different individuals understand the world differently. In education and other social activities, it is argued, it is futile to try to discover universal laws. It is more useful to study the different ways people make sense of situations, through language and other symbolic systems. Interpretivists maintain that the way individuals make meanings is not purely subjective or idiosyncratic. The focus in the interpretive framework is on the interaction of self and social structure and culture. It is by studying these interactions that we can come to understand how people make sense of, and act on, the world. There is often a strong emphasis in this framework on communication, on how people's interactions are mediated through language and other symbolic systems (Carr & Kemmis 1986: 83–94; Usher & Bryant 1989: 23–40).

It is possible that the interpretive paradigm is now dominant in Western adult education. Two of the most influential theoretical developments in adult education of the past 40 years—self-directed learning and reflection-on-action (see chapter 3)—are both located within the interpretive paradigm. Both these theoretical 'products' emphasise the way individuals make meanings and the capacity of individuals to become more proficient learners by 'learning how to learn'—by coming to understand and act on their own learning processes.

The critical paradigm

Although the interpretive paradigm recognises that individual understanding is shaped by culture and social structure, the emphasis in the interpretive framework is still on the way *individuals* construct meaning. A third framework, the critical paradigm, places a much greater emphasis on the *social context* of knowledge and education. Critical theory focuses on the relationship of knowledge, power and ideology.

According to Jürgen Habermas, different ways of understanding the world represent different social interests. Habermas (1971) identifies three ways of knowing the world. The first of these he calls the technical or instrumental. Here the interest is in knowledge that will help people to control nature and society.

The second way of knowing Habermas calls practical (and we have called interpretive). Knowledge of this kind serves a 'practical interest' in the sense that it facilitates practical judgment, communication and action by enabling people to understand their own and others' ways of knowing. According to Habermas and other critical theorists, the limitation of the interpretive framework is that it overemphasises the subjective dimension of knowing and learning, and it pays insufficient attention to the ways in which our understandings are shaped by the structure and culture of the institutions in which we live and work.

Habermas argues that there is a third or emancipatory knowledge-interest, which arises from 'a basic human interest in rational autonomy and freedom'. This universal human desire causes people to demand 'the intellectual and material conditions in which non-alienated communication and interaction can occur'. This emancipatory drive means that people need both subjective knowledge (i.e. understanding of their own and others' processes) and social knowledge (i.e. understanding of political, economic and cultural processes). According to Habermas, critical theory takes us beyond the relativism of the interpretive framework, which simply helps us to understand that different people see things differently, and helps us to realise that our understandings are socially constructed, often in distorted ways. Such distorted understandings, Habermas and other critical theorists argue, can be systematically exposed, explained and eliminated through a process called ideology critique. This notion of critical and emancipatory theory and practice has been influential in adult education over the past century at least (Carr & Kemmis 1989: 137).

The strength of the critical paradigm lies in its recognition of the connections between theory, ideology and power relations. For example, if we are to understand the radical changes currently taking place in workplace education around the world, we certainly need to understand the ideas behind these changes, which are now part of educational discourse. But we also have to understand the historical and social context of these ideas—the political and economic dynamics that have led to workplace education becoming the major current issue in adult education in most countries (see chapter 6 and Part II).

Critical theories and adult education
For the past 50 years adult education theory in the English-speaking world has been dominated by the US literature. The overwhelming majority of US adult education scholars work within the positivist and/or the interpretive paradigms. Only compara-

tively recently has a significant number of critical scholars written within the critical paradigm, which nevertheless continues to be extremely marginalised in the US adult education academy. Further, US critical scholars and those they have influenced tend to work with theory that emphasises culture, ideology and discourse rather than politics and economics.

In other parts of the world, including Europe and Latin America, there is a much more developed body of critical adult education scholarship, much of it springing from the work of activist adult educators. This tradition of activist scholarship informs many of the chapters in this book, as does the more recent, more scholastic writing.

The radical changes underway globally in the economy and adult education make it likely that over the next decade critical adult education scholarship will make a more significant contribution to the field than it has done in the past. For this reason the concluding chapter of this book (Chapter 18) discusses three varieties of critical theory that are currently being applied in adult education scholarship.

The uses of 'paradigm'

As John McIntyre notes in Chapter 6, 'paradigm' is a rich and at times confusing concept. Bearing in mind this quite valid warning, I still find 'paradigm' a most useful heuristic (explanatory) device. It helps me to identify the theoretical and value assumptions of different writers in adult education and other fields, and so enables me to better understand and make judgments about scholarly claims and debates. It also helps me to understand the development of adult education as a field of study.

CONCLUSION

Adult educators and trainers need to develop theoretical frameworks which are:

- *holistic*—that is, they comprehensively account for the contextual and ethical factors which shape adult education;
- *coherent*—that is, they give a clear account of the ways in which these different factors interact in particular situations;
- *strategic*—that is, they help adult educators to act at both the micro or local level (e.g. in training rooms, workplaces, communities) and at the macro (e.g. social-movement, state, national, international) level.

Such frameworks develop from analysis of practice, informed by insight drawn from formal theory. The other chapters in this book will discuss how such frameworks can be developed in relation to a range of central issues in contemporary adult education and training.

NOTE

1 Boud and his colleagues (1985) have developed the action–reflection notion in relation to adult education. Carr and Kemmis (1986) have argued for a similar view of the relationship of action and reflection in school education. Brookfield (1995) works the concept through in a very thoughtful and readable way.

FURTHER READING

Brookfield, S. 1995 *Becoming a Critical Reflective Teacher.* San Francisco: Jossey-Bass.

Carr, W. & Kemmis, S. 1986 *Becoming Critical: Education, Knowledge and Action Research.* Geelong: Deakin University Press.

Schon, D. 1983 *The Reflective Practitioner: How Professionals Think in Action.* New York: Basic Books.

Welton, M. 1987 'Vivisecting the nightingale: reflections on adult education as an object of study'. *Studies in the Education of Adults,* 19: pp. 46–68.

2

Understanding adult learners

Philip Pogson & Mark Tennant

Just who is the adult learner and how is that learner best understood? Are adult learners defined by their intelligence (IQ), practical skills, knowledge, expertise or wisdom? What impact does stage of life and past experience have on the learner and learning, and just what status should be given to the prior learning adults bring? What distinguishes the adult learner from the child and at what point (if any) can we confidently separate our conception of the two? How do adults approach learning and in what ways might the findings of disciplines such as lifespan-development psychology and sociology inform the work of adult educators and trainers? These and other similar questions provide an introduction to the project of understanding the cognitive and developmental attributes of the adult learner, an essential study for those who wish to facilitate learning in the post-school years. As lifelong learning becomes the norm, the issue takes on an increasing urgency.

In attempting to further the understanding of the adult learner, this chapter examines recent research on the nature of adult intelligence, the acquisition of expertise and adult life-span development psychology. First, we explore the development of adults' capacities as learners, outlining the cognitive dimensions of adults, including the psychometric and cognitive structuralist views on adult intelligence. We then discuss more recent formulations of adult cognitive abilities, including the development of expertise, so-called 'practical intelligence' and wisdom. Our fundamental conclusion here is that adults' thinking and cognitive structure are far more complex than was once commonly accepted. In the following section, we explore the conceptions of adulthood and life stages as social constructions. In the conclusion, we draw together these strands and provide some suggestions for further research.

UNDERSTANDING THE DEVELOPMENT OF ADULTS' CAPACITIES AS LEARNERS

In the past it has been customary to distinguish between two domains of theory and research in adult development: the development of intellectual or cognitive functioning and the development of personality and social roles. In the former domain two models dominated in early research: the first, the 'stability' model, assumed that adult cognition remained essentially the same after the attainment of maturity; the second, the 'decrement' model, assumed a gradual decline in ability, probably due to biological effects of ageing. Neither promised a basis on which a robust postadolescent learning theory could be built. Recent theory and research reject both these models and advance a far more complex view of adult learning capacities. It is these findings which we examine first.

THE ADULT LEARNER AND IQ TESTS

It has been understood for quite some time that psychometric, or IQ, tests are culture-specific, largely school-based, measure academic prowess and are even racially biased, but there is a growing view that they are also age-specific. Early studies postulated a decline in adult intellectual capacity with age. The work of Baltes (1968) and Schaie (1975) has shown that the supposed decremental differences in intelligence from younger to older age groups found by earlier researchers were in fact generational differences. That is, the negative findings were the result of measuring extraneous factors such as education, whose availability has grown over the past 50 years. The increase in the level of education is a key point, as there is a direct correlation between level of education and IQ. When Schaie and his colleagues designed studies which controlled for age, cohort (year of birth) and time (the year the tests were administered), they found that intelligence does decline with chronological age, but not until relatively late in life. In addition, it was found that such a decline could generally be reversed with training (Baltes & Willis 1982; Schaie & Willis 1986).

Along similar lines, Cattell (1971) and Horn (1970, 1982) separated intellectual abilities into two general clusters, which they labelled 'fluid' and 'crystallised' intelligence. The fluid component

24

of intelligence revolves around the capacity to process information in the form of complex reasoning, memory and figural relations, while crystallised intelligence is measured by tests of information storage, verbal comprehension and numerical reasoning. From the teenage years, there is a decline in fluid intelligence and a concurrent rise in crystallised intelligence. Howard (1988) notes similar independence between the functions of explicit and implicit memory among the aged: explicit memory declines with age while implicit memory remains stable.

A parallel concern with the inadequacy of past formulations of adult cognitive development is reflected in the writings of cognitive structuralists such as Piaget (1972). Piaget's earlier work theorised six stages of cognitive development through which every person was said to progress, the penultimate stage being 'formal operations', which commences in early adulthood. At the achievement of formal operations, thinking is characterised by the ability to reason and think abstractly. The available data on the acquisition of formal operations would suggest that it is not a single unified capacity operating independently of content and context, but may in fact be acquired in certain domains and not others, depending on the individual. Thus, as with IQ, formal operations has come to be seen as abstract and removed from the everyday nature of problems and problem solving. In response to this dilemma, there have been attempts by cognitive structuralists to extend the six-stage model. For example, Kohlberg & Ryncarz (1990) posit a seventh 'metaphoric' stage. On the whole, though, cognitive structuralism has not been successful in providing a convincing account of postadolescent adult cognitive development.

In summary, adult intelligence as measured by IQ tests does appear to decline with age, but not until relatively late in life. Remedial training can reverse such decrements. In comparison, those components of intelligence that are based on learning from experience are maintained or even developed with age, an issue that is discussed further when we examine practical intelligence and expertise.

ALTERNATIVE ACCOUNTS OF ADULT INTELLECTUAL DEVELOPMENT

From around 1970, dissatisfaction with the IQ-based model of adult intelligence generated a renewed interest in alternate views of cognitive functioning. The results of empirical research into such diverse models as insight, practical intelligence, wisdom, creativity, tacit knowledge and expertise have created a whole new field of study. For the greater part of this century the term 'intelligence' was so closely linked to the results of IQ tests that new terms such as non-academic intelligence, practical intelligence, everyday cognition and practical thinking were coined in an attempt to describe the newly emerging cognitive constructs. The underlying thread in this debate, which is reflected in the choice of terminology, is the belief that academic intelligence as conventionally understood did not account for the full range of adult cognitive abilities—that there existed non-academic intelligences and cognitive skills which functioned independently of IQ.

Whereas most IQ-based testing is firmly situated in the classroom or university, much of this new research took place in 'real life' environments such as the workplace. It is now well-established that many adults act intelligently despite an IQ test result that predicts otherwise. Adulthood is not a period of static or declining intellectual competence but of ongoing, qualitatively different, intellectual and cognitive growth. The nature and diversity of this growth are illustrated in the following examination of three alternative cognitive constructs to IQ.

The adult learner and practical intelligence
The concept of the existence of practical as opposed to academic intelligence is relatively new in the psychological literature. Academic intelligence relates to performance on abstract, theoretical tasks, while practical intelligence underlies skill in everyday tasks. Several recent publications have challenged previously held assumptions about the nature of adult intelligence and established practical intelligence as a legitimate field of study. Most of these studies were conducted on real-life tasks and not in a laboratory, school or university. Ceci and Liker (1985), for example, studied the intelligence of professional punters. They found no correlation between the ability to consistently predict winning horses and IQ. Dube (1982) found high levels of memory and reasoning among illiterate people. In addition, he found that capacity for story recall was higher among illiterate Africans than among comparable American students. Several studies have found that practical intelligence functions best in real-life situations. Lave et al. (1984) studied grocery shoppers and the processes they used to make mathematical calculations. They found that shoppers averaged 98 per cent correct answers on 'situated' calculations when actually shopping, and only 59 per cent on identical pen-and-paper problems. Carraher et al. (1985) found similar results when studying the mathematical abilities of Brazilian street children. Others have argued that practical intelligence strongly correlates with the ability to form relationships and build social networks. Ford (1982) suggests that social competence represents a domain of human functioning that is at least partly distinguishable from

a cognitive or general competence domain. Goodnow (1985) found that one of the general features of practically intelligent persons is the ability to organise and reorganise plans that enable them to go about their everyday lives efficiently.

The cross-cultural psychologist Sylvia Scribner (1984, 1985) investigated and documented the practical thinking of workers in her pioneering studies of everyday thinking in a milk factory. She found that practical thought has five distinct features: it is marked by flexibility; it incorporates the external environment into the problem-solving system; expert practical thinkers adopt effort saving as a higher-order cognitive strategy which informs the way they work; practical thought is highly reliant on domain specific knowledge; and practical thought actually reformulates and redefines problems for ease of solution.

The exploration of the nature of practical intelligence makes fascinating reading. However, little of this literature is available in conventional sources on adult education and training. Those wanting to pursue an interest in practical intelligence should initially consult Resnick (1987) and the edited volumes of Sternberg and Wagner (1985), Rogoff and Lave (1984), and Chaiklin and Lave (1993). Research into practical intelligence and practical thinking has extended our previously restricted view of the cognitive skills of adults. The study of uneducated, practical or non-academic thought in context has broadened the conventional picture of adulthood and presents adult educators with a richer and more complex view of adults than was previously conveyed in the psychological literature.

The adult learner and the acquisition of expertise

Practical intelligence, when applied in the context of a particular domain of work or knowledge, is often referred to as expertise. As noted above, many studies of expertise have been conducted independently of any theory of adult development or learning. Further, Stevenson (1994: 8) remarks ironically that the study of cognitive development (expertise) in the vocations is leading reforms in general education but is not being applied in vocational (and, in our view) adult education.

The most commonly used method in the study of expertise is the comparison of expert and novice performance at a particular task or in a certain domain. Expertise research has been carried out in many diverse areas, including taxi-driving (Chase 1983); baseball (Spilich 1979); judicial decision making (Lawrence 1988); bartending (Beach 1984) and medical expertise (Schmidt et al. 1990). Recent research (Stevenson 1994) has extended the expertise model into the milieu of vocational education in a series of

27

studies, including the development of expertise in apprenticeship courses, technical and further education colleges and problem-based learning.

The original and classic experiments on expertise remain the chess studies of de Groot (1966) and Chase and Simon (1973), who looked at the thinking of chess masters and novices. One of the most interesting findings in this work concerned what eventuated when the researchers asked players to memorise and reproduce the positions of chess pieces from set plays. All players were unfamiliar with the layout of the boards, but the layouts were all of a type that might be played by masters. It was found that experts could reproduce the boards almost without fault, while novice players wavered. Apparently, when memorising, chess masters 'chunked' together groups of pieces to relieve the load on their short-term memory. Novices had not developed such skills. The follow-up studies of Chase and Simon added a new twist: instead of asking players to memorise a board with the pieces logically set out, they asked them to memorise 'scrambled' or meaningless boards. The memory performance of the experts then plummeted to almost the level of the novices. Robert Sternberg's (1990a) studies of bridge yielded similar results.

What expertise research tells us is that expert knowledge is often domain-specific: when operating in the environment they know best, experts excel. When significant details change, their performance declines. Experts in one domain are not necessarily experts in another. Neither does expertise appear to be correlated with IQ (see Ceci & Liker 1985). The construct of expertise thus appears to complement that of practical intelligence in offering a favourable theoretical underpinning for the efforts of adult educators.

Chi et al. (1988) summarised the research findings on expertise as follows. Experts:

- excel mainly in their own domains;
- perceive large, meaningful patterns in their domain;
- are faster and more economical;
- have superior memory, but memory is restricted to their particular domain;
- see and represent a problem in their domain at a deeper, more principled level than novices;
- spend a good deal of time analysing a problem qualitatively— this is especially the case with ill-structured problems;
- have strong self-monitoring skills—that is, they are aware of their mistakes and of the complexity of problems facing them.

Limitations of the expertise model

Although the expertise model generates positive data on adult learning and performance which are of considerable interest to adult educators and trainers, it does have limitations. First, the findings of various expertise researchers, although largely complementary, can be contradictory on specifics. Chi et al., for example, claim that experts reason and present problems at a deeper level than novices, while Schmidt et al.'s study of expertise in medicine seems to cast some doubt on this. Second, in real life the pool of genuine experts in specific domains is limited, and often not easily accessible for research purposes. Third, in some domains, expertise seems to take a lifetime to develop, and little is yet known about how it develops over the lifespan of an individual. Fourth, much expertise research has not addressed or answered some significant questions on adult development. For example, continuing to frame research as a comparison between experts (much experience) and novices (little experience) ignores the problem of non-experts (those whose level of expertise does not appear to have profited from considerable experience). Finally, Sternberg (1990a) notes that there appears to be a cost of expertise, in that the very procedure-bound routines that experts develop can blind them to the insight of relative novices. Clearly, the challenge for adult educators is to draw on the considerable literature now available on teaching for the transfer of expertise (e.g. Stevenson 1991; Beven 1994) so as not to narrowly confine the cognitive and/or technical skills gained by learners. The complexity of this task is, however, beyond the scope of this chapter.

THE ADULT LEARNER AND THE GETTING OF WISDOM

Wisdom has traditionally been thought of as more interesting to philosophers and theologians than a subject for scientific investigation. Wisdom stimulated the interest of Jung in the early part of this century, and the psychologist Erikson made the attainment of wisdom the emerging value of the eighth and last stage of his lifespan system; this final stage he titled 'integrity versus despair (and disgust)'. Neither writer advanced empirical evidence supporting the existence of wisdom as a separate entity. In recent years, however, the concept of wisdom has undergone something of a renaissance and generated continuing interest among research psychologists.

Contemporary views as to the nature of adult wisdom are varied. Some see wisdom as a high-level, peak form of expertise (Baltes & Smith 1990); wisdom is of interest to these writers both as an indicator of the positive aspects of ageing (the attainment of wisdom and advancing years are almost inextricably linked) and as a challenge to the past dominance of intelligence testing (1990: 93). Others, such as Chandler and Holliday (1990), reject the notion of reducing wisdom to another psychological construct, fearing the loss of the deepest sense of what wisdom is. Labouvie-Vief (1990, 1994) understands wisdom to be the integration of *mythos,* represented by speech, narrative and dialogue, and *logos,* that part of knowledge which is arguable and can be demonstrated.

Evidence for a distinct construct of adult wisdom is provided by Sternberg (1990b). In a major study, he investigated the similarities and disparities between wisdom, intelligence and creativity. To Sternberg, wisdom has most to do with understanding; intelligence with the recall, analysis and use of knowledge; and creativity with going beyond the conventional and redefining the permissible.

As a psychological construct, wisdom complements IQ, practical intelligence and expertise, in that it furthers our understanding of the adult learner in a number of ways. First, wisdom provides a positive state to which a learner can legitimately aspire regardless of level of education or IQ. Second, wisdom provides something of a link between postmodern Western society and the historical roots of cultures, both Western and otherwise. Modern adult education and training risks drowning in the instrumentalist rush to prepare the learner for participation in society as skilled workers, parents, activists, teachers and so on. Wisdom reminds us that there is still a place in adult learning for *being,* not just *doing*—for personal growth that has no necessary extrinsic value.

THE ADULT LEARNER AND THE IDEA OF ADULTHOOD AS A SOCIAL CONSTRUCTION

As a balance to our emphasis so far on understanding adult learners in terms of cognitive constructs, we should like to probe the nature of the adult life course itself. The idea that one's personality or identity changes and/or develops during the adult years is now generally accepted. In this sense, the developmental literature parallels the cognitivist and structuralist views we discussed above. Each takes the stance that cognitive development continues apace in adulthood. Further, the developmental psychological literature contains a number of propositions about the attributes of the various phases of life, many of which have become premises or rationales for adult education practice. For example, the use of experiential and group techniques is based on the notion of the cumulative experience of adults; the use of learning contracts is related to the idea that adults desire to be autonomous and self-directing.

The developmental literature proposes a number of models of adult development, which can be broadly divided into those which take a position that the life course is normative, age-related and stage- or phase-based, and those which recognise the significance of non-age-related, non-normative events. Of the former group, those most frequently cited are Havighurst, Maslow, Erikson, Levinson, Gould, Loevinger and Valiant (see Tennant & Pogson 1995). Each of these authors advances an account of development that has as its end-point the mature, psychologically healthy and balanced person. All posit life stages or phases through which they envisage adults passing on the journey to maturity.

The second group of writers point to the tremendous variation in adult experience, and are not content with invariant sequences. Baltes and his colleagues, for example (Baltes 1987; Baltes et al. 1980), recognise three influences on development: those which are normative and age-related; those which are normative and historically graded such as epidemics, wars and depressions, which may influence entire generations; and non-normative influences, such as parenting a child born with a disability, or winning a lottery. Riegel (1976) argues for a dialectical understanding in which there is a constant interplay between the changing and developing person and the changing and evolving society. A third view holds that the life course itself is a social construction: that is, that the way in which we frame and understand the very notion of life course cannot be removed from the time, place and culture in which we live. For example McAdams (1996) sees identity as reflexively self-authored or constructed. This leads him to examine the life course as a narrative or story. He defines the life story formally as: 'an internalised and evolving narrative of the self that incorporates the reconstructed past, perceived present, and anticipated future' (1996: 307) McAdams thus sees identity as a psychosocial construction, jointly authored by the person and his or her defining culture. Life stories are based on fact but they go beyond mere facts by rendering past, present and future meaningful and coherent in sometimes imaginative ways. The basic function of a life story is integration—it binds together disparate elements of the self. Contrast this conception with the more postmodern view of selves as residing in narratives which surround and define them (Gergen 1997).

The significance to the adult educator of developing an understanding of the life course and its social construction cannot be overestimated. First, we need to recognise that certain adult education practices are based on what are often unspoken suppositions about the nature of adulthood. When working, say, with persons from non-Western cultures, such assumptions could bring educators unstuck. Second, adult educators need to distinguish between significant life events which are normative and age-related and those which are not. Finally, an understanding of the adult life course and its social construction can help the educator to frame learning more appropriately and to respond with grace and wisdom to the variety of experiences adults bring to any learning environment.

CONCLUSION

In an overview of complex fields such as those we have scrutinised in this chapter, it is difficult to do justice to the subtlety and diversity revealed in the literature. We hope that adult educators will be stimulated to continue developing their understanding of the adult learner. In the past 20 years or so the scientific understanding of adulthood has undergone a profound and radical shift. No longer constrained by the IQ paradigm, adulthood is now understood as a period of ongoing, constant growth and change. In addition, some formerly 'commonsense' appreciations of adults have been confirmed. It has always been recognised that some adults have a practical rather than a theoretical bent. Now studies of everyday skills and everyday thought have opened up the ordinary aspects of life and disclosed complexity and creativity in the execution of even simple tasks. As a result, the unfortunate historical bias towards the theoretical and academic aspects of cognition has been somewhat redressed.

Much of the research we have drawn on in our exploration of adult intelligence, the development of adult cognitive skills (including the development of expertise) and lifespan-development psychology comes from the USA. To complement this work there is a need for a serious commitment among adult educationalists to undertake original work on their local situations. For example, edited volumes such as those of Stevenson (1994) on the development of vocational expertise, and Evans (1991) on learning and teaching cognitive skills, go some way to filling the gaps in our knowledge, but much more systematic investigation is needed.

It is also likely that there is much relevant research on adult intelligence, the nature of adult learning, and the nature of adulthood itself being conducted in the psychology and sociology departments of universities around the world which is not necessarily contributing to the knowledge of adult education practitioners. In addition, the body of work undertaken for Masters' and PhD theses is not being accessed and applied. The dissemination of these data is a challenge for the future.

In an era of radical economic and social change, the workplace is once again becoming a place of serious and important learning. So far it is one about which we know too little, although interest is growing (see Goodnow 1990; Billett 1993, 1994, 1996; Stevenson & McKavanagh 1992). In addition, there is the question as to how effective vocational education and other professional development providers are in preparing employees to grasp the cognitive demands of the workplace of the future. Such questions provide a starting point for developing and enhancing our understanding of the adult learner.

FURTHER READING

Chaiklin, S. & Lave, J. (eds) 1993 *Understanding Practice: Perspectives on Activity and Context.* Cambridge: Cambridge University Press.

Chi, M.T.H., Glaser, R. & Farr, M.J. (eds) 1988 *The Nature of Expertise.* Hillsdale, NJ: Lawrence Erlbaum.

Gilligan, C. 1986 *In a Different Voice.* Cambridge: Harvard University Press.

Stevenson, J. (ed.) 1994 *Cognition at Work.* Adelaide: National Centre for Vocational Education Research.

Tennant, M. 1997 *Psychology and Adult Learning, 2nd edn.* London: Routledge.

3

Teaching adults
Griff Foley

Real teachers are those who think and act strategically and with commitment. These teachers are technically proficient: they can present a lively and interesting session, or effectively facilitate a discussion. When we watch such teachers we can see, and admire, their grasp of technique. But these people are much more than a bundle of skills. They think, and act, at a number of levels. They have a deep understanding of themselves and their students, and of the organisational contexts in which they work. They think strategically—they 'think on their feet', and they have a long-term view of their work. They also relate their teaching to some sort of 'bigger picture', or, to put it another way, their work is determined by particular values. These values may be individualistic or collectivist, conservative or radical, altruistic or hedonistic. But whatever their values are, these teachers are passionate about them.

Technique, context, strategy, values: these concepts provide a framework for understanding teaching, but they are not a recipe for success. The first thing to understand about teaching, or any educational activity, is that there are no formulas. Teaching is far too complex for that. But what we can do is build up our picture of teaching. This chapter surveys some of the research and scholarship that have influenced adult educators' and trainers' understanding of teaching. While the major schools of thought are covered, the survey is inevitably selective. The literature of teaching is huge, and what is included here is shaped by my experience and values.

The chapter is divided into two parts. The first looks at some of the ways in which classroom research has illuminated our understanding of teaching. The second examines insights into teaching drawn from psychological and social theory.

UNDERSTANDING TEACHING FROM CLASSROOM RESEARCH

RESEARCH ON TEACHING

It seems logical to begin a discussion of teaching by looking at what research tells us about it. But for the adult educator there are a number of problems with research on teaching: much of it examines the teaching of children and youth in classrooms, and so does not reflect the diversity of student ages and classroom settings that is found in adult education; teaching is such a complex activity that it is difficult to devise reliable and valid ways of researching it; there is so much research on teaching that it is difficult for the practitioner to get access to it, and to know what is useful in it; the endless debate among researchers about their findings makes it difficult for the practitioner to make judgments about the soundness of research; much teaching research has been constructed around a quite narrow notion of 'teacher effectiveness'.

Teachers, administrators and policy makers want to know what works in teaching. So it is understandable that the bulk of research on teaching has been into teacher effectiveness—into what teachers can do to help their students to learn. This research tries to establish links between what teachers do in classrooms (the processes of teaching) and the product or outcome of the teachers' work (student learning). The assumption is that differences in teacher skills (e.g. clarity of presentation, structuring of lessons, verbal fluency) and qualities (e.g. enthusiasm, warmth, confidence) will have different effects on student learning. The researcher's task is to carefully study classroom behaviour, using categorical observation scales to record what the teacher does (Shulman 1986: 9–10). In this way, it is argued, teacher behaviour that leads to student learning can be identified and teachers systematically trained to master these behaviours. The preferred form of training is 'microteaching': that is, laboratory practice of particular teaching techniques, such as introducing or concluding a lesson or questioning students, and supervised practice in real classrooms.

The results of this work give rise to pessimism. The Canadian adult educators Brundage and Mackeracher concluded in their survey that research on teacher effectiveness showed only that 'most teaching behaviour is unrelated to learner outcomes' (1980: 20). The findings of the massive Coleman Report on educational opportunity in the USA (Coleman et al. 1966) appear to support this view, implying as they did that there was no relationship between quality of teaching and student achievement. Biddle and Dunkin (1987: 121) conclude that 'most studies of teaching effects provide little evidence that the effect in question was produced by teaching and not some other causative factor'. But teachers and students *know* that there is a relationship between the way teachers teach and what students learn. The crux of the problem is the way teacher effectiveness research is constructed. Teaching and learning are such complex and context-specific activities that it is impossible, as we soon see, to reach any but the most general conclusions about what constitutes effective teaching behaviour. Consider these findings:

- class size and student achievement are, 'on average', negatively correlated (Biddle & Dunkin 1987: 122);
- 'lecturing is at least as effective as other methods at presenting information and providing explanations' (Brown 1987);
- effective teachers are those who do the most teaching (Barr & Dreeben 1978).

My favourite finding from teacher effectiveness research comes from a survey of research on the teaching of adults (Pratt 1981), which concluded that an effective presenter of knowledge (measured by student satisfaction, and increase in student knowledge and understanding) was one who was precise and clear in her presentations, and alive and moving (Pratt used the more 'scientific'-sounding term 'high teacher animation') (see Figure 3.1).

The fairly meagre findings of the teacher effectiveness research program fit the experience of most adult educators. Their implications for practice are clear. Thorough preparation and careful structuring of sessions will help precision and clarity in presentation. (The emphasis on the systematic structuring of educational experiences is associated with the 'objectives' approach to course design, which has been enormously influential in adult education: see chapter 4.) The more time you spend with each student, and the more lively and engaging you are, the more effective your teaching will be. But these findings merely confirm teachers' experience. The effectiveness paradigm leaves out so much. It says nothing about the content of teaching, or about how teachers and students make sense of their work, or about the ways teaching and learning are affected by social and cultural factors. For insight into these issues, we have to turn to other writers.

One group with useful insight are those experienced adult educators who have drawn on their experience to write practical

Figure 3.1   The effective presenter

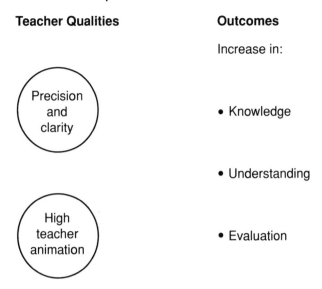

Teacher Qualities	Outcomes
	Increase in:
Precision and clarity	• Knowledge
	• Understanding
High teacher animation	• Evaluation

'handbooks'. Mike Newman's *Tutoring Adults* (1986) is a practical and clear guide to session preparation and teaching. A comprehensive US manual, by Malcolm Knowles, is *The Modern Practice of Adult Education* (1980), which is heavily influenced by the humanistic approach to education (see below). The English adult educator Jennifer Rogers' *Adults Learning* (1989) is also systematic, but less like a manual. It begins with three chapters on learner characteristics and learning styles and then has a number of 'how to' chapters. In the same vein, see Alan Rogers' *Teaching Adults* (1990), and Barer-Stein and Draper's *The Craft of Teaching Adults* (1994). Julius Eitington's *The Winning Trainer* (1989) is a trainers' manual that emphasises small-group and experiential techniques.

TEACHING FUNCTIONS

Possibly the most useful outcome of the teacher effectiveness research was that it documented some of what teachers actually do. It showed that they do not just present information but perform a number of roles or functions. The teacher effectiveness work also showed that what researchers called 'indirect teaching' (student work organised by teachers) contributed more to students' learning than direct (didactic) teaching (Shulman 1986: 12). This insight has been developed by other educators. Ira Shor (1980),

Table 3.1 Heron's six-category intervention analysis

Styles	Category	Descriptions
Authoritative	Prescribe	Advise, judge, criticise, evaluate, direct, demand, demonstrate
	Inform	Be didactic, instruct/inform, interpret
	Confront	Challenge, feedback, question directly, expose
Facilitative	Be cathartic	Release tension in
	Catalyse	Elicit information, encourage
	Support	Approve, confirm, validate

Source: Heron 1975

who teaches working-class students at the City University of New York (and to whose work we refer later in this chapter), says that in his classroom work he performs the following nine roles:

* convenor
* facilitator
* advocate (of missing perspectives)
* adversary (of oppressive behaviour)
* lecturer
* recorder
* mediator
* clearing house
* librarian.

John Heron, who trains adult educators and other professionals in England, has developed the notion of teaching functions in an interesting way. Heron argues (1989, 1993) that there are only six 'authentic interventions' that a teacher or a therapist, working with clients one-to-one or in groups, can make. Three of these interventions Heron calls 'authoritative', because they involve the practitioner in trying to directly influence the individual or group. The other three interventions are 'facilitative', or indirect (see Table 3.1).

For Heron, a skilled practitioner is one who can move from one intervention to another as the developing situation and the purposes of the interaction require. Heron has found that most practitioners use only a small number of the six categories. He and his colleagues conduct workshops in which practitioners are given opportunities to use the six categories and to expand their repertoire of interventions.

A more conventional development of the insight that teachers perform various functions is in work with US teachers: Finkel and

Monk (1981) maintain that teachers have an 'atlas complex'—that is, they feel they have to control and be responsible for everything that goes on in their classrooms. The way out of this trap is for teachers to identify the teaching and learning functions associated with particular pieces of learning and work out which of these functions can be performed by the students and which can be performed by the teacher. Through such means as worksheets, readings, question-and-answer sessions and small-group work, teachers can move away from reliance on didactic teaching methods.

THE SOCIAL DYNAMICS OF CLASSROOMS AND SCHOOLS

Dissatisfaction with quantitative, one-dimensional studies of teacher–student interaction led in the 1970s to a spate of studies, generally carried out in school settings, which tried to capture more completely the dynamics of teaching and learning. Approaching classrooms, schools and groups of students open-mindedly, as anthropologists would approach people in another culture (see Delamont 1983), researchers used methods of participant observation to discover both how students and teachers made sense of educational situations and the social outcomes of those situations. Many of these studies (see Shulman 1986: 17–23 for a survey) show that students often see education as a matter of completing set work and achieving grades, rather than as the attainment of understanding. Other researchers have dug into the deeper dynamics of institutionalised education, showing how it often reproduces relationships of exploitation and oppression.

Out of many such studies, a few will illustrate the dynamics of social reproduction. In the late 1960s Ray Rist, a black sociologist, studied the first eight days of classroom life for a group of black kindergarten children in Harlem. Within a few days their black, university-educated teacher had streamed the children according to their racial and class characteristics, and had them reproducing, or failing to reproduce, the roles of white middle-class families (Rist 1970). In the mid-1970s Paul Willis spent a year with a group of northern English teenagers in their final year of high school. The coherent working-class culture of these 'lads', centred around alcohol, tobacco, girls and 'having a laugh', so successfully resisted the attempted imposition by the school of an academic and achievement-oriented middle-class culture that the boys all did badly scholastically and wound up in low-skilled, low-paid jobs (Willis 1978). Spender & Sarah (1980), and many others (see especially Belenky et al. 1986), have shown how patriarchal practices and ideologies suffuse education and work against women.

The idea of social reproduction was central to these studies. It was argued that, whatever the intentions of educators, in any society education reproduced social relationships. In traditional societies education focused on such things as productive work, respect for age and the primacy of maintaining good relationships among people in communities. In these ways education helped to reproduce the economy, society and culture. In contemporary society, it is argued, education helps to reproduce capitalist social relations by socialising students and allocating them among jobs. Bowles and Gintis (1976) maintained that the authoritarian, teacher-dominated approach to education produces obedient and passive workers who expect to be disciplined from without. Newer, child-centred approaches to teaching also domesticate students, but they do so by getting students to internalise such norms as the importance of working without supervision, behaving predictably, and knowing what is expected without having to be told (Bowles & Gintis 1976: 298–303; Keddie 1971; Sharp & Green 1975).

Bowles and Gintis's 'correspondence' theory, arguing that the social relations of education mirror those of the workplace, has rightly been criticised for being overdeterministic (e.g. Sarup 1978: 172–81). Educational institutions in our society certainly do socialise students in ways of thinking and acting that help to maintain capitalism, but they do so in more subtle ways than Bowles and Gintis realised. Later work has shown that the dynamics of reproduction are complex, contradictory and open to resistance (or 'contestation') and change. This work shows that an understanding of these dynamics requires analysis at many levels, including:

- *the political economy.* How is education shaped by the economy and by politics? How does education help to reproduce and/or alter economic and political relationships?
- *educational institutions.* How do the practices and ideologies of institutions (sometimes called the 'hidden curriculum') reproduce or alter relationships of class, gender and race?
- *teacher–student relationships.* What shapes these? How do they affect educational processes and outcomes?
- *teacher ideologies.* How do these affect educational processes and outcomes?
- *the curriculum.* How is knowledge constructed in education? How is the construction of knowledge legitimised and/or

challenged? What are the social outcomes of the ways in which knowledge is constructed?

The complexity of the analysis is accentuated by the fact that each of these levels has a history through which the contemporary reality must be understood, and by the possibility that behaviour has an unconscious dimension. We not only need to understand what appears to be going on now, we also have to understand how things got to be the way they are, and that there may be an unconscious psychological dynamic in teaching and learning.

UNDERSTANDING TEACHING FROM PSYCHOLOGICAL AND SOCIAL THEORY

In the 1960s and 70s, in adult education and to some extent in school education, the attention of researchers and practitioners moved from trying to develop more effective teachers to trying to produce more effective learners. This change in the way we look at teaching and learning has been of enormous importance to adult education, and has a number of theoretical strands, which we now examine.

COGNITIVE PSYCHOLOGY AND ITS PEDAGOGIES

A major contribution to the interpretive understanding of learning and teaching has been made by cognitive psychology. Studies by German *Gestalt* psychologists early this century showed that people, constantly confronted as they are with a mass of stimuli, impose order on it in predictable ways. In other words, people have cognitive frameworks which help them to make sense of the world (Mayer 1981). This finding has significant implications for teaching. It means that learners are active: they do not passively absorb information but process it in their own ways. It follows from this that it is important for teachers to understand how students think and learn.

Apart from the work of US progressive educators (notably John Dewey) and Russian cognitive psychologists (notably Lev Vygotsky) in the 1920s and 30s (see Youngman 1986: 82–7; Kolb 1984), the insights of the gestaltists were overwhelmed by behaviourist psychology until the 1950s, when the development of computers revived interest in how people process information and there was a surge of research in cognitive psychology (Youngman 1986: 133–4).

41

From the perspective of the adult educator, one of the most interesting cognitive development theories is that of William Perry. Perry, through interviews with Harvard undergraduates in the 1950s and 60s, showed that they moved through nine 'epistemological positions' or 'ways of knowing'. Perry maintains that in their cognitive development students move from seeing knowledge as something that is handed down to them by authorities to seeing knowledge as relative (everyone has the right to their own opinion), to seeing that knowledge is constructed by people in particular social contexts, in accordance with particular values (Perry 1970; Belenky et al. 1986: 9–10).

In recent years a lot of work has been done on cognitive and learning styles—the distinctive and varied ways in which people think and learn. (For a review of this work, see Tennant 1997.) Probably the best-known of the learning-style theorists is David Kolb, who, with his colleague Ronald Fry, developed a 'learning-style profile', a way of identifying people's learning styles. Underlying Kolb's understanding of learning style is a sophisticated theory of experiential learning which attempts to integrate insight from cognitive psychology (Piaget, Vygotsky), educational theory (Dewey), social psychology (Lewin), psychoanalysis (Jung) and Buddhism. Kolb's theory can be summarised in the following eight propositions:

1. People's primary mode of adaptation to the world is learning (Kolb 1984: 31).
2. Learning involves two basic processes:
    *   grasping (prehension);
    *   transformation.
3. People learn in four ways:
    *   through immediate concrete experience (apprehension) (the affective mode);
    *   through observation and reflection (the perceptual mode);
    *   through abstract conceptualisation (comprehension) (the symbolic or thinking mode);
    *   through active experimentation (the behavioural mode).
4. Effective learning is cyclical (beginning with concrete experience) and holistic (involving all four learning modes).
5. Learning is developmental. People go through three stages in their learning:
    *   acquisition—birth to adolescence;
    *   specialisation—midlife, adulthood;
    *   integration—later in life.
6. Learning is social. The sort of life experience people have shapes the way they learn. People are likely to develop one

mode of learning more than another: they develop dominant learning styles. People's education and occupation particularly influence their learning styles.

7. Learning is interactive. It involves 'interactions between individuals with their biological potentialities and the society with its symbols, tools and other cultural artefacts' (Kolb 1984: 133, after Vygotsky).

8. Learning is a dialectical process. It involves people acting on and reacting to their environment.

(For more on Kolb's experiential learning theory, see Kolb [1984]. For a critique of Kolb, see Jarvis [1983: 16–20].)

Ausubel (1963, 1968) and others (see Entwistle 1984; Marton et al. 1984) have examined the relationship between learning context (the way knowledge is presented to learners) and learning strategy (the way learners learn). A distinction is made between *reception learning*, in which what is to be learned is taught directly to the learner, and *discovery learning*, in which learners are able to inductively build up their own understanding. It is argued that either of these types of learning can be rote (or 'surface' or 'reproductive') or meaningful. Meaningful learning occurs when learners are able to relate new knowledge to their existing cognitive frameworks. When learners cannot do this they must learn by rote. Whether meaningful or rote learning occurs depends both on how knowledge is presented to students and on the sorts of learning strategies used by students (Wittrock 1987: 72; Entwistle 1984; Gibbs 1996; Candy 1991).

A general understanding of such concepts as learning style, epistemological position, discovery and reception learning, meaningful and rote learning can help us to become more sensitive to how our students learn. At a more systematic level, understanding of the ways learners think enables educators to help students develop learning strategies, ways of understanding and acting on their learning. For example, by asking open-ended rather than closed questions, a trainer can give learners opportunities to develop a meaningful rather than a surface or reproductive orientation to learning. Again, by encouraging the use of 'mind maps' (Buzan 1978), adult educators can encourage students to develop their own ways of grasping and using knowledge. To take a third example, in the 1980s many adult students learning English as a second language were taught in ways that enabled them to understand their own learning styles and to expand their repertoires of learning strategies (Willing 1985).

HUMANISTIC PSYCHOLOGY AND ASSOCIATED PEDAGOGIES

Cognitive psychology has encouraged educators to shift their attention from developing direct teaching techniques to understanding how learners learn, and to facilitating that learning through teaching, course design and encouraging learners to understand and develop their own learning strategies. The movement of attention from teaching to learning has also been encouraged by humanistic psychology. The roots of this psychology lie in the existential philosophy of writers like Kierkegaard and Buber, who maintained that individuals are both free to choose which course of action they will take and responsible for their actions. This philosophy contrasted with the determinism of behaviourist and Freudian psychology, and much of sociology (Youngman 1986; Kovel 1987).

Humanistic psychology flowered in the optimistic atmosphere of the postwar United States. There, and particularly in California, a range of alternative therapies dedicated to the development of 'human potential' emerged, ranging from the *Gestalt* psychology of Fritz Perls to the body work of Patricia Rolfe (Rowan 1976). Humanistic psychology has also made a great impact on education, in particular through the work of the therapist and educator Carl Rogers. If one figure can be said to have influenced contemporary adult education in English-speaking countries more than any other, it is probably Rogers. His notions of 'meaningful learning' and 'facilitation' turned conventional wisdom about teaching and learning on its head, and encouraged a shift from direct teaching to teaching learners how to learn.

CARL ROGERS: 'MEANINGFUL LEARNING', AND 'FACILITATION'

Rogers saw therapy and education as potential agents of individual and social change. He distinguished between meaningless, oppressive and alienating learning, which he maintained constituted the bulk of the formal education curriculum, and 'significant, meaningful, experiential learning', which was self-initiated and involved the whole person (Rogers 1969: 5). The dilemma for the humanistic educator, as Rogers saw it, was to devise alternative ways of working within an education system characterised by 'a prescribed curriculum, similar assignments for all students, lecturing as the only mode of instruction, standards by which all students are externally evaluated, and instructor-chosen grades as the measure of learning', all of which precluded meaningful learning (ibid.).

Rogers' critique of the dominant 'telling' mode of teaching was one strand in a radical analysis of education that developed in the late 1960s and early 70s. Notable among the critics were Paulo Freire, who contrasted 'banking' and liberating education; Ivan Illich and Paul Goodman, with their ideas of replacing oppressive institutionalised education with voluntary learning networks; John Holt, with his practical ideas for more creative and participatory classroom teaching; the accounts of the difficult and inspiring work in 'liberatory classrooms' of Kohl, Kozol, Henry, Serle and others; and Postman and Weingartner's devastatingly funny critique of conventional education as answering the questions learners have not asked, and their idea of replacing it with an open-ended-question curriculum. (For a survey of these and other radical educational works, and bibliographical details, see Wright 1990: 114.)

Although the critique articulated by this body of work is now part of the thinking of many educators, some of the 1960s ideas are still directly relevant to the project of moving from a dominating to a liberating form of education, one which encourages individual development and contributes to the building of a more just society. Rogers' idea of the facilitation of learning is particularly important here. Rogers starts from the position that the focus of work in learning groups should be 'the honest artistry of interpersonal relations', and not the facilitator's predetermined aims for the group. Rogers maintains that he 'usually' has 'no specific goal for a particular group', although he hopes for 'some sort of process movement in the group'. In working with a group, Rogers trusts it to grow in a healthy direction and to recognise and eliminate unhealthy elements in its process. This trust in the group is symptomatic of the optimism of Rogers' humanism, reflecting as it does the confidence of the postwar USA, and contrasting with psychoanalytic theory, which focuses on both the destructive and constructive potential of the unconscious, and which digs deeply and critically into the dynamics of learning and teaching. (For applications of psychoanalytic theory to teaching and learning, see Salzberger-Wittenberg et al. 1983; Foley 1992c.)

Rogers also aims 'to become as much a participant in the group as a facilitator', willingly carrying his share of influence in and responsibility for the growth of the group but not wanting to control it. In the course of doing this he seeks to present his authentic self, his whole personality, and to allow others to do the same. Rogers hopes that his lack of precise aims, and his trust in the group process, will create a climate of openness in the group, allowing people to express their feelings and to learn from their experience. He seeks 'to make the climate psychologically safe' for group members. He listens carefully but selectively to what people say, focusing on the meaning experiences have for people and the feelings they express. In this way he aims to affirm and validate people, and to be a companion to them as they experience both joy and pain (Rogers 1973). Rogers spoke directly from his position as a therapist. For him most of what went on in education—the transmission and acquisition of skills and knowledge, the vocational and intellectual dimensions of education—were unimportant. Important learning was that which heightened your awareness of yourself and others, and which gave you the option of changing your behaviour. Nobody could tell you about such learning—you had to experience it, as a person does in psychotherapy.

Rogers' critique of conventional teaching and his concept of facilitation have been a dominant influence in adult education for the past 30 years: most adult educators now see themselves as facilitators of learning rather than as didacts. Rogers' educational theory also helped to generate a whole literature on experience-based learning (see chapter 14). The influence of Rogers' ideas can be seen in two other major contemporary developments in adult education: 'self-directed learning', and 'adult learning principles'.

SELF-DIRECTED LEARNING

The idea of learning being facilitated rather than taught has been linked in adult education theory and practice to the notion of adults directing their own learning rather than having it directed by teachers. It is now accepted that the bulk of adult learning is informal and self-directed. There is a long tradition of autonomous adult learning, stretching back to working-class autodidacts and beyond (Johnson 1979). US data from the 1970s suggests that more than two-thirds of total adult learning efforts are self-directed (Brookfield 1986: 150). Research conducted by the Canadian adult educator Alan Tough (1979) revealed that adults spent around 700 hours each year on learning projects—systematic learning activities planned and conducted by the adults themselves.

Tough's findings have been supported by numerous studies of mainly middle-class learners, in a range of occupations (Brookfield 1986: 149). This research, together with the 'human potential' and 'empowerment' ideologies already referred to, and the adult education profession's desire to stake out a distinctive territory (Harris 1989: 103), led to self-directed learning becoming the adult education fad of the 1970s and 80s. For many educators, self-direction came to be seen as an inherent cognitive and/or personality characteristic, whose emergence was to be facilitated by the adult educator, through a process which Knowles (1978, 1984) popularised as andragogy. (For critiques of Knowles' notion of andragogy, see Tennant 1997: 144–6, and Brookfield 1986: 90–102.) Instruments were developed which purported to measure the readiness of people to undertake self-directed learning. To date, research on the characteristics of self-directed learners has told us little, and the validity of measurements of readiness for self-directed learning has been questioned (Field 1989; Harris 1989).

Despite these doubts, the commitment of many adult educators to the notion of self-directed learning remains strong. There is now a large literature on the theory and practice of self-directed learning (Candy 1991 has a comprehensive review). For many adult educators, the most interesting question about self-directed learning is: How can teachers devise ways of giving students greater control over their learning? To do this is much harder than it may at first appear. Particularly important factors working against self-directed learning are the structure and culture of institutionalised education and workplace training (in turn shaped by broader social and cultural forces), which support teacher or trainer direction, and the resistance of students schooled to the 'telling mode' of teaching and learning. The challenge for the educator interested in promoting self-directed learning is to create spaces in which it can develop, within largely hostile environments. Studies of self-directed learning in adult education and training (see Foley 1992b) show that essential to its success are:

- adult educators' ability to understand learning and teaching from the learners' perspective;
- provision of clear procedures and support to enable learners to move from teacher-directed to self-directed learning;
- development of honest and caring interpersonal relationships, allowing all issues to be discussed and acted on;
- development of a 'learning–teaching dialectic', enabling learners to direct their learning while at the same time being challenged and extended, rather than indulged, by their teachers;
- a deep understanding on the part of adult educators of the structure, culture and dynamics of the organisations in which they work.

ADULT LEARNING PRINCIPLES

Another adult education concept that is shaped by humanistic psychology, but is also influenced by cognitive psychology and by research into teaching and learning, is the notion of adult learning principles. These are principles to guide adult educators when they work with learners. They are based partly on evidence of what constitutes effective and satisfying learning and teaching, but they are just as much statements of the value positions of particular adult educators.

There have been various explications of adult learning principles. (For a survey see Brookfield 1986: 26–33.) Probably the most comprehensive is Brundage and Mackeracher's 1980 survey of literature on teaching, learning and program development, in which they identify 36 learning principles and discuss the implications of each for teaching and program planning. Another interesting statement of adult learning principles is that of Scott (1985: 8–13), which draws on both the North American literature and the experience of Australian adult educators. Also of interest is Brookfield's (1986: 9–20) discussion of six 'principles of effective practice in facilitating learning'. These six principles (voluntary participation, mutual respect, collaborative spirit, action and reflection, critical reflection, and self-direction), while greatly influenced by the humanistic and cognitive psychology that we have been considering, move beyond them and demonstrate an awareness of the importance of social context, and human agency, in adult education. We now turn to a consideration of more contextual and critical pedagogies.

CRITICAL THEORY AND CRITICAL PEDAGOGIES

Critical pedagogy

'Critical pedagogy' developed out of the radical critique of education of the 1960s and 70s discussed earlier in this chapter, but rejects the determinism of that critique. Critical pedagogy also finds fault with both the teacher effectiveness and humanistic approaches to teaching because of their failure to address social and ethical issues related to teaching and learning.

The main theoretical tenets of critical pedagogy, and their implications for the practice of teaching, can be summarised as follows:

- Critical pedagogy places teaching and learning firmly in their social context. Particular attention is paid to the interaction of teaching and relations of class, gender and race.
- Critical pedagogy is concerned with the ways in which 'meaning is produced, mediated, legitimated and challenged' (McLaren 1988: xiv) in a wide range of formal and informal educational settings.

48

- Critical pedagogy focuses on relations of domination, on the ways in which, in capitalist society, culture, ideology and power intersect and control people in such sites as the workplace (through the hierarchical management of work), the marketplace (through consumerism, facilitated by advertising) and educational institutions (through teaching methods, the overt and hidden curricula, teacher ideologies etc.).
- Critical pedagogy seeks to help students to see through and challenge dominant (or 'hegemonic') meanings and practices. It also seeks to identify, celebrate, critique and build on popular and subordinate cultures, and a common democratic culture.
- This inductive and democratic pedagogy works from students' experience, but moves beyond it to expose the dynamics of everyday social reality and to offer learners choices for action.
- With critical pedagogy, the mode of teaching is dialogic. The teacher puts the students' experience back to them in ways which enable them to analyse and discuss the reality critically, and consider ways in which they might act on and change the reality.
- The critical teacher both supports and challenges her students. The teacher, as Belenky et al. (1986: 217–18) point out, can be seen as a *midwife*.

Midwife teachers are the opposite of banker teachers. While bankers deposit knowledge in the learner's head, midwives draw it out. They assist students in giving birth to their own ideas, in making their own tacit knowledge explicit and elaborating it. They support their students' thinking, but they do not do students' thinking for them or expect students to think as they do.

There are some detailed accounts of critical teaching with adults: for example, Shor's (1980) analysis of his New York University English classes; Lovett's (1975) discussion of his community development work in Liverpool, England; Wallerstein's (1983) account of teaching English to immigrants in California; and Mike Newman's (1993) account of his experiences in Australian trade union education.

Feminist pedagogies

The development of feminist scholarship has been one of the most significant intellectual developments of the late 20th century, an aspect of the 'second wave' of feminism that emerged in the 1960s and which has been concerned with 'enlarging the concept of politics to include the personal, the cultural and the ideological' (Marshment 1997: 125). From the 1960s onwards in many countries women's studies courses were established in adult and higher education, often developing from informal consciousness-raising efforts in women's groups. As the discipline of women's studies was established in universities from the 1970s onwards, important pedogogical issues had to be confronted. Primary among these was the relationship of teacher and student. Women wanted to move away from the dominant hierarchical pedagogical relationship, which involved teachers in transmitting their knowledge to students and then assessing whether the students had absorbed the teaching.

The great contribution of feminist pedagogy to adult education theory and practice has been its problematising of the hierarchical teacher–student relationship and its experimentation with alternative practices such as joint essays and presentations, team teaching, autobiographical writing and collective marking (see Robinson 1997: 11–12 for further reading on these innovations). Feminist educators have sought to build 'safe spaces' in which women students can analyse their experience and find their 'authentic voices' (see chapter 15 for detailed discussion of these efforts). As they have done this, teachers and students have had to work through difficult issues. How can such work be done in male-dominated, hierarchical, rationalising, certifying institutions? How to reconcile a desire to work in women-centred, cooperative and nurturing ways with a desire to make your way in a patriarchal, competitive world? How to work in classrooms with differences among women by class, race, sexuality, ability and age? Women's struggles with these issues have produced a large body of literature (see chapter 15; Maher & Tetreault 1994; Thompson 1997; Bhavani 1997). It has also (as we see in the next section) generated a challenge to the very notion of critical and feminist pedagogy.

The critique of critical and feminist pedagogy
In 1989, in a detailed case study of a media studies course in a US university, Elizabeth Ellsworth pointed out that students can experience as oppressive attempts by teachers to 'empower' them. Ellsworth's critique resonated with many feminist educators, and there is now a developed critique of critical and feminist pedagogy (e.g. Lather 1989: Luke & Gore 1992; Lee 1994; Durie 1996). To date, probably the most developed argument is that of Jennifer Gore (1993), who, using Foucault's concept of 'regime of truth', examines in great detail the theoretical and value assumptions, the techniques and practices, the institutional relationships, the mode of knowledge formation and the ethical effects of these pedagogies. Gore concludes that these pedagogies:

- see power as a property that can be conferred by teachers on students;
- are based on abstract philosophical assertions about such qualities as 'female experience' and 'authentic womanhood' rather than on 'empirically-developed and context-specific evidence' (121);
- have regulatory, supervisory and 'self-styling' effects on both students and teachers;
- demonstrate little or no awareness of these potentially domi-native effects—'we [teachers] have constituted ourselves as bearers or holders of knowledge . . . [rather] than as agents subjected to knowledge' (131).

While some readers may be repelled by Gore's dense poststructuralist language, I find her argument compelling, echoing as it does earlier reflections of adult educators (discussed below) on the unintended and potentially oppressive outcomes of their attempts to 'liberate' or 'improve' students. Her critique also connects with some recent writing on workplace change and learning, which 'deconstructs' (i.e. subjects to critical scrutiny) taken-for-granted terms and practices like 'empowerment', 'teams', 'quality' and 'the learning organisation' (see Field 1997; Garrick & Solomon 1997) and which proposes approaches that take account of and harness diversity rather than seeking to impose a vision or strategy (Gee et al. 1996; Rhodes 1997; Cope & Kalantzis 1997).

Reflection, and critical reflection
In the field of professional development over the past two decades, there has been a growing interest in the concept of reflection. Donald Schon, his colleague Chris Argyris and others have argued that in their practice professionals are faced with messy problems and contexts. These are best dealt with by people who can flexibly and intuitively draw on their knowledge of practice (or their informal theory) rather than try to apply rules drawn from formal theory.

The notion of reflection is often linked to the idea of practitioners as action researchers who plan, act, reflect on their practice and plan, act and reflect again, in a continual spiral. Heron, Boud and others advocate practitioners' learning to 'monitor' their 'interventions' and expand their repertoire of inter-ventions. They argue that as professionals act, they should strive to be continually aware of the impact of their actions. This, they maintain, can be achieved by asking oneself questions like:

- What happened?
- What does it mean?

• What can I do?

Reflection can also be a retrospective process, in which practitioners return to the experience, attend to their own and others' feelings about the experience, and re-evaluate the experience. (For some examples of extended reflection on practice, see Boud & Griffin 1987.)

This approach to examining practice is proving to be of great use to adult educators. It enables us to look at our practice as something that is continually in process and can be acted on. Our teaching, then, becomes something that we are continually examining and learning from, and is no longer seen as a bundle of skills to be 'mastered'.

A distinction needs to be made between, on the one hand, reflection and the associated concepts of 'action learning' and 'action science' as they are used in human resource development and professional development and, on the other hand, reflection as it is used in critical pedagogy. The former emphasis, generally referred to as 'reflection-on-action', tries to work out how people make meaning in situations and devise strategies for acting on them. It is concerned with effectiveness and 'manageable change' within existing institutions, rather than with radical institutional or social change. It is often coupled with 'problem-based' learning (see Boud et al. 1985; Boud & Feletti 1991). It is informed by the interpretive paradigm, and to some extent by the behaviourist framework (e.g. Heron's six categories).

Critical reflection, conversely, has as its aim the identification and challenging of people's assumptions, and radical social change, in a democratic and often socialist direction. Work such as that of Brookfield (1987) on critical thinking goes part way in the direction of critical reflection, concerned as it is with encouraging people to:

• analyse the assumptions underlying their 'traditional beliefs, values, behaviours and social structures';
• be aware that these assumptions are 'historically and culturally specific';
• explore 'alternatives to the current ways of thinking and living'; and
• be sceptical of claims to universality.

Brookfield considers the political implications of teaching people to think critically (1987: 51–68), and how educators might contribute to the political education of citizens by teaching them to think critically (1987: 162–83). In doing so he considers the possible revolutionary outcomes of such work, but stops short of articulating a strategy for linking education to movements for radical social change. (For more on the distinction between reflection and critical reflection, see Boud, Cohen & Walker 1993.)

Teaching and social movements

The concepts of critical reflection and critical pedagogy are attractive to educators with an interest in social justice and radical social change. But there are many barriers to the implementation of these ideas, such as the isolation in which many educators have to work, the individualistic and competitive nature of institutionalised education, and the messages of the dominant culture transmitted through the mass media, the family, and most education. It is interesting, then, and heartening, to find teachers who manage despite all the constraints to teach critically. It is also stimulating, and sometimes inspiring, to explore the theory of critical pedagogy, which takes us into such areas as socialist theory (e.g. Youngman 1986) and feminist theory (see chapter 15), and brings to our attention the optimistic notion of popular education.

Popular education emerged from people's struggles and mass movements in Latin America in the 1960s and 70s and, in a sense, is the educational equivalent of the liberation theology of that era. Its methods are those of critical pedagogy, with an emphasis on working from the learner's experience, locating that experience in a broader social context, and devising collective strategies for change (see Arnold & Burke 1984; for further discussion of educational programs for critical thinking and social action, see chapter 17).

But in our society the impact of critical pedagogy has been relatively minor, and is likely to remain so for the foreseeable future. This is not to say that critical pedagogy is futile. But it does mean that radical educators need to develop a sophisticated and realistic analysis of the social context of their work. It is also clear that critical pedagogy will make a significant contribution to struggles for social justice only when it moves beyond its current situation of being practised in isolated pockets and becomes a dimension of the work of social movements with a real interest in radical social change, such as the working-class, women's, Aboriginal, gay, disabled and environmental movements.

The democratic imperative

If critical pedagogy is to be emancipatory, it must be democratic: it must entail a genuine sharing of power among learners and teachers. To build genuinely democratic processes in societies and institutions in which there is so much that is undemocratic and exploitative is a constant struggle. Fortunately, we have some detailed accounts of democratic educational work. One of these relates to the work of Myles Horton, who founded Highlander Folk School, a residential college in Tennessee which for more than 60 years has provided education for trade unionists, civil rights workers and environmental activists. Horton and his colleagues appear to have developed a genuinely democratic way of working with adult learners. Their starting point is a deep respect for learners and their life experience. Highlander's historian, Frank Adams (1975), writes of the 'one axiom that never changes at Highlander: learn from the people; start their education where they are'. Horton himself put it like this (Moyers 1981):

> You have to know that working people—the uncommon common people—have a past . . . Adults come out of the past with their experiences so at Highlander you run a program based on their experiences . . . Our job is to help them understand that if they can analyse their experiences and build on those experiences and maybe transfer those experiences even, then they have a power they are comfortable with.

When they come to Highlander, learners have experience but lack techniques for analysing it. The educators teach the learners how to develop these techniques (Moyers 1981):

> One of the things we have to do . . . is to learn how to relate our experience to theirs and you do that by analogy, you do that by storytelling. You don't get off and say: 'Look, here are some facts we're going to dump on you.' We say: 'Oh, you might consider this. Now this happened to somebody kinda like you in a different situation.' So we get them to do the same thing, with each other—get peer teaching going.

What is developing in this sort of education is a genuine dialogue, in which each party listens to and learns from the other. This is real, and difficult, educational work. The difficulties and gains in this sort of work, and the unresolvable tensions that arise in it, are explored with great honesty and sensitivity by David Head in an account of his work with doss-house dwellers at Kingsway Day Centre in London in the 1970s. Head begins by confronting educators with an unpalatable fact about their work: 'Education is invasion'. We educators, Head notes, like to believe that our 'interventions' are 'friendly invasions'. But our work inevitably carries with it 'overtones of occupation, cultural imposition . . . the territory of the learners is occupied by change-bringing forces' (Head 1977: 127).

Head then outlines the intricate dynamics of educational work with fragile and wounded learners, learners who will flee at the first hint of condescension. In the course of his account, he affirms the truths about democratic teaching discovered by the Highlander educators. 'If we are to avoid the worse aspects of invasion', Head writes, 'our aim must be to begin where people are and discover with them where it is worth going' (Head 1977: 135). This will involve educators in recognising the invasiveness of their work and struggling with learners to build a different sort of relationship—one that is based on a notion of solidarity rather than on a patronising notion of service.

For an adult educator to work with learners 'in solidarity' means to support and provide resources for learners, to challenge and extend them, but never to patronise or try to control them. It means educators using their power to create educational situations in which learners can exercise power (Gore 1992: 62). This is the most useful meaning of the much-abused and coopted notion of 'empowerment'. Empowerment is not something that educators can do to or for learners. Nor is it a withdrawal by the educator, an abandonment of power. This has been one of the great confusions in adult education over the past 30 years. It has arisen primarily, I think, from a misreading of Carl Rogers' approach to facilitating learning groups. Rogers' condemnation of conventional teaching, his faith in the capacity of groups to develop in healthy directions, and his commitment to working with groups in non-directive ways, have been misinterpreted as a refusal to use power. In fact Rogers, like Horton, used his power as a counsellor, teacher and administrator to enable clients, learners and staff to exercise theirs. (A reading of Rogers' accounts of his struggles to develop facilitative teaching and administration in the university department he chaired is instructive here: see Rogers 1978: 69–104.)

What distinguishes Rogers the humanistic educator from Head and Horton the critical and radical educators is the latter's social analysis and political commitment. Both Head and Horton, in their different ways, see their learners as being oppressed. Both direct their educational efforts to helping learners act collectively on their oppression. Both have asked, and loudly answered, the question posed by the old union song: 'Whose side are you on?'. Both have, in Amilcar Cabral's (1974: 50–1, 57, 59) vivid sense, committed 'class suicide': they have decided that they want no future in an oppressive social order and have turned their backs on the privileges that accrue to the middle class in that order. And in making that step they have developed a democratic approach to teaching. They have ceased to assume that their expertise is of use to people, and instead of making pronouncements about what they can do *for* learners have come to ask themselves, and their learners, 'What can we do *with* you?' (Gore 1992: 62).

Discussion groups

A common thread in the various forms of critical pedagogy is the use of discussion. Facilitation, self-directed learning, andragogy and adult learning principles all focus on the importance of developing a teaching and learning process that supports and encourages adult learners. This humanistic tradition in adult education has been criticised for its lack of interest in the content of education and its consequent naivety about the social and ethical outcomes of education. An examination of the discussion group tradition in adult education helps us to see that in teaching and learning both content and process are important.

In an excellent article on discussion as an educational method, Brookfield (1985) points out that for many adult educators discussion is seen as the 'education method par excellence'. Two features are generally seen to be central to the concept of discussion in adult education: 'purposeful conversation . . . about a topic of mutual interest', and a notion of equal participation, a roughly equal sharing of conversational time. The goals of discussion are both cognitive and affective: the development of participants' analytical capacities, their increased appreciation of the complexities of issues, their increased identification with subject matter, and their increased tolerance of opposing viewpoints. Brookfield, drawing on studies of discussion groups in action, emphasises that, particularly in our competitive and individualistic culture, the attainment of these goals is problematic. As he notes, discussion groups often become 'an arena of psychodynamic struggle', in which 'students will be alternately defensive and aggressive'. Brookfield argues that meaningful and productive discussion is more likely to take place if the following four conditions prevail:

- the discussion topic is stimulating;
- the group leader is well versed in both group dynamics and the topic under discussion;
- group members possess reasonably developed reasoning and communication skills;
- group members have devised and agreed on 'an appropriate moral culture for group discussion'.

For Brookfield, this last condition is crucial. It 'means that the group must spend some time agreeing on a set of procedural rules concerning the manner in which equity of participation is to be realised'. These procedural rules will in turn be based on the sort of ethical principles identified by Bridges as being essential to the functioning of discussion groups: 'reasonableness (openness to others' arguments and perspectives), peaceableness and orderliness, truthfulness, freedom, equality, and respect for persons'.

There are some lively accounts of discussion groups in adult education. One of the most interesting of these is Lovett's (1975: Ch. 5) account of the operation of discussion groups in a range of sites (community centres, a mothers' club, a pub bar) in a working-class area in Liverpool, England. Lovett's analysis distinguishes between what he calls 'social group work' and educational discussion. The goal of the former is social and therapeutic; the goal of the latter is to 'develop understanding, to help people make up their minds about a variety of issues, to assess evidence, to formulate conclusions'. The intention is to *extend* the learners' 'understanding, cognitive ability and linguistic resources'.

Real teachers

There are some good teaching autobiographies and biographies. Adams (1975) is an excellent educational biography of Myles Horton. Horton's autobiography, *The Long Haul*, was published just before he died in 1990. There is also a two-hour videotaped interview with Horton, in which he talks at length about his approach to education.

Other interesting autobiographies are Jane Thompson's (1983) account of her work with women in Southampton, Mike Newman's (1979, 1993) lively accounts of his experiences as a tutor and organiser of adult classes with the Inner London Education Authority in the 1970s and with Australian trade unionists in the 1980s, and David Head's (1977, 1978) analyses of his work with homeless and working-class people in London during the same period.

Accounts of the work of educators like Horton and Head, and the recollections and polemics of the radical educators of the 1960s and 70s (see above) and of teachers from an earlier generation (e.g. A.S. Neill, Sylvia Ashton-Warner), have confirmed for me that good, great, excellent or real teachers—call them what you will—are those with honesty, compassion, humour and passion. It is also clear to me that in teaching, as with any other human activity, the sum is greater than the parts. While it is useful to analyse what, say, Myles Horton does, and to examine the theory behind his practice, Myles Horton, the teacher and the human being, is more than technique and theory. This is an optimistic realisation, and one of its implications is that, while we can learn a lot from studying real teachers, we should not try to model ourselves on them. We should be ourselves.

CONCLUSION

The material referred to in this chapter has helped to develop my understanding of teaching. If you were to speak to another educator of my generation you would get a different collection. Learning about teaching is a complex process, involving a mixture of solitary reflection, reading, and discussion with colleagues. The important thing for each of us is to develop our own ways of understanding teaching, to realise that we will never fully understand it, that all we can do is try to develop a fuller and more sensitive awareness of what happens when people teach.

FURTHER READING

Brookfield, S. 1986 *Understanding and Facilitating Adult Learning.* San Francisco: Jossey-Bass, Chs 1–6, 12.
——1990 *The Skilful Teacher.* San Francisco: Jossey-Bass.
——1995 *Becoming a Critical Reflective Teacher.* San Francisco: Jossey-Bass.
Candy, P. (1991) *Self-Direction for Lifelong Learning.* San Francisco: Jossey-Bass.
Connell, R.W., Ashenden, D.J., Kessler, S. & Dowsett, G.W. 1982 *Making the Difference.* Sydney: Allen & Unwin.
Gore, J. 1993 *The Struggle for Pedagogies: Critical and Feminist Discourses as Regimes of Truth.* New York: Routledge.
Head D. 1977 'Education at the bottom', *Studies in Adult Education* 9(2) pp. 127–52.
Heron, J. 1989 *The Facilitator's Handbook.* London: Kogan Page.
Horton, M., Kohl, J. & Kohl, H. 1990 *The Long Haul.* New York: Doubleday.
Newman, M. 1993 *The Third Contract: Theory and Practice in Trade Union Training.* Sydney: Stewart Victor.
Rogers, C. 1983 *Freedom to Learn for the 80s.* New York: Charles E. Merrill.
Shor, I. 1980 *Critical Teaching and Everyday Life.* Boston: South End Press.
Thompson, J. 1997 *Words in Edgeways: Radical Learning for Social Change.* Leicester: NIACE.
Willis, P. 1978 *Learning to Labour: How Working-Class Kids get Working-Class Jobs.* London: Saxon House.

4

Program development in adult education and training

Michael Newman

Program development is an art, not a science. Learning is a mysterious process and deciding on, designing and then conducting a program of learning for a group of adults will require imagination, flexibility and willingness to take risks. Some adult education and training theorists have attempted to tie the process down by developing sets of guidelines or lists of steps to follow, but in doing so they deny the magic of the process. Program development in adult education and training is much more like the production of a piece of theatre in which, if everything goes well, ideas, people, resources, organisations and environments coalesce. A lot of hard work and clear thinking are needed. There are accepted and proven ways of doing things, but there are very few absolute rules.

In this chapter we look at some of the ideas, people, resources, organisations and environments that coalesce into a learning program, and at how adult educators and trainers might play a part in managing and directing this process. We look at examples of educational programs, and define the term 'program'. We look at how programs come into being, at the various players in the design and implementation of a program, and at the contexts in which the development of a program of learning can take place. We then discuss a number of approaches to program development, identifying key theorists, discussing the strengths and weaknesses of the various models of program development they have put forward, and examining how the various theories of program development have changed in emphasis over the years.

PROGRAM: DEFINITION

Definitions are difficult. In adult education and training, the word program has a wide range of applications. It can denote a single educational or training event, a formal course, a collection or set of courses, an individual learning project, a workshop, a colloquium, a conference, or a public education campaign. Educational programs may be difficult to define but there are a number of features that are common to them all. People have come together for a purpose and, for some at least, that purpose is to learn. What these people are doing has an order and sequence. And what they are doing has a time limit, in that the program has a discernible beginning and end (Brookfield 1986: 204). In short, we are talking about learning that has been consciously entered into and consciously organised, as opposed to all the other learning that we engage in incidentally, unconsciously or unintentionally as we go about our lives.

PROGRAM DEVELOPMENT

Adult education and training programs come into being in many different ways. Some grow out of an idea: the coordinator of a community adult education centre, after a conversation with her teenage son about his new interest in science fiction, tries a course on the subject. Some programs might be designed around a particular person with a particular interest, skill or background: a university department of French, hosting a writer from France who is researching a novel he wants to set in Australia, prevails on the writer to conduct a series of public seminars on current intellectual debates in France. And some programs grow out of a local issue: a local politician, looking for ways of defusing a confrontation between the environmentalists and loggers in her town, sets up a meeting with several expert speakers, followed by discussions and feedback, on possible ways of diversifying the economy in the region.

Some programs pick up on fads or fashions: researching family histories becomes a popular pastime and the continuing education department of a university runs a course on genealogy. Some reflect social changes: a neighbourhood house organises meetings examining the struggle for women's equality. And some are in response to a crisis: following the brutal bashing of a gay man in a suburb of a large city, a number of organisations and local authorities organise a range of meetings, activities and the making of a video aimed at combating prejudice against gay men and lesbians.

Some programs grow out of the nature and purpose of the centre or organisation sponsoring them: the Family Planning Association provides courses on human sexuality. Some respond to the need of an organisation to continue, grow or renew itself: a trade union provides training for its organisers in the procedures of recruiting new members. Some programs come about because of government decisions and government policy: jobs are analysed in terms of competencies, and training for those jobs is reorganised in competency-based modules, in response to urging from centralised agencies promoting the government's training reform agenda.

Some programs are set up to meet needs, interests and demands: adult education and community centres run courses on communication skills, self-assertion and personal growth to meet people's individual needs. A local public library runs a program of films and lectures to meet an interest in another country generated by increased trade links and the arrival in that area of immigrants from that country. Following bitter industrial action in an isolated, single-industry town, a peak union body demands that the management pay for a series of meetings to be conducted by educators and counsellors aimed at bringing the community back together.

In essence, each program has its own story, and the program developer—the educator or trainer—enters the story at some point, often after it has started; plays a major part in writing the story for a while by designing and coordinating the program itself; and then at some stage eases out of the story, leaving others to take it on. The adult educators and counsellors who were invited to enter the single-industry town and run those meetings entered a story that was well underway. They learnt about the dispute and the tensions in the town both during the dispute and in its aftermath, then designed and conducted a number of meetings bringing together strikers, strike-breakers and representatives of management in roughly equal numbers, letting them talk out the events they had been through, express their feelings and learn from each other. At the end of an intensive week of meetings, the educators left and the townspeople went on with the process of dealing with, and perhaps healing, their community's wounds.

THE PLAYERS

Learning programs can involve a number of players. There will be the learners, of course, and in most cases also the helpers of learners—the facilitators, teachers, tutors, counsellors or trainers. There are likely to be administrators, organisers, managers or supporters of some kind. And there are likely to be organisations, governments, or authorities which house, provide, finance or sponsor the program in some way.

There may be occasions when there is only one player—the learner. In this case an individual adult engages in a program of learning independently, identifying what she or he wants to learn and deciding how to go about learning it. The learner may use community facilities such as libraries, museums and other public bodies, bookshops, the mass media, friends, and experts she/he makes contact with. The learner may also use existing programs, such as short courses, learning kits, educational video programs or instructional computer programs. But in selecting and using all these resources, the learner develops an individually designed learning program and is answerable to no-one but her/himself. One of the major researchers into adults conducting their own learning, Alan Tough (1979), indicates that adults spend hundreds of hours a year engaged in learning projects that they have planned by themselves.

There will also be occasions when there are two players in a learning program—the learner and the tutor. The learner is likely to have approached the tutor—to learn piano, or to be put through a personal get-fit program, for example—so is seeking the tutor's knowledge or skill. But as the learner has engaged the tutor, she/he will be constantly judging whether what the tutor is providing is worth going on with. This kind of learning program, then, will be continuously evaluated and renegotiated.

We might describe most individualised learning and one-to-one learning as belonging to the informal arena of education and training. In most formal contexts there will be three distinct players—the learner, the teacher or trainer, and an organisation controlling, requiring or providing the program.

Often in this case it is the organisation or wider political and economic forces that set the policy and the parameters, allowing only so much room for the educator and the learners to vary the program. Governments, for example, can control educational programs through selective funding. Certain money is made available for disbursement to community colleges whose programs until recently have been dominated by enrichment and leisure-oriented courses, but this money can be used only for the provision of *vocational* courses.

In such cases the educator responsible for delivering the educational program will be constrained in the way she/he can develop and design the learning. Part of the educator's skill will be to operate creatively within those constraints. Policy may be set, and so may the educational program's broad objectives. The format may in part also be prescribed, in that it must relate to an occupation that has been analysed in terms of competencies. However, the educator may have more control over the design and delivery of sections of the program, and in the encounter with the participants there will inevitably be adjustments and renegotiation of the curriculum relating to the individual and collective needs of those participants.

CONTEXT

Program development takes place within a context, and so the educator must take notice of, adjust to, react against, or make use of that context. The contexts are many and most are interrelated. They are industrial, political, economic, social, organisational, aesthetic, moral, spiritual and historical (see Case 4.1).

CASE 4.1

In a steel city between 1988 and 1992 an adult educator was involved in developing training programs to introduce consultative practices in a steel-industry company, in a port authority, and in a state government department. In each case the broad objectives of the programs were the same: to provide workers and management with a background to the changes deemed necessary in work organisation; to provide a rationale for the introduction of consultative committees; and to provide initial training for members of the newly formed consultative committees. However, although the aims were the same, the programs in each case reflected the very different contexts in which the organisations operated.

In the steel company, personnel came from many different cultures, their average level of formal schooling was low, and a number had histories of escape from hardship in their countries of origin, and struggle to establish themselves in their new country. Many were self-made people. This was a union town, so these individualists were also members—often active members—of a union. The design of the program of meetings and courses took these factors into account. Some of the meetings were held at a union centre, others on site at the company plant. Sessions were structured so that time could be given over to discussion and the exchange of ideas, personal stories and opinions. And in the final four-day course in the program, the trainers delegated much of the design and running of the course to the participants.

In the port authority, the workforce was responsible for the management of the port and the traffic through that port, the maintenance of docking facilities, the crewing and maintenance of emergency vessels, and monitoring the environment. Many from senior management and from the workforce were former seafarers, and an egalitarian culture prevailed as a result. The average level of education or training was reasonably high, with some of the crew on the vessels holding masters tickets. Many of the workers lived in portside suburbs and identified with the leisure activities as well as the business of the port. The workforce in effect formed a kind of industrial community within the portside community. Courses were held in a large motel, or in a club that served as a community focus in one of the portside suburbs. The program took account of the common seafaring history in its case studies and, although following a set timetable, allowed for a considerable amount of fairly loosely structured group work and general discussion.

In the government department, the industrial climate was poor. The department had been 'downsizing' at the time it wanted to introduce consultation. The majority of people involved in the setting up of consultative processes held white-collar posts. The program was in the form of a one-day briefing on work reorganisation and a one-day training program in group problem solving, both held in a formal training room attached to the department. To make the program possible, the trainer built in an opening session in which people were able to express their anger at the current state of the department, and in which he then sought their agreement to go on with the program. The program that followed was tightly designed, with a series of structured exercises and some of the key input in printed form.

PROGRAM DEVELOPMENT MODELS

A number of writers on adult education and training have tried to detail the complex process of devising, designing and implementing an educational program, and have developed models to follow. Some of these models are overly mechanistic, unrealistic, or simply too complex, but many contain excellent ideas and offer guidelines for a practitioner to follow—so long as he/she is ready to act not so much as a technician but as an artist.

I want to look at influences that have played a part in the formulation of some of these models, describe some of the most important models and, by looking at them in a roughly chronological order, identify some of the differences between them.

Four major influences

Some teaching programs are structured on a body of knowledge. The liberal tradition in adult education draws on the 19th-century university practice of dividing knowledge into disciplines. A course therefore would be defined by an academic discipline and taught by an expert in that discipline, and its structure would be based on the given wisdom among scholars about how that discipline was normally organised when taught. The process would be seen as transferring a body of knowledge in an orderly way from the expert to the students, and at the same time gradually initiating the students into the critical and research processes associated with that discipline. In the adult education context there might be some negotiation about the curriculum with the students (Albert Mansbridge, who founded the Workers Educational Association in Britain in 1904, encouraged the practice of the teacher discussing the curriculum of a course at the first meeting), but the image of this kind of adult education is still that of the lecturer addressing a body of students, the lecturer active and the students attentive but essentially passive recipients. As the teacher possesses the knowledge to be taught, he or she possesses the authority, designs the course according to the dictates of the subject and the traditions of the discipline within which that subject falls.

Some teaching programs are structured around the transfer of a skill. As the USA began asserting itself towards the end of the 19th century and into the 20th as the dominant industrial nation, North Americans were influential in developing industrial work structures and the kind of training that might go with it. Frederick Winslow Taylor developed his concepts of scientific management in the 1890s, breaking skills down into their component actions, developing new kinds of supervision and decision structures, setting standards for work, and developing forms of bonuses and piece rates. Training was reduced to an absolute minimum. As there was no need for them to know what happened further up the line or further down the line, in its extreme form this kind of induction into a factory was a form of training in a number of predetermined and prescribed actions without reference to any knowledge at all.

I have depicted here an extreme example of this kind of reductionist training, but an emphasis on actions rather than knowledge (behaviour rather than cognition) could be given a kind of respectability in contexts beyond the factory floor by reference to behavioural psychology, with its interest in stimulus and response and its emphasis on observable behaviours and measurable outcomes.

Some educators sought to wrest control of learning from the authority of the subject, the dehumanising influences of some kinds of industrial training, and the reductionist nature of some behavioural training. John Dewey (Cross-Durrant 1987) was one of the most prominent of these: he was responsible, through his writings and teaching during the first four decades of this century, for shifting some of the attention away from outcomes or bodies of knowledge and back to the learner as a person who has feelings, interests, needs and preoccupations and in whom learning is a phenomenon of lifelong growth. In the 1920s to 40s in the USA, Eduard Lindeman (Brookfield 1987) argued for adult education to be an act of free will, emphasised discussion as a method, and articulated a vision of a democratic society informed and safeguarded by networks of neighbourhood discussion groups.

These four influences, then—the liberal tradition's emphasis on knowledge and the subject, the Taylorist or behaviourist emphasis on performance and outcome, Dewey's focus on the learner as a person, and Lindeman's emphasis on society and community—are all to be seen in the first, and in many ways most influential, program development model I want to examine.

FROM PURPOSE TO NEED

In 1949 Ralph Tyler published a small but influential book called *Basic Principles in Curriculum and Instruction.* The book is in four major chapters, which in effect outline a four-stage model for planning an educational program:

* deciding on educational purposes;
* selecting learning experiences to achieve those purposes;
* organising the learning experiences for effective instruction;
* evaluating the effectiveness of the learning experiences.

Tyler calls his first chapter: 'What educational purposes should the school seek to attain?', and proposes that the source of educational objectives should be the learners themselves, contemporary life outside the school, the institution's and educator's philosophies, and subject-matter specialists. From the outset, therefore, Tyler is arguing that we should take account of people, society and the intellectual climate, as well as the experts in the subject, in deciding on our educational purposes and setting our course objectives.

In Tyler's second chapter, 'How can learning experiences be selected which are likely to be useful in attaining these objectives?', he makes the point that it is the experience the learner goes through that counts. The trainer may provide information, instruction and exercises and in effect create a complex environment for the participants, but it is in the participants' interaction with that environment that the learning takes place. Tyler states categorically that it is what the learners do that they learn, not what the teacher does (1949: 63). From this principle flow a number of others—that the participants must be given an opportunity to practise the kind of behaviour implied by the objective, that the practice should be satisfying, and that it be appropriate to the participants' present 'attainments' and 'predispositions'.

The third chapter, 'How can learning experiences be organised for effective instruction?', develops this theme of relevance to the learner when he warns us against designing programs or courses according to the apparent 'logic' of a subject. Tyler draws a distinction between logical organisation, which he describes as 'the relationship of curriculum elements as viewed by an expert in the field', and psychological organisation, which he describes as 'the relationship as it may appear to the learner' (1949: 97). He warns, for example, against automatically organising history courses chronologically. This may seem 'logical' but may not be the way a learner comes to grips with the meaning of history. The learner might actually see the relevance of historical analysis better by starting with an examination of a current state of affairs and then tracking back in various ways.

If we follow Tyler's reasoning, we release ourselves from the tyranny of the academic subject and can look for other ways of organising learning. Tyler suggests several ways of structuring a program. These include using a chronological order, increasing the application of a process or principle, expanding the breadth and range of an activity, starting with description followed by analysis, providing information followed by intellectual principles, and presenting a unified world view. However, he argues that whatever form the organisation of learning might take, three criteria should be met. These criteria are continuity, sequence and integration. Continuity, Tyler says, is achieved by the reiteration of major elements in the curriculum. If a skill, principle or concept is taught, then the course should provide 'recurring and continuing opportunity' for the skill, principle or concept to be practised, applied or dealt with 'again and again'. But *continuity*—simple reiteration—is not enough. A program of learning should have *sequence* as well: each experience should lead the learner to a higher level of study and understanding. Tyler's third criterion is *integration*: elements of learning should be organised in a way that allows the learner to develop a unified view, to integrate what has been learned into her or his behaviour as a whole.

In his fourth chapter, 'How can the effectiveness of learning experiences be evaluated?', Tyler argues that our purpose in education is to bring about a change in the behaviours of our participants and that to evaluate a learning program we need to 'appraise the behaviour' of our participants at an early point in the training, at a later point, and some time after the training has been completed.

It is in discussing evaluation that Tyler clearly demonstrates that he is still drawing on behaviourist ideas. Objectives, in a sense, frame his model, being both the starting and finishing points, and those objectives are to be expressed in terms of change in the learners' behaviours. Evaluation is achieved by observing those changed behaviours and checking them against the program's stated objectives. Despite his emphasis on the learner, his challenge to the authority of the subject and the subject specialists, and his argument that the program designer should take account of 'contemporary life', Tyler restricts his model by locking it into objectives. Once the objectives are set, and with evaluation relying on meeting those objectives, the educators and learners will be less likely to explore, take risks, go off at tangents, pursue their own interests, and engage in the kinds of learning that might take them into unexplored territory.

Inevitably some of Tyler's examples are dated, but his ideas are still current and many of the curriculum design models at present in use, particularly in institution-based adult education and training, could be said to be 'Tylerian'. It has to be noted, however, that Tyler's model differs in one significant way from many of these later models. Tyler discusses concepts of need, but understanding need is subsumed within the process of defining educational purposes; and his model does not, as many later models do, include the assessment of needs as a clearly articulated and significant first step in the process of developing a learning program.

Cyril Houle, in his book *The Design of Education* (1972), expands Tyler's model and interprets it into a specifically *adult* educational form. Houle envisages adult learning taking place in such places as 'the factory, the community, the labour union' as well as more conventional educational settings, and he argues that educational responses in 'natural settings' will need to be many-faceted (Houle 1972: 20):

> For example, a safety specialist acting as a change agent may reduce the highway accident rate by better law enforcement, improved engineering, and more effective education. He may apply this third remedy in many ways: mass campaigns to inform drivers of the rules of the road, stringent training programs for those who want drivers' licences, instruction of engineers on appropriate standards of high-way construction and of law enforcement officers on how to carry out their duties, and special courses required of habitual breakers of traffic laws.

This leads Houle to argue that there will be different categories of program, and that the differences between them will be defined by which players hold the authority and control over the program and whom the program is intended for, rather than by the subject matter or methods used. Houle presents his model as a number of decisions to take rather than steps to follow, and accompanies each decision-point or component in his model with detailed discussion and examples.

Houle does not highlight the concept of need. It is Malcolm Knowles who places the concept of need firmly in a program development model for adult education and training. Knowles' book, entitled *The Modern Practice of Adult Education*, was first published in 1970, revised and updated, and published in its definitive form in 1980. The book has been hugely influential, particularly in adult education and training in the USA. Knowles' model involves the following steps:

1. *Creating a climate conducive to learning.* Here he discusses ways of establishing an educative environment within an organisation that is built on a democratic philosophy and a recognition of the need for change and growth.
2. *Establishing a structure.* Here he discusses ways of creating the right kinds of committees or other structures to support and promote adult education within the organisation.
3. *Assessing needs and interests.* Here he examines different kinds

of needs and interests that individuals, organisations and communities might have, and then outlines a number of ways of identifying them.

4. *Translating needs into program objectives.* Here he discusses how the needs that have been assessed should be screened through three filters: the purposes of the institution; feasibility; and the interests of the clientele.

5. *Designing a program.* Here he discusses various principles of program and course design, and processes for selecting different formats for learning.

6. *Operating the program.* Here he discusses the practicalities of implementing and managing a program, including recruitment of teachers, promotion, recruitment of participants, and management of finance and facilities.

7. *Evaluating the program.* Here he discusses purposes and methods of evaluation, and the uses to which the findings can be put.

Knowles' book is filled with useful guidelines, practical hints, case studies and examples. His particular contributions are an emphasis on establishing a climate and structure conducive to adult learning, the highlighting of the concept of need, and his attempts to reconcile the needs of the individual with those of the organisation.

AN INSTITUTIONAL MODEL

Tyler, Houle and Knowles are all American. Other North Americans, such as Patrick Boyle and Roby Kidd, have offered their versions of a program development model, but as Boone (1985) and Brookfield (1986) both point out, most of these models derive from Tyler's and resemble each other quite closely. Brookfield identifies a pervasive 'institutional model of program development' in the literature on program development, and suggests that it comprises five stages (1986: 204):

> Identify needs, define objectives (preferably in behavioural terms), identify learning experiences to meet these objectives, organise learning experiences into a plan with scope and sequence, and evaluate program outcomes in terms of the attainments specified in stage two.

Brookfield (1986: 206–32) then mounts a detailed criticism of this model. He notes that in his own experience and in the views of adult educators he has trained, life simply is not like that. The model, with its emphasis on objectives, is inflexible and derivative of a Taylorist concept of work organisation and training. It does not take account of the adventure and unexpectedness in learning, and ignores or makes difficult to foster any 'significant personal learning' that might be unrelated to the objectives of adult educators or organisations. If locked into objectives, the parties involved cannot continually renegotiate the curriculum. Variation and flexibility become difficult. Brookfield questions the ascendancy of the concept of need, suggesting that this has become something of an adult education shibboleth, and that basing program development on a response to the felt needs of learners 'condemns education to an adaptive, reactive mode and turns educators into mere providers of consumer goods' (1986: 222). He argues that the model ignores the contextual factors that can play such a powerful part in defining the form a program will finally take. And he maintains that, in providing a formula to follow, the model offers the promise of success—'the chimera of perfectability', as he calls it—and does not acknowledge the possibility of failure.

FROM LEARNER TO ORGANISATION

In *Developing Programs in Adult Education* (1985), Edgar Boone proposes and outlines a model which is clearly an attempt to break free of the 'institutional' model Brookfield identified. Ironically, Boone's model actually marks a move during the 1980s away from a concern with the learner and the learner's needs back to a concern with the organisation. The three major subprocesses are: planning; design and implementation; and evaluation and accountability. Under *planning* there is a whole section made up of five tasks, all concerned with understanding and developing commitment to the organisation and to its renewal. In another section there are four tasks aimed at linking the organisation to its public. Under *evaluation and accountability* there is a task concerned with using evaluation findings for organisational renewal.

Boone's model is clearly located in an organisational context, and appears to be based on the assumption that one of the main reasons for conducting educational programs is the development and renewal of the organisation. Boone provides a bridge, then, between the Tylerian models of the 1950s, 60s and 70s with their interest, in part at least, in individual learners and their needs and interests, and those human resource development and industrial training models developed in the 1980s to 90s that are concerned with the training of functions and the promotion of organisational interests.

71

FROM PEOPLE TO HUMAN RESOURCES

In Australia until the 1960s, most training for work was done either at an educational institution, generally through an apprenticeship system that involved some training at work and some training in an educational institution, or simply in an ad-hoc way on the job. By the 1960s a growing number of enterprises were providing some kind of in-house training for their employees. In larger enterprises training units or departments were set up, and by the 1980s these units were being given briefs that went beyond providing in-house training courses. They were being made responsible for coordinating all the teaching and learning that might go on in the enterprise, whether it was induction, formal in-house training, on-the-job training, mentoring, or the referral of personnel to training outside the enterprise.

This expanded responsibility for training and learning in an enterprise was called human resource development (HRD), and the term means what it says. People are seen as resources, and it is argued that by putting them through a program of learning the enterprise can add value to them and so can improve the quality of its resources and enhance its 'human capital' (Nadler & Wiggs 1986).

The HRD models that emerged during the 1980s are Tylerian, but with certain significant differences. Those concerned with training, supporting and developing executives and middle managers use processes influenced by Knowles' model, as his model allows for the mixing of the personal development of the individual with the requirements of the organisation and society (see Knowles and Associates 1984).

In HRD models concerned with industrial training and aimed at the line worker, the focus is shifted away from individual or organisational need to task. Training is concerned with enabling employees to perform their tasks and roles efficiently, in order to make the organisation's processes and structures function effectively to achieve the organisation's goals. The dominant and most influential steps in the program development process in this context, therefore, are an analysis of the structure and functions of the organisation and an analysis of the tasks and roles of personnel within the structure. Attention is not on people with needs but on functions that can be broken up into tasks, skills and, more recently, competencies.

Other differences flow from the concern with organisational goals and the focus on tasks. Objectives are likely to be concerned with the more limited idea of improving a standardised performance rather than the larger idea of changing behaviour. And

72

judgment of the program is more likely to be based on assessment and testing of the participants in the program than on evaluation—that is, examination of the worth—of the program as a whole.

Laurie Field, in *Skilling Australia* (1990), applies a Tylerian model to the world of industrial training. He draws his examples from the training of hairdressers, road tanker-drivers, draftspeople, bank clerks, car mechanics, chemical workers, telecommunications technicians, retail industry workers and workers in the food industry. His model consists of the following stages:

1. *Investigate skills and training issues.* Here he discusses how the trainer might enter a workplace, carry out an exploratory study, and then use different kinds of research to understand the workplace and identify the problems that can be tackled through training.

2. *Analyse competencies for a job.* Here he discusses the concept of skill, and offers a schema for describing occupations and jobs and then developing comprehensive lists of competencies necessary to perform those jobs.

3. *State performance objectives.* Here he discusses how to write performance objectives that state the activity, the conditions under which the activity must be performed, and the standards that must be achieved for each competency identified.

4. *Structure a training program.* Here he examines different ways of building a sequence into a training program, and the different ways skills training can be provided. These include off-site training in a college, in-house training, simulator training (often using computer models), and on-the-job training.

5. *Deliver the training.* Field then provides a number of chapters looking at different methods of delivering training. There are chapters on the design and use of job aids such as reference guides, user manuals and computer aids; on-the-job training; the use of computers in training; and modularised training. He also devotes a chapter to the processes involved in explaining and demonstrating a task.

6. *Supervise practice.* At several stages in the book Field discusses the processes of transferring skills learnt to the actual job. In one chapter he examines ways of providing the learner with structured and supervised practice in the skills learnt.

7. *Assess skills.* Here he discusses ways of testing learners' competence, and assessing the change in their skills and knowledge as a result of the training.

As even this brief summary indicates, Field's model is concerned with getting people to *perform* more skilfully to make the organisation more efficient and more productive. He argues that organisations can and should be changed to increase efficiency, and that there should be moves towards a 'more cooperative, participative relationship between workers and management' (1990: 8). But there seems little room in the model for providing opportunities in training to enable people to think and behave differently and therefore significantly to alter the goals and structures in the organisation (but see Field's work on the 'learning organisation', chapter 10).

COMPETENCY-BASED CURRICULUM

Field's model assumes that the task and competency analysis will be done in house and the process controlled by the trainer or human resource developer in consultation with the organisation. However, in the 1990s this part of the program development process for industrial and workplace training is increasingly being taken out of the hands of the locally based trainer and placed under the control of national, state or industry-wide bodies.

Starting in the mid-1980s, concerted efforts were made by unions, managements and government to develop manufacturing industries, reorganise the way people worked, restructure industrial relations awards and agreements, and make career paths available to all workers. As part of this complex process, trades, occupations and professions were analysed and described in terms of competencies. By 1994 a number of national and industry-wide bodies had been established to oversee what became known as the training reform agenda (see chapter 6). Some of these bodies were responsible for commissioning analyses of jobs and occupations in terms of competencies, others to establish and apply a standards framework, and still others to design competency-based curricula and oversee the granting of credentials to competency-based training in both private and public sector training and in educational agencies.

In a sense we could argue that this constitutes the most recent program design model in the Tylerian mode. Experts, in consultation with practitioners, analyse an occupation or profession, identifying and describing the competencies needed to perform that occupation or profession effectively, and then educators and trainers design programs covering those competencies. The organisational analysis, the identifying of needs, and the setting of objectives are conducted at an industry-wide, state or national level, and in some cases these centralised bodies may also design training kits, modules and courses. The role of the individual educator or trainer at the local enterprise level is diminished and the opportunities to develop original and creative educational and training programs reflecting and responding to local conditions are severely curtailed. (For further discussion of competency-based education, see chapters 7, 10 and 12.)

FORMS OF DELIVERY

Many educational programs are delivered by educators, trainers, instructors or facilitators dealing directly with groups of participants in classrooms, training rooms or workshops. But there are other ways of delivering educational programs. From the days of adult schools and mechanics institutes in Britain in the 1820s, and Charles Knight's *Society for the Diffusion of Useful Knowledge*, forms of correspondence course have been employed. Since then correspondence courses have been used in many countries, especially where large distances made conventional forms of program delivery difficult. Other forms of 'correspondence course' delivery include the study circle, developed in Sweden but now used in many countries around the world (by several Indian trade unions, for example); and discussion groups backed up by 'book boxes' and discussion notes delivered to the group. With the advent of television, and then the video recorder, 'open learning' methods of program delivery were developed, perhaps the best-known being the Open University established in the UK in the 1970s. Open learning made use of spare time on TV channels to provide lectures and instruction, and these were backed up by notes and readings sent out in the correspondence mode. Later forms of open learning simply included the videotape with the other course materials. In the 1980s and then into the 90s, with the development of other forms of electronic communication such as fax, e-mail and the Internet in its current worldwide form, a wide range of modes of program delivery have been developed, and the generic term now in use to describe this proliferation is 'flexible learning'.

EXPERIENTIAL LEARNING PROGRAMS

Not all educators or trainers look to the Tylerian family of program development models for guidance. There are other modes of operation and other theoretical frameworks.

Most Tylerian models owe something to behavioural psychology, and educators and trainers using them are more likely to be managing instrumental kinds of learning. But there are educators and trainers who, in the course of designing programs of learning, draw their inspiration from the fields of developmental and humanistic psychology. These educators and trainers are less likely to be concerned with instrumental learning, and so less concerned with identifying and achieving objectives and with the didactic forms of teaching and instruction that may be used to achieve those kinds of objectives.

Carl Rogers, whose influence on some areas of adult education has been enormous, rejects the teaching role (1983: 120):

> So now with some relief I turn to an activity, a purpose, which really warms me—the facilitation of learning. When I have been able to transform a group—and here I mean all members of the group, myself included—into a community of learners, then the excitement is almost beyond belief. To free curiosity; to permit individuals to go charging off in new directions dictated by their own interests; to unleash the sense of enquiry; to open everything to questioning and exploration; to recognise that everything is in the process of change—here is an experience I can never forget.

Within this statement are two important ideas about the organisation and management of learning. One is concerned with group process and the creation of a community of learners, and the other is concerned with facilitation and the opening of everything to questioning and exploration.

Some educators and trainers, then, develop learning programs based on various ideas about group process. They bring people together and then, through different kinds of leadership, management or facilitation, help that group pass through a series of stages in which the members of the group learn about and from each other and so learn about themselves. In some cases the purpose of the learning program is experiencing and coming to understand the group process itself. One of the most often-quoted descriptions of group process is that of Tuckman (1965), whose stages are forming, storming, norming, and performing. These four stages can be used as a basis for organising and managing an experiential learning program.

Other educators and trainers may use the group process as a form of program design but more actively facilitate the process (Heron 1989), or offer as part of the process specific exercises and experiences on which the learners can then be encouraged to reflect in order to learn (Miller 1993). These facilitated experiences may be games, role-play, and exercises of various kinds such as metaphor analysis or critical incident analysis. The learning program in this case is built around organising the experience, debriefing and reflecting on the experience, and identifying the learning achieved through the process.

Boud et al. (1985) construct a model to explain the process of helping turn experience into learning through reflection, and this model can serve both as an examination of the process of learning and as a guide for the design of a learning event or program. The model contains three clusters of activities: *experiences*, under which they list behaviour, ideas and feelings; *reflective processes*, under which they list returning to experience, utilising positive feelings, removing obstructing feelings, and re-evaluating experience; and *outcomes*, under which they list new perspectives on experience, change in behaviour, readiness for application, and commitment to action.

These kinds of experiential program are rarely constructed on detailed, identified needs. More often they seem to be based on the general assumption that all human beings have a need for 'growth' or 'self-actualisation'. Objectives are similarly vague or unspecified, often including such goals as helping people to know themselves better, learn more about the human condition, interact and relate better, and develop empathy. Evaluation, therefore, will have to rely to a large degree on the reported feelings of satisfaction or dissatisfaction of the participants. Indeed, experiential programs often appear to be based on the belief that within all of us there is some essential human essence, which is good; and that, if the program helps people come to know themselves better and understand that internal essence, although the process might be confronting and painful, the outcomes will be beneficial.

There is another model of experiential learning that can be used in the development of educational programs but that tends to be more contextualised and therefore concerned with more outward-looking kinds of learning. This model has its origins in the work of Lewin and then Kolb. Kolb (1984) describes a learning cycle that includes concrete experience, followed by observation and reflection on that experience, followed by the development of hypotheses and concepts from that reflection, followed by the testing of those concepts, followed by more concrete experience, and so on around the cycle (see chapter 3). This cycle is taken and adapted by people concerned with action research, and it is in this form that a model for developing educational programs arises.

Action research is located in a social or organisational context. It normally arises out of a dissatisfaction and a sense that a system or situation or organisation or context could be improved. A researcher then plans a change, implements the change, observes and reflects on the results of this experience, draws conclusions and hypotheses, plans further changes based on what has been learnt, implements these new and perhaps better-informed changes, and the process continues. The process is commonly depicted as a spiral (see chapter 1), with the spiral continuing until the changes are deemed satisfactory, perhaps on the basis of criteria that have been developed and clarified during the process (Kemmis 1980; Field 1990).

As action research normally takes place in a 'real-life context', a workplace or a community for example, the researcher is likely to involve some at least of the people in that context, making the process a collaborative one. Groups of workers or community members will share in the planning, the experience, the reflection and drawing of tentative conclusions, the planning of the next experiences and so on. In this form, they become both researchers *and* learners within the action-research project. And in this form the action-research project becomes a model for a vital, active, 'organic' kind of educational program. (For further discussion of experience-based learning, see chapter 14.)

PROGRAMS FOR CRITICAL THINKING AND SOCIAL ACTION

Action research is a structured process with clearly defined phases. But there are other kinds of educator who intervene in people's lives with little or no predetermined structure in mind. These educators adopt principles and make use of processes derived from the fields of adult education, community work, community development, political organisation and social action (Lovett 1988; Newman 1993). They are often activists themselves, guided by their own ideologies, beliefs and visions. Often their objectives are to redress inequities and to help people who do not have a voice gain some control over their own affairs. Their methods are to engage in the lives of their learners, to listen and learn, to ask questions and, through the example of their own questioning and learning, to encourage the people they are with to begin asking questions and learning themselves. These educators are likely to share their vision with their learners but, if they are committed to helping people take control of their own lives, will offer it as an example for the learners to consider and not as a prescription. And they will evaluate their work not in terms of the individual learning achieved but in terms of the social change that has occurred.

There is a growing body of writing on adult education in social action (see chapter 17) in which the work and writings of Paulo Freire (see Taylor 1993) remain hugely influential. Freire's approach is as much a philosophical framework as a methodology, but within it we can identify a number of principles and processes. Freire began his particular form of educational work in his native Brazil with shanty-town dwellers and peasant villagers in the early 1960s. The educators would seek entry to a village or community, and engage in a period of listening and learning. Through dialogue they would try to establish themes that recurred in the discourse of the villagers or shanty-town dwellers and that had real significance in their lives. As the program developed, the educators would begin feeding back to the learners codified versions of the themes, often doing this in the form of line drawings or photographs. Through dialogue and discussion centred on the drawings or photographs, the educators would encourage the learners 'to name their world'; that is, they would help the learners to begin articulating their lives and the context in which they lived in terms of problems and challenges that they could tackle. In this way the educators and learners worked together to change the learners' perception of the world, from a given they must fatalistically accept to a world on which they could act in order to bring about change. The educators did not instruct, but asked questions; they became problem posers rather than problem solvers; and, if the process was successful, the learners began changing from being 'objects of social history' to 'subjects of their own destiny' (Freire 1972a & b, 1976).

Through his work and his writing, Freire has provided inspiration for educators developing programs of learning in many parts of the world (see chapter 17; Newman 1993: 218–43, 1994: 35–6, 142–4). We end this chapter on three examples of such programs. A trainer constructed a week-long residential course for officials of a national union in the finance sector around a series of scenarios, all expressed in terms of problems and reflecting themes which, he had established through preliminary discussions, were important to those officials (Newman 1993). A teacher of English to speakers of other languages at a TAFE college developed a whole program aimed at helping women learn English through the use of posters, poems, discussion and dialogue, which focused on the kinds of pressures, inequalities and challenges they faced as migrant women at home, at work and within the broader national culture (Bee 1982, 1984). And during 1993 at Tranby Aboriginal Cooperative College, a teacher devised a combined literacy and photography program towards the end of which she and the participants travelled to a coastal indigenous community and, through photography, visits, discussion and writing, compiled a report on the Aboriginal people of that region, their history and

79

present-day enterprises and communities; and then, by using the text and images they had compiled, reflected on their own Aboriginality and their place in contemporary society.

CONCLUSION

The literature of adult education and training may contain ideas and models for those developing programs to draw inspiration from and to follow, but there are no hard and fast rules. The educator must approach the design of learning as a creative endeavour. And as the learners are adults, and the learning takes place in social and organisational contexts which the learners may be able to change, there will be times when the design of an educational program becomes a political endeavour as well.

FURTHER READING

Brookfield, S. 1986 *Understanding and Facilitating Adult Learning*. San Francisco: Jossey-Bass, Chs 7–10.
Field, L. 1990 *Skilling Australia: A Handbook for Trainers and TAFE Teachers*. Melbourne: Longman Cheshire.
Houle, C. 1972 *The Design of Education*. San Francisco: Jossey-Bass.
Knowles, M. 1980 *The Modern Practice of Adult Education*. Chicago: Association Press, Follet.
Newman, M. 1993 *The Third Contract: Theory and Practice in Trade Union Training*. Sydney: Stewart Victor Publishing.
——1994 *Defining the Enemy: Adult Education in Social Action*. Sydney: Stewart Victor.
Tyler, R.W. 1949 *Basic Principles of Curriculum and Instruction*. Chicago: University of Chicago Press.

5

Evaluating adult education and training

James Athanasou

Evaluation has a place in every field of human activity. It is especially relevant in education or training in order to ensure: that the needs of learners are being satisfied; that there are benefits to the organisation; that the instructional approach is efficient; that the most effective learning methods are being used; and that the rights of all interested parties are being maintained. Evaluation is seen as one practical step to improving education or training. Its aim is to help us make judgments about the appropriateness, merit, worth, effectiveness and efficiency of a program.

The purpose of this chapter is to provide an overview of issues in the evaluation of adult education and training. The introductory section surveys the relevance and nature of evaluation as a field of practice in education or training and outlines some of the main developments in evaluation approaches. The second part provides a framework appropriate for use in adult education settings. The focus is on public, structured, formal and summative evaluations, and on the key steps for evaluating a program or service in adult education and training and other human services.

NATURE AND PURPOSE OF EVALUATION

Evaluation encompasses the word 'value', and is distinct from the testing or assessment of learning (see Athanasou 1997: 3). It is sometimes confused with research or inquiry because it involves a variety of research methods, but unlike pure research it has an applied and policy emphasis. The greatest benefit of evaluation for those involved in training or education is that it helps us to

Figure 5.1   The foundations of educational evaluation

PURPOSES OF
EVALUATIONS

• to improve
• for decisions
• as a response to controversy
• to compare
• to judge
• as a management requirement
• to determine effectiveness
• to assess quality
• to determine performance

EVALUATIONS

THE OBJECTS OF
EVALUATIONS

• programs
• policies
• initiatives

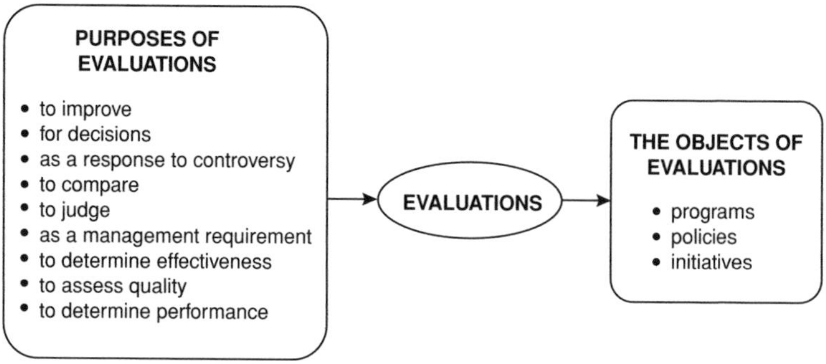

think critically about what we are doing, and this critical thinking is based on empirical observations and evidence.

The word 'evaluate' comes from the French *valuer*, meaning to value, and also from the Latin *e*, meaning from, and *valuere*, to be strong and to be worthwhile. The commonsense meaning of the word is to determine the worth of something or to appraise it, in the sense of calculating its value. In social and educational contexts, then, evaluation has the formal meaning of determining the value of a program or service, policy or initiative. A US joint committee on standards for evaluation defined it as 'the systematic merit or worth of some object' (Joint Committee 1994). Figure 5.1 lists some purposes of program evaluation.

Educational evaluation is a natural response to improving any learning and instruction. Over the past 150 years, evaluation as a discipline has developed as a formal way of examining the impact of public educational practices, programs and policies. Its initial inspiration was the positivist assumption that 'the methodology of science can be harnessed for the improvement and effective management of social affairs' (Norris 1990: 11). Related assumptions were: (a) that research is more authoritative or trustworthy than individuals' judgments; and (b) that the knowledge of experts will lead to better decisions. The conviction was that evaluation served a vital and practical end—the improvement of educational practice and outcomes (Popham 1993: 5).

DEVELOPMENT OF EDUCATIONAL EVALUATION

The early history of formal education was not characterised by the need for evaluations as we know them today. In 19th-century

mass schooling, fairly fixed beliefs about the purposes of education and about how people learn controlled the delivery of
instruction. Educational evaluation was originally equated to the
grading of students and testing: around 1845, the Boston School
committee developed the Boston surveys, which were printed tests
for the large-scale testing of pupils. It was also exemplified by
the introduction of a spelling test to some 30 000 pupils in
American schools by Joseph Rice late in the century. His purpose
was to evaluate the routine spelling drills that were common in
schools. The idea that testing was the most important way of
evaluating education has a long history, and is still evident in the
community through basic skills testing or performance in statewide
examinations.

In the first half of the 20th century the technology of
psychometrics (i.e. psychological testing) became influential in
many industrialised countries. Tests were often used to evaluate
the effectiveness of educational treatments. This approach is
related to the still influential view that testing is 'objective' and
outcome data are indicators of teacher or school effectiveness.

OBJECTIVES AND GOALS AS A BASIS FOR EVALUATION

Ralph Tyler, who considered evaluation as the examination of a
program's quality, brought about an important shift in the concept
of evaluation in the 1930s. Tyler was invited to direct the
evaluation staff of the 'Eight Year Study' (1932–40), which compared conventional and progressive schools. This study arose from
concern that some colleges were not admitting the graduates of
progressive schools. These were schools that were developing
educational programs appropriate to the needs of their students,
without regard to certification or accreditation. Tyler was among
the first to apply evaluation to programs rather than to the mere
testing of students' learning.

At the time this was a significant development. A program
would now be judged successful according to the extent to which
the objectives had been met. Tyler (1949) stated these objectives
in observable terms, and developed measures and collected data
in order to make recommendations concerning the program goals.
The objectives model of evaluation offered a rational approach to
education and training. While it was suited to some programs with
very specific outcomes, it took no account of differences in
students' backgrounds or experiences, and was unsuitable as an
all-purpose evaluation model. Moreover, Scriven (1967), in his
paper *The Methodology of Evaluation*, emphasised the importance
of rational (scientific) judgment, and argued that another failing

of the objectives model was that there were no procedures for judging the worth of the goals themselves: ' . . . it is obvious that if the goals aren't worth achieving then it is uninteresting how well they are achieved'. He distinguished the formative and summative roles of educational evaluation. A formative evaluation is conducted during a program in order to bring about changes, if required; a summative evaluation summarises evidence, and occurs mainly at the conclusion of a program.

OTHER PERSPECTIVES ON EVALUATION

In the USA, another important impetus for the role of evaluation was the Elementary and Secondary Education Act (1965), which introduced mandatory evaluation of projects, programs and instructional materials. At that time the favoured method of evaluation was some type of comparison (e.g. with control groups). Evaluation projects were treated as experiments (e.g. with hypothesis testing), but this type of design was not always capable of dealing with the complexity and specificity of learning.

In a 1963 paper, Cronbach argued that evaluation should deal less with program comparison than with the extent to which a program promoted its desired consequences. For Cronbach the outcomes of instruction were always multivariate, and his concern was to: (a) extend the range of evidence that was collected to describe an educational program and; (b) pinpoint the features of an education program that required further attention and revision. Cronbach made other points that are still relevant to evaluators, namely: (a) that there are links between evaluation and decision making; (b) that evaluation performs a number of functions (e.g. course improvement, overhaul of administrative policies); (c) that follow-up or longitudinal studies are extremely important in determining the lasting effects of educational programs; (d) that learner performance and/or experimental studies should not be the only focus and method of evaluation; and (e) that measurement approaches to evaluation should be broadened to include the sampling of items (i.e. specific instances) and matrix sampling (i.e. avoiding the need to assess every outcome with every person).

Other perspectives on evaluation built on Cronbach's insight. Scriven (1967) advocated a form of goal-free evaluation. In this approach the evaluator recorded the major effects of a program, which could then be compared with its original purpose. It was a significant learner-centred innovation that acknowledged the unplanned results of education. Performance data were gathered to establish the merit or worth of educational activities, and the evaluator was responsible for judging the merit of the goals. The strength of this approach was that it encouraged educators to systematically investigate educational processes and to critically examine the value of educational goals.

Stake (1967), in a seminal paper, went on to tackle the important question of what kind of evidence an evaluator should collect. He focused on the functional goal of evaluation—namely, its attempt to judge the worth or merit of something. He noted: 'Both description and judgement are essential—in fact they are the basic acts of evaluation'. This approach involved the description of a program, reporting the description to relevant audiences, obtaining and analysing their judgments, and reporting the analysed judgments back to the audiences.

At about the same time the 'decision-management' approach to evaluation emerged. For Stufflebeam (1971, 1983), the evaluation of a program was linked to decision making about four dimensions of the program: context, input, process, and product. This approach encouraged educators to systematically generate criteria by which educational programs could be evaluated: context criteria for planning; input criteria for programming; process criteria for implementation; and product criteria for prediction or recycling decisions. The value of this model lay in its recognition of the need for holistic evaluation. A program needed to be evaluated in its context and through its different phases.

Objectives, judgmental and decision-making models were developed largely for school contexts. Although these approaches contributed to an awareness of the merit of program goals, they did not always provide the comprehensive basis required for program evaluation in adult education settings. A comprehensive approach that is particularly suitable for adult education is Kirkpatrick's (1996) hierarchy of evaluation, which focuses on four levels of program outcome:

1. *reaction*: program participants' estimates of satisfaction provide an immediate level of evaluation;
2. *learning*: the extent of learning (i.e. skills acquisition, attitude change) that has been achieved is also of interest;
3. *behaviour*: the extent to which learning has generalised (e.g. to the work situation), or there has been a transfer of skills is assessed at this level through follow-up after a program;
4. *results*: the wider impact of a program in the community or the organisation is assessed at this level in the hierarchy.

Kirkpatrick's approach offers a straightforward, pragmatic and initial basis for an evaluation. It is multidimensional, integrated, and especially suited to those training contexts where specific

Table 5.1   A tentative classification of the predominant characteristics of evaluation approaches

Approaches	objective vs subjective	standard vs varied	analytical vs descriptive	social vs technical	specific vs wider	explicit vs implicit
Objectives-based evaluation	objective	standard	analytical	technical	specific	explicit
Evaluation for decision making	subjective	standard	analytical	technical	specific	implicit
Context–input–process–product	subjective	standard	analytical	technical	wider	explicit
Cost–benefit analysis	objective	standard	analytical	technical	specific	explicit
Judgment of worth and merit	subjective	varied	descriptive	social	wider	implicit
Outcome- or output-oriented models	objective	standard	analytical	technical	specific	explicit
Illuminative approaches	subjective	varied	descriptive	social	wider	implicit
Community impact of a program	subjective	varied	descriptive	social	wider	implicit

outputs are of interest right from the outset. A general principle of integrated evaluation is that it must be conceived comprehensively, even if only a part of the total process is being evaluated.

In summary, there are now more than 20 major educational evaluation approaches from which to choose, including:

- objectives-based evaluation (Tyler 1949);
- evaluation for decision making (Cronbach 1963);
- context–input–process–product (Stufflebeam 1971);
- community impact of a program (Stake 1967);
- expert judgment (Eisner 1976);
- cost–benefit analysis (Levin 1983);
- evaluation as a judgment of worth and merit (Scriven 1967);
- outcome- or output-oriented models (Kirkpatrick 1996);
- illuminative approaches (Parlett & Dearden 1977; Kemmis 1980).

The plethora of evaluation models reflects the diversity of the contexts in which adult educators and trainers work and the variety of views they hold about education. One way of making sense of these diverse evaluation models is to categorise them according to a number of dichotomies: objective versus subjective; standardised versus varied; analytical versus descriptive; social versus technical; specific group interest versus wider social interest; explicit ideology versus implicit ideology (see Table 5.1).

Evaluation of education and training can thus take many forms.

Figure 5.2   The ECCOES evaluation framework

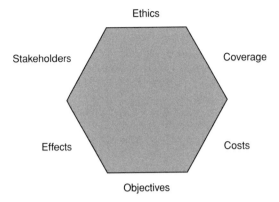

Ethics

Stakeholders   Coverage

Effects   Costs

Objectives

It can be formal or informal in nature (i.e. for organisational or personal use); it can be internal or external (i.e. conducted by yourself or consultants); formative or summative. The complexity of educational issues and their uniqueness is such that specific models or 'cookbook' approaches to evaluation are not always helpful. It is doubtful that one approach is sufficient for all circumstances, and a general strategy that is eclectic in nature is required. Experience in evaluations and research quickly reveals that these activities can be highly subjective, ideological and political. I favour an integrated and multidimensional view of evaluation, believing that this is more likely than others to capture the complexity of educational processes and outcomes.

HOLISTIC EVALUATION OF A PROGRAM

Practitioners looking for some way of deciding the worth and merit of a program, policy or other initiative may want to consider a holistic approach that encompasses many of the features of these earlier evaluation models. The particular approach to be considered here is the 'ECCOES' model, which generates information about six dimensions of a program (see Figure 5.2). These are, reading clockwise from the bottom of the hexagon: the objectives of the program, its effects or outcomes, the stakeholders or interest groups involved, ethical issues raised by the program, the coverage or reach of the program, and cost issues.

    ECCOES provides a framework and a structure for decision making in evaluation. In this approach six broad questions, each

Table 5.2 Checklist for holistic evaluations of training services

---

Issue 1. Is the program or service ethical?
Ethics/morality
Social and political implications
Legality
Any harmful ecological issues
Any impact on privacy or confidentiality
Any abuse of privilege
Reasons for the evaluation
Whether human ethical guidelines have been satisfied
Whether evaluation standards have been satisfied

Issue 2. To what extent does the program or service cover those who are most in need?
The incidence of the educational or training need
The numbers of people who are at risk
The prevalence of the educational or training need
The sensitivity of the program
The specificity of the education or training
The attendance and completion rates for any course

Issue 3. What are the costs, benefits and utilities of the program or service?
Cost feasibility
Cost-effectiveness
Cost–utility
Cost–benefit

Issue 4. Did the program or service achieve its key objective(s)?
Reactions
Learning
Behaviours
Results

Issue 5. What is the net effect of the program or service?
Comparison with other programs
Comparison with predetermined standards
Determining statistical effect size (if relevant)

Issue 6. To what extent have the perspectives and interests of all stakeholders been considered and met?
Why was the program, policy or initiative introduced?
What are its intended educational outcomes?
How do people feel about the program?
Who are the key stakeholders?
What are the social costs and benefits of the program?
What constraints are operating?
What aspects will influence decision-making?
How will these evaluation findings be used?

Source: Adapted from Athanasou (1998a: 102).

of which generates a number of more specific issues (see Table 5.2), guide the work of evaluators. ECCOES is a synthetic and individualistic approach, because each evaluator is required to combine the information from these six areas in order to determine the merit or worthiness of any program or service. Some users will emphasise questions of ethics or stakeholder involvement, others might focus mainly on costs and effectiveness. These six dimensions provide a framework that will help in making decisions about the worthiness of programs, policies or services. ECCOES does not advocate a single correct way of conducting an evaluation; rather, it suggests a variety of ways of gathering and analysing data—empirical as well as naturalistic, descriptive as well as phenomenological.

Once all the information is assembled, the evaluator has to decide the basis on which the judgment of overall merit will be made. For instance, a program may have wide coverage and be overly expensive at the outset yet very effective in the long-term; the same program may be popular with consumers but opposed by some stakeholders; and it may have some questionable short-term social implications, and so on. Each evaluator will bring to these issues his/her values and perceptions, which must ultimately influence any reporting as well as decision making on the evaluation. Thus, evaluation can never be 'objective', and there is no 'right' answer (Athanasou 1998: 101):

> Some criteria will be more relevant to you than others but all need to be weighted appropriately for your decision. Such decisions involve complex judgements about each educational program or service. Maybe the best that we can hope for is to provide information that confirms our ideas about the potential of a program or that refutes claims about the value of a program. In this way educational and training evaluations will add to our store of knowledge about what works and what does not work in education and training and how well it works.

Case 5.1 provides the results from the judgments of one evaluator, which suggest that evaluation judgments are highly idiosyncratic.

CASE 5.1 A QUANTITATIVE CASE STUDY OF THE COMPONENTS OF A HOLISTIC JUDGMENT

This case study uses what is called a lens model analysis to determine the reliability of one evaluator's pattern of judgments (Cooksey 1996).

Method

An independent judge was asked to evaluate the overall worth or merit of each one of 60 adult training programs on a scale from 0 (low) to 9 (high). The programs were rated randomly from 0 (low) to 9 (high) on each of the six features of ethics, costs, coverage, objectives, effects, and stakeholders. The mean value of the features was 4.6 (SD=1.6). The features were independent, and the inter-correlation between them ranged from –023 to +0.20.

Results

The overall multiple correlation between the six cues and the subjective judgment of worth of a program was 0.85. The pattern of regression weights for each of the cues indicated that judgments were based largely on the effectiveness, ethics and coverage of the program. Costs and objectives were only a minor influence in the making of judgments of merit or worth. (These regression weights are estimates of the influence of each feature holding all other features constant, whereas the correlations do not take all other factors into account.) Results indicated that this evaluator's pattern of judgments was relatively predictable.

Features	Correlation between each feature and judgment	Regression weights for each feature on the overall judgment
Ethics	0.27	0.61***
Coverage	0.35	0.53 **
Costs	–0.29	–0.04
Objectives	0.33	0.12
Effectiveness	0.61	0.78 ***
Stakeholders	–0.08	0.10

Before any evaluation of learning and instruction, there are some design features of the learning context that may need to be considered. Some of these are listed in Table 5.3 and may themselves be the subjects of a technical investigation of the instructional processes. For instance, internal learner characteristics such as prior knowledge and interest have an impact on learning in multimedia environments, together with external features such as learner control or instructional design (Lawless & Brown 1997).

It is important to distinguish between microevaluations, or investigations that focus on one or two aspects of a program, and macroevaluations, which consider the overall merit or worth of a program. Microevaluations might consider only one or more of

Table 5.3   Some design features to be considered within or before any evaluation of instruction

- General mode of delivery (e.g. flexible delivery, classroom instruction)
- Internal structure of the instructional process (e.g. experiential learning, problem-based, didactic)
- Social relationships within the instructional setting
- Relationship with the other component of training/instruction
- Impact of technology or other media in the learning process
- Stage of development in the assumed learning sequences (e.g. novice, competent, proficient, expert)
- Nature of any feedback and reinforcement processes
- Extent of interactivity, self-pacing and self-direction
- Extent of subject-matter interest

the six features (e.g. cost-effectiveness) of the ECCOES framework, but they do not really make a judgment of overall value. An example of a micro- or quasi-evaluation is a study by Johnson and Geller (1992), which compared the effects of computer-assisted instruction and conventional teaching on 5379 Job Corps trainees. In this study, the achievement gains were small after some 60 hours of instruction. Any judgment from a microevaluation based on comparisons of effectiveness assumes that all the five other factors in the ECCOES framework are held constant.

JUDGING EVALUATIONS

By what standards should an evaluation be judged? The Joint Committee on Standards for Educational Evaluation identified four primary criteria by which evaluations should be judged: utility, feasibility, propriety, and accuracy. Some criteria by which evaluations can be considered were outlined by Rachal and Courtney (1986), who proposed three criteria for judging the worth of adult education research: (a) practical application, (b) contribution to understanding, and (c) universality.

First, it is obvious that there are multiple approaches to evaluating adult education programs, and that using an integrated framework will enhance valid judgments and decisions. The characteristic of an integrated evaluation is that it is conceived comprehensively, even if only one aspect of a program is ultimately evaluated. Second, a key factor to be considered is that evaluation in adult education must be congruent with adult learning principles (see chapter 3). The methodology, therefore, tends to be naturalistic and/or heuristic. Third, there are no rigidly prescribed procedures for adult education evaluations. Techniques can come from a variety of disciplines, but they must be capable of providing authentic findings and confirming or disconfirming hypotheses. Finally, the two fundamental guidelines in designing an evaluation are that (a) the results must be reproducible, and (b) the findings must make some statement about the content and process of the program and its present and future impact. With regard to the latter, follow-up or longitudinal studies are extremely important in determining the lasting effects of adult education programs.

Evaluation of education or training is a multifaceted endeavour, covering almost every aspect of programs, policies and services in the area of instruction and learning. Many students take courses on research methods yet overlook the stimulating field of evaluation activity, which involves the application of critical thinking to the solution of social problems and which also develops expertise in a variety of research methods. Those interested in examining further aspects of evaluation in greater depth are referred to Owen (1993), Walberg and Haertel (1990), Rossi and Freeman (1993) and Popham (1993). The writings of Parlett (1990) offer a useful guide to illuminative evaluation. Specialist journals in the field include *Evaluation Journal of Australasia, Educational Evaluation and Policy Analysis, Evaluation Review, New Directions for Program Evaluation,* and *Studies in Evaluation.*

ACKNOWLEDGMENTS

The helpful comments of my colleague Griff Foley and the contributions of Master of Education in Adult Education students to refining my views on evaluation are gratefully acknowledged.

FURTHER READING

Athanasou, J.A. 1997 *Introduction to Educational Testing.* Wentworth Falls: Social Science Press.
——1998 'A framework for evaluating the effectiveness of technology-assisted learning'. *Industrial and Commercial Training,* 30, pp. 96–103.
Cooksey, R.W. 1996 *Judgement Analysis: Theory, Methods and Applications.* San Diego: Academic Press.
Cronbach, L.J. 1963 'Course improvement through evaluation'. *Teachers College Record,* 64, pp. 672–83.
Joint Committee on Standards for Educational Evaluation 1994 *The Program Evaluation Standards.* Newbury Park, CA: Sage.
Johnson, T.R. & Geller, D.M. 1992 'Experimental evidence on the impacts of computer-aided instruction in the Job Corps program'. *Evaluation Review,* 16, pp. 3–22.

Kirkpatrick, D.L. 1996 *Evaluating Training Programs: The Four Levels*. San Francisco, CA: Berret-Koehler.

Lawless, K.A. & Brown, S.A. 1997 'Multimedia learning environments: issues of learner control and navigation'. *Instructional science*, 25, pp. 117–31.

Levin, H.M. 1983 *Cost-Effectiveness: A Primer*. Beverly Hills, Ca: Sage.

Norris, N. 1990 *Understanding Educational Evaluation*. London: Kogan Page.

Owen, J.M. 1993 *Program Evaluation*. Sydney: Allen & Unwin.

Parlett, M. 1990 'Illuminative evaluation', in H.J. Walberg & G.D. Haertel (eds) *The International Encyclopaedia of Educational Evaluation*, Oxford: Pergamon Press, pp. 68–73.

Popham, W.J. 1993 *Educational evaluation, 3rd edn*. Boston: Allyn & Bacon.

Rachal, J. & Courtney, S. 1986 'Response: focus on adult education research questions'. *Adult Education Quarterly*, 36, pp. 157–65.

Rossi, P.H. & Freeman, H.E. 1993 *Evaluation: A Systematic Approach, 5th edn*. Newbury Park, CA Sage.

Scriven, M. 1967 'The methodology of evaluation', in R.W. Tyler, R.M. Gagne, & M. Scriven (eds), *Perspectives of Curriculum and Evaluation*. Chicago, IL: Rand McNally.

Stake, R. 1967 'The countenance of educational evaluation'. *Teachers College Record*, 68, pp. 523–40.

Stufflebeam, D.L. 1971 *Educational Evaluation and Decision Making*. Itasca, IL: FE Peacock.

——1983 'The CIPP model for program evaluation', in G. Madaus, M. Scriven & D.L. Stufflebeam (eds), *Evaluation Models: Viewpoints on Educational and Human Services Evaluation*. Boston: Kluwer-Nijhof.

Tyler, R.W. 1949 *Basic Principles of Curriculum and Instruction*. Chicago, IL: University of Chicago Press.

Walberg, H.J. & Haertel, G.D. 1990 *The International Encyclopaedia of Educational Evaluation*. Oxford: Pergamon Press.

PART II
CONTEXT AND CHANGE

Introduction to Part II

A central assertion of this book is that adult learning and education are contextual, complex and contested activities. To understand a particular adult education policy or practice, therefore, it is necessary to examine both its relationship to broad political, economic and cultural influences as well as the microprocesses of policy construction or adult education practice in particular places—how people act and how they explain and justify their actions. Each of the four following chapters illustrates this theme. A variety of theoretical perpectives is employed to analyse differing perceptions of adult education research (chapter 6), directions in adult education policy (chapter 7), flexible delivery of courses (chapter 8), and the discourses of adult literacy teaching (chapter 9).

Chapter 6 examines the meaning of research in adult education and training, focusing on a number of themes—the divergence of research traditions, the role of underlying paradigms of research, and the need to see research in relation to practice. The central theme is that research takes place in context and needs to make its context visible. The chapter begins by critiquing the notion that research is a purely scientific and rational process, arguing that it is also a social and value-laden one. Four factors that have shaped practice and debate in adult education research are then discussed: the influence of research on school education, the tension between an institutional perspective and a learner-centred perspective, economic restructuring, and the variety of forms and contexts of adult education and learning. A number of factors that adult educators and trainers should take into account when they engage in research are then canvassed, including the context of inquiry, the researcher's assumptions, and the problem that is being investigated. The way in which these factors are worked through in practice is demonstrated through an examination of four research studies: an empirical study of how adaptability in the workplace is learned and taught in vocational education; an interpretive study of the relationship of a priest and his Aboriginal parishioners in northern Australia; a participatory and policy-oriented study of learning in women's community centres; and ongoing action research in a public sector organisation. The chapter ends by affirming the inevitability, and the value, of diversity in research practice.

Chapter 7 begins with a discussion of the political and economic context of contemporary adult education policy. Particular attention is paid to the impact on adult education of the restructuring of economy and state that has occurred over the past 30 years and the discourse of economic rationalism that has accompanied that restructuring. It is argued that the contemporary restructuring constitutes the latest in a long line of economic reorganisations, all of which are generated by a drive to maximise profit. In the current reorganisation, government attempts to withdraw to some extent from its role of social service provider and to concentrate its energies on supporting locally based business in its efforts to compete in the global marketplace. Education becomes both an instrument of economic policy and a commodity to be bought and sold. To illustrate this thesis, two recent developments in adult education policy are examined: the emergence of a particular conception of vocational education, and the general direction for adult education policy articulated at a recent UN congress. The chapter concludes with an examination of the tension between the state's focus on educational outcomes and the creation of an educational market on the one hand, and the access and equity function of adult education on the other, and by making suggestions about how the latter function may be promoted.

Chapter 8 critically examines the growing interest in 'flexible learning'. The notion of 'flexibility' is analysed as an example of a 'governing metaphor', chanelling people's efforts in particular directions. The tendency is to present flexible learning unproblematically as a new technology for the delivery of learning, which improves overall access to the system and 'choice' for the individual within it. Access and equity are held to be promoted most efficiently through curriculum and institutional flexibility, in particular through the deployment of new information and communications technologies. With this comes changed working practices and recognition of a growing number of learning settings.

Flexibility then is taken up in ways which attempt to conceal its significance and effects and 'normalise' it as having a particular meaning. It becomes known as something about which there needs to be no further discussion. The notion of 'flexibility', thus, comes to drive changes in education and training in particular directions as though they were the only possible ones.

Chapter 8 examines three aspects of the deployment of the governing metaphor of flexibility in education:

- the emergence of flexibility as a powerful metaphorical resource to be deployed by governments and others in support of specific forms of change;
- likely effects of the implementation of flexible learning strategies on curriculum, pedagogy, teachers' working conditions and learner identity; and
- some of the ways in which the meanings invested in flexible learning can be and are being contested.

Chapter 9 also looks critically at a particular set of discourses, those of basic education teaching. Examination of teacher talk, policy documents and professional publications reveals four major discourses in literacy teaching in recent times. The first of these, and the dominant one until recently, is a humanistic discourse, which emphasises the needs of learners and argues for equality between teachers and learners. The second is an emancipatory discourse, which sees education as a vehicle for social change through consciousness-raising linked to community development and political action. A third discourse, which shares some of the values of the second, focuses on the implications for adult literacy teaching of cultural and social difference, and issues of access and equity. A fourth discourse, that of economic restructuring and economic rationalism, defines learners as 'human capital' and defines adult literacy teaching in terms of its capacity to contribute to economic production. The chapter analyses policy texts and developments in terms of these four discourses, pointing out that adult literacy teachers will have more control over their work if they understand the ways in which these discourses influence the way they think and act.

6

Research in adult education and training

John McIntyre

This chapter assesses the meaning of research in adult education and training, exploring a number of themes—the divergence of research traditions, the role of underlying paradigms of research, and the need to see research in relation to practice. The underlying theme is that research takes place in context and needs to make this context visible. The chapter examines, too, some of the tensions that occur when research, in the academic sense, is broadened to include other kinds of inquiry. Research, indeed, is treated as a problematic notion.

RESEARCH AS SCIENCE

Unfortunately, the idea of research as science pervades our educational thinking. Textbook passages like the following still call up images of white coats and laboratory mice (Kerlinger 1994: 16):

> Let us summarise the so-called scientific approach to inquiry. First there is doubt, a barrier, an indeterminate situation crying out, so to speak, to be made determinate. The scientist experiences vague doubts, emotional disturbance, inchoate ideas. He struggles to formulate the problem . . . He studies the literature, scans his experience and the experience of others. Often he simply has to wait for an inventive leap of the mind. Maybe it will occur; maybe not. With the problem formulated, with the basic question or questions properly asked, the rest is much easier. Then the hypothesis is constructed, after which its implications are deduced, mainly along experimental lines. In this process the original problem . . .

100

may be changed. It may be broadened or narrowed. It may even be abandoned. Lastly, but not finally, the relation expressed by the hypothesis is tested by observation and experimentation. On the basis of the research evidence, the hypothesis is accepted or rejected. This information is then fed back to the original problem and it is kept or altered as dictated by the evidence.

In this view, research is mechanical, male and rather melancholic. The 'problem' is like a key that unlocks a particular rational process, one which is abstract and impersonal. The researcher struggles in isolation to state the problem, and there is little sense of him engaging much with other people. With precision and control in mind, the researcher acts from outside on the educational field. He alone appears to have the power to bring a 'problem' into being.

This model for research has been called the positivist, empirical-analytic or 'natural science' model (Usher & Bryant 1989: 10–14), and has, through its grip on education and the social sciences, dominated adult education and training. It continues to be recommended to students as the most respectable approach to research, at least in the USA (Deshler & Hagan 1990; Merriam & Simpson 1989). However, it has been vigorously criticised as being based on limited assumptions about science, persons and society that deny the power of human beings to make meanings and create a social world (e.g. Usher 1996) or to imagine human inquiry as a collaborative activity of research participants (Reason & Rowan 1981; Robinson 1993).

Thus, for several decades there has been a challenge to the domination of empirical-analytic science and a search for alternative paradigms (see Neville et al.; Willis & Neville 1997; Higgs 1998). In the liberation from the straitjacket of the natural science model, there is room for more choice but also great potential for confusion. If now there are different frames of reference for inquiry, it is all the more necessary to make explicit the underlying assumptions of our work. In fact, if research includes inquiring into our practice as adult educators and trainers, can we avoid examining our deeply held beliefs about our practice and its contexts? And perhaps also what we believe about 'inquiry'?

This chapter aims to explore some of these questions by:

- briefly clarifying some meanings of the concept of paradigm;
- exploring some dynamics of research in the field of adult education and training;
- exploring selected examples of research drawn from different contexts of adult education and training.

PARADIGMS

The term 'paradigm' is used in multiple senses in both educational research (e.g. Carr & Kemmis 1986; Merriam 1991) and the wider literature (Reason & Rowan 1981). Though there are no definite schools of thought about paradigm, three main meanings can be identified:

* *The social organisation of science.* In this view, the paradigm is the key concept in a complex sociological account of the way science is institutionalised. It refers to typical methodologies, their associated disciplines, and the social relationships and world view that underlie, for example, Western behavioural science. This is the rich meaning of paradigm that emerged from the work of Kuhn (see Usher & Bryant 1989: 15–16; McIntyre 1993).
* *A broad 'philosophy of science'.* Here, the paradigm is seen as a set of philosophical beliefs supporting a broad approach to research. It is a way of expressing a philosophical alternative to empiricist science, for example Lincoln and Guba's naturalistic inquiry paradigm (1985) or the 'new paradigm inquiry' of Reason and Rowan (1981). Thus, it is argued, there are many methods but two competing paradigms. Another version of this approach understands 'qualitative research' and 'quantitative research' as opposing paradigms, with paradigm being represented in many comparable traditions (Denzin & Lincoln 1994).
* *Types of science.* This is a view of paradigms associated with critical theory (Habermas 1971; Bredo & Feinberg 1982; Merriam 1991). There are three forms human inquiry can take, according to the dominant knowledge-interest. These are empirical-analytic, interpretive, and critical science (see chapters 1 and 17). This is the view Carr and Kemmis develop (1986) when they argue that a critical educational science, going beyond both empiricist and interpretive science, is necessary if practitioners are to achieve a better relationship between theory and their professional practice.

The advantage of the above first and third views is that they emphasise that knowledge is always constructed in a social context. They assume there are no absolute answers as to what 'research' is. Activity deemed as research is legitimate when it conforms to the practices, ideals and values shared by a 'community' of researchers (Usher & Bryant 1989: 16). This view is of great significance to adult educators and trainers. It makes the context of inquiry—and the values and interests that make the context what it is—fundamentally important. Because there is such a variety of contexts in adult education and training, this view of the research in the field will lead us to relish, rather than regret, the uncontrolled diversity of research practice in adult education and training.

We will, then, be able to identify a range of research traditions, perhaps in different kinds of organisations and settings. A given paradigm will be accepted in one place but rejected in others. History, culture and location will affect what paradigm surfaces in an organisation (see Burrell & Morgan 1986). We might ask, for example, how research is seen by computing professionals, tele-communications technicians, vocational education planners, community development workers, Greenpeace activists or Catholic missionaries. What conflicts about inquiry emerge among practi-tioners when such organisations are challenged or changed?

The concept of paradigm thus provides us with a way of understanding research and inquiry in our field of practice. (The term 'inquiry' is added here to suggest that a range of investigative activity can count as research.) Paradigm leads us to greater awareness of our deeper assumptions about such matters as knowledge, human learning, self and society. Thus, there is a connection between the researchers' understanding of research and their view of the field.

'Paradigm' points to the differences in the way that people understand adult education and training—to the fundamental differences in world view, institutional linkages, political and social values that underlie beliefs about what should be researched and why it should be researched—and how in fact 'the field of inquiry' is seen. For this reason, a paradigm is something more than the philosophical preference for one research methodology over another.

To reiterate an important point, the term 'paradigm' is used in a range of ways and at different levels of analysis. Ongoing debates about educational research have not really clarified these meanings. Three difficulties are worth noting. First, there is a problem of different levels of analysis of paradigm: scholars are often unclear whether they mean a specific methodology, an institutionalised research tradition or a broad world view. The concept can be used validly in each of these ways, although equally paradigm is best not reduced to any one of them. Second, there is a tendency to refer to 'qualitative research' as a paradigm, to denote its difference from quantitative methodologies (although what is usually meant is their difference from a 'scientific' approach). This is the problem of equating paradigm to a type of methodology, obscuring the important aspect of research as institutionalised power. It also obscures important differences among diverse research traditions that are 'qualitative' (see Lancy 1993). Thus, it ignores such differences between interpretive research and the ideology critique of social critical theory we are suggesting in this chapter. Third, the very abstractness of the concept of paradigm can lead to an exaggerated emphasis on the 'philosophical' basis of research compared to political, ethical and pragmatic considerations. This is precisely what was wrong with the idealised model of scientific research referred to earlier: it neglects the way assumptions actually construct the research process. Thus, it is important to ask in what sense or senses an author is using this rich but troublesome idea of 'paradigm'.

ADULT EDUCATION AS A FIELD OF INQUIRY

The deep differences among adult educators and trainers about the nature and uses of research can be seen in a number of key areas: (a) the influence of school education on thinking about educational research; (b) the conflict between institutional and learner perspectives on adult education and training; (c) the domination of research by the intervention of the state in economic 'reform' and educational restructuring; and (d) the importance of the context of inquiry on what is researched, who does the research, and to what ends.

Research on adult education and training has been overshadowed by school education. Education is still often thought of in terms of *schooling*, and it is only quite recently that TAFE, workplace training and adult education have become 'researchable'. Academic research in adult education and training is not well-developed, and perhaps scholars therefore tend to exaggerate the special features which separate 'adult education' from education and the social sciences in general (see Deshler & Hagan 1990). This can cut off inquiry from rich sources of theory to be found beyond the field of practice. Moreover, the 'schooling' influence over-emphasises institutional or formal adult learning, such as in TAFE systems. This is unfortunate, because some of the most interesting research questions in adult education and training are about the informal learning in workplaces, community organisations and other settings (see Marsick & Watkins 1991; Foley 1991a, b, 1993a, b, c, 1994).

TAFE

Technical And Further Education

There is a tension between an institutional perspective and a learner perspective on adult education and training. Tension exists between a perspective which emphasises formal learning in courses and one which emphasises the need to understand the experiences of adult learners. This tension is seen in different scholarly research traditions. Research is still dominated by participation in course-taking: who participates, why they come, how much they participate, and what they gain (Courtney 1992; McGivney 1990; Sargant et al. 1997; McIntyre & Crombie 1996). This research is often empirical-analytic, often uses a national sample-survey approach, and may emphasise the distribution of adult learning opportunities and barriers to participation. Others, working in an interpretive tradition, have reacted against this focus and explored how adult learning is distinctive, how it can be understood, and how it can be theorised as an aspect of life experience (Boud & Griffin 1987; Brookfield 1984; Mezirow et al. 1990).

But neither the 'participation' nor the 'adult learning' research perspective provides a framework that helps us to understand how institution and learner interact in context. A further tradition can be identified, which engages critically with social and economic institutions, analysing how they determine radically different opportunities for learners. Research in this tradition is participatory, it goes on as part of social action, and it is often critical of the failure of academics to speak of social injustice, power and oppression (Hall & Kassam 1988).

We can thus see that adult education research is not a unified field in which the goals and methods of research are settled among experts. There are deep ideological differences about adult education and training that affect what is seen as the meaning and purpose of research (see McIntyre 1993).

The state is intervening to reform education and training, transforming the practice of adult educators and trainers. In the past decade, adult educators and trainers have been affected by a continuous restructuring of educational institutions. The contemporary state has taken a much more direct role in shaping educational directions, under the political-economic pressures of the shift to global capitalism (Yeatman 1990, 1993). This has had several consequences. In particular, the state has employed strategic research to engineer policy changes—for example, in making vocational education and training respond to the needs of industry or learner 'clients' through competition policy and drawing private and community providers into a national training system. Educational policy has itself become an important focus of research and critique (Peters & Marshall 1996; Marginson 1993; Halpin & Troyna 1995; Taylor et al. 1997).

Thus, important questions for researchers are: In what directions are the policy interventions of national governments driving both practice and research? How far do researchers respond to policy agendas and to what extent do they challenge and critique those agendas? How they respond will largely depend on how they see themselves as researchers. Are they objective observers, measuring and communicating information about policy impacts? Are they insightful interpreters of the meaning of change to those it affects? Or are they change managers, dancing with the demons of organisational restructuring? Or do researchers see themselves as representatives of those oppressed by change?

The practice of research and inquiry is always situated—it always takes place in particular organisations or settings. We have already suggested that it is too limiting for adult education and training research to take either an institutional perspective or a learner perspective as an exclusive frame of reference. Research needs to explore how learning occurs in context, because the settings of adult education and learning can differ greatly from each other. Where something is learned (in TAFE, community adult education, HRD, through informal learning in an environmental campaign), how it is structured, the relative power of participants, and the kind and degree of coercion, all define the kind of experience the learner will have. Thus, to inquire into practice leads to analysis of context and its structuring of learning.

One assumption of the development of the professional field of adult education and training is that there might be theories of 'adult learning' which can apply irrespective of the nature of the setting in which learning occurs. Should research in the field be limited by such frameworks? Or are some of the eminently researchable things in the field to be found in what is distinctive about the context of practice? If so, the researcher's framework for understanding the context becomes important. Researchers need to analyse their assumptions about the context that lie perhaps unconsciously in their thinking—affecting, for example, what they take to be a 'problem' for research, for whom it is a problem, and how it might be approached through research.

FRAMEWORK, PROBLEM AND PROCESS

The view of inquiry I am suggesting is that any adult educator

Table 6.1   Aspects of inquiry in adult education and training

Area of inquiry	Key issues
Context of inquiry	What is the setting for the research? Is it a formal educational institution or another type of practice? Is the research policy-driven, academic or practitioner based?
Framework	What are the main assumptions the researcher is making about adult education and the kind of research that is appropriate to the context? How are these assumptions reflected in the inquiry process?
Problem-taking	What is the problem that is the focus of the inquiry? Who defines this as a problem? How is the problem formulated by the researcher, and how does it reflect the framework of assumptions?
Theorising	How is the problem understood? What theorises—either formal or informal—are being used to grasp the problem? What key concepts guide inquiry, or emerge from reflection on the process?
Research method	To what extent is research seen in terms of applying a method or technique to the problem? Is the researcher aware of the limitations of the technique? What justifies the use of the method?
Negotiation	How will the interests of other people be affected by the research? How far does research involve collaboration with its participants, rather than coercion? What are the ethical issues?
Meaning of data	In what form is the information collected and from what sources? How are categories of 'data' developed, understood, validated and reported on?
Interpretation	What meanings are made out from the inquiry? What is claimed for the research? What conclusions are communicated to others?
Critique	How is the research used by the researcher or by other interests? For whom is the inquiry significant? What were its strengths and limitations?

or trainer has a framework for understanding research in the field. This is a long way from the textbook approach which equates research with *formal inquiry* for scientific and scholarly purposes (see Merriam & Simpson 1989). In this alternative view: (a) research can take quite different forms, in which research 'method' may be less important than in scholarly research; (b) the form of research will depend greatly on the context, the researcher's framework and the kind of problem that arises; (c) research is seen as a political and practical process in which the researcher pursues inquiries into a problem through a range of activities; (d) there are then a wide range of issues that impinge on the researcher: issues of power and relationship with others, of ethics and negotiation with participants, of naming and theorising concepts, of design and method, of project management, writing up and reporting.

This view of adult education research directs our attention to the sorts of issues researchers need to be aware of when they undertake inquiry. These are summarised in Table 6.1. Cases 6.1 to 6.4 show how these aspects of inquiry are worked through in practice.

CASE 6.1 ADAPTABILITY IN TAFE

A study that took place in Queensland illustrates the strengths of empirical-analytic research. Stevenson (1986) explored adaptability in a study of trainees undergoing formal vocational education and training. A decade of education and training reform has made adaptability a key objective in achieving a more flexible and productive workforce, as there will not be much 'working smarter' unless learners can apply their knowledge in new and complex work situations.

This study illustrates an interesting combination of factors driving research. There is clearly a strong use of theory in analysing a 'problem' for research, in conceptualising 'adaptability', but there is also a strong policy interest at work. Stevenson was at the time a director of TAFE curriculum services in Queensland. He used cognitive theory to understand adaptability as higher-order procedures which enable learners to apply existing lower-order knowledge (e.g. facts or techniques) to new situations. In other words, adaptability is 'knowing how to apply what you know' to unfamiliar situations. Interestingly, this study anticipates the policy forces of training reform, such as competency-based instruction, which have been reshaping technical and further education (TAFE).

Stevenson argued that an 'open environment' is necessary for adaptability to be learned (Stevenson 1986). Higher-order procedures must be 'compiled' through challenging experiences—as, for example, when electrical apprentices crawl in underfloor spaces to locate wiring circuits, or hairdressers razor-cut hair to an unfamiliar style without prior instruction. Though there are currently pressures on vocational providers to develop flexible delivery of training, in the past few classes were set up for problem-based learning to deliberately foster this kind of

---

higher-order cognition. They were typically formal and content-centred, and gave little play to active learning strategies.

Stevenson's work implies that formal institutions may have difficulty in responding to the demands of policies encouraging more deregulated and flexible training, because their educational culture has grown out of content delivery and examination. To achieve 'adaptability', educators will need to take the adult learners' perspective and learning environments which can build in some of the factors that press learners into higher-order learning in the workplace. By the same token, such studies have raised questions about what factors are important in bringing about that kind of 'situated learning' (see also Stevenson 1994).

In Case 6.1, the TAFE classrooms where the research took place appear as a kind of background to the main focus of the study—the psychological complexity of adaptability. To reveal the nature of contexts in adult education and training, it is necessary to go to more interpretive research that brings the social setting and its participants into the foreground.

CASE 6.2 PATRONS AND RIDERS: ABORIGINAL–WHITE RELATIONS

Such an interpretive study is Peter Willis's analysis of the hidden structure of Aboriginal–White relationships in Northern Australia (Willis 1988). In *Patrons and Riders* Willis insightfully explores his experiences as a Catholic missionary working in the Kimberleys in the 1970s, and attempts to understand the failure of a community development project on an Aboriginal reserve.

Willis shows how his Aboriginal congregation included him in their kinship relations (he was self-defined 'Father') but refused to become obedient clients in response to his assumed 'patron' role when he acted on their behalf. The Aboriginals went along with his attempt to start a market garden and gain a government grant to buy a large truck. They exercised their independence by using the truck mainly to transport numbers of people to ceremonies.

Willis suggests the Aborigines in his care adopted a 'kinship-rider' role, in which they went along with his attempts to achieve community self-determination so long as this served their objectives too—getting transport to remote places, controlling disturbance from 'young fellas' and getting more cash and goods for the reserve.

Willis arrives at the view that Aboriginal people, made economically dependent on Whites by dispossession, had nonetheless developed strategies to manage White control of their lives on remote cattle stations run by all-powerful managers who, while 'protecting' the Aborigines, were actually dependent on their cheap labour. The strategies of 'kinship-riding' continued to be useful in dealing with White welfare and church agencies, despite the rapid social and economic changes of the 1970s. The walk-offs from stations, the introduction of award wages, the coming of mission education, the citizenship referendum, legal alcohol, and the shift from assimilation policies to self-determination—all are seen by Willis as instances of Aboriginal resistance to White colonial domination.

The context here could not be more different from that of vocational education and training in an urban centre. Here Willis, in his role as adult educator, looks reflectively into a past experience of practice full of conflict and attempts to understand its deeper meaning. He struggles to understand how the context, in its cultural complexity, constrained the educational outcomes he wanted from his community development activity.

This (Case 6.2) is interpretive, not participatory research. There is no specific research technique here, as there is with Stevenson's empirical-analytic study. But there is a distinctive process of inquiry that emphasises not technical control over the means of producing data but the depth and power of interpretation applied to past events. Participatory research, in further contrast, takes as its basic concern the means by which people can own a process whereby they together discover information with the potential to change their situation (Hall & Kassam 1988).

Interpretive research can take many forms. Among the best-known is educational ethnography (Hammersley & Atkinson 1995), which takes as a problem how participants make sense of their social world (the classroom, a workshop, a community group, a learning team). Among the best-known research of this kind is Walker's *Louts and Legends* (Walker 1988). Over three years, Walker studied the life of several groups of young men at a Sydney high school. These young men are understood as inhabiting 'worlds' constructed by male youth culture and those cultures with which it interacts—the culture of the school, of ethnic and language communities, and social class. The identities of young men are shaped by the youth culture and its interactions, but at the same time the boys are shaping the youth culture by imposing themselves on it or resisting its values and understandings.

CASE 6.3 OUTCOMES OF ADULT COMMUNITY EDUCATION

Adult community education (ACE) refers mainly to learning that is organised in self-managing community organisations such as evening colleges, neighbourhood houses or adult learning centres. The vocational emphasis of education reform has challenged community adult education (see chapter 6). In the mid-1980s, policy researchers in ACE were forced to justify the value of their literacy, leisure and bridging courses to the TAFE funding body.

A well-known Victorian study, the 'Outcomes Report' (Kimberley 1986), used both survey and case histories to document the outcomes of short courses. The researcher developed a Freirean framework that looked for evidence of participants becoming more conscious of themselves as learners through courses and other activities organised in neighbourhood houses (Kimberley 1986: 31):

> Community providers understand education as the recognition, valuing and promotion of learning. They seek to develop the individual's consciousness of learning so that the learner is proactive (the agent) rather than reactive (the recipient) . . . education is about discovering the means by which learning may be directed. It is not only learning how to learn but discovering what uses may be made of one's learning.

It is difficult to demonstrate such processes through empirical-analytic research. Kimberley understood that the real problem of the study was persuading TAFE managers that 'community' access courses had valuable vocational outcomes not easily quantifiable in terms of specific job skills.

Underlying this kind of negative perception of adult community education courses is the assumption, at the core of the institutional perspective, that less formal learning is not really worthwhile. The challenge to the researcher was to counter this view by demonstrating the hidden educational values of such courses. She constructed a research process which allowed participants' voices to be heard by including case studies as part of the documentation.

To achieve this, the researcher had to negotiate the participation of people in the Victorian neighbourhood houses, who had a vital interest in the funding outcome. This kind of hidden work of negotiation is rarely acknowledged as part of inquiry—particularly in the natural science model, where researchers can often simply impose on participants their own construction of reality (see Reason & Rowan 1981; McIntyre 1993).

The support of providers ensured that a wealth of case studies was collected. The researcher was able to claim, for example, how these courses could lead to further education or training by developing self-confidence and self-esteem. The learners' stories illustrate the specific consequences courses often had for their life experience, including reorientation to study and work. But the meaning of such stories is not self-evident. The researcher places them in an interpretive frame that challenges us to see the processes of lifelong learning or 'conscientisation' they are meant to represent.

In empirical-analytic studies, such voices (Case 6.3) are not heard. Human complexities are purged of their subjective qualities. For the behavioural scientist, such anecdotal data is inadequate, because it is not a 'scientific' understanding. It does not isolate and quantify the factors which prompted learning, such as course or teacher qualities, the learners' own readiness to change, or the effects of other activities associated with the centre. The scientist does not deny that the stories are moving, but simply says we do not know what they represent because there has not been a controlled analysis of the various factors involved.

We could leave the issue there, but for a crucial point: such case-history evidence is now less politically compelling, as the vocational education and training agenda (see chapters 6, 7) demands more sophisticated analysis of outcomes (see McIntyre et al. 1995; Bagnall 1994). The corporatisation of public education institutions, the emphasis on outcomes-driven activity, favours highly instrumental research. Empirical-analytic science is attractive to the corporate managerialism of the contemporary state, because it ties down the object of study and restricts the meanings in play when controlling the communication of evidence becomes a priority. The tendency of positive science to reduce complex information to simplistic generalisations becomes a virtue rather than a vice. The new public sector managers are less concerned with real-life complexities of adult learners than with controlling the policy agenda, assessing policy impacts, and limiting demands on the public purse (Yeatman 1990).

Thus the policy interest of government has led to a resurgence of participation studies, but in a very different form from the North American tradition of motivational research, which aimed to develop theory, not influence social policy (see Darkenwald & Merriam 1982; Long 1983; Courtney 1992). The new wave of policy research demands social and political relevance from researchers and a robust engagement with social policy debates (see Griffin 1987; Jarvis 1993). This social research is not simple surveillance by governments of the educational effort of their populations but is partly shaped by the advocacy of such public-interest organisations as the National Institute for Adult Continuing Education in the UK, which through such national surveys as the 'Learning Divide' study (Sargant et al. 1997) has shown the extent of the social inequalities that challenge the rhetoric of 'lifelong learning for all'.

CASE 6.4 INQUIRING PRACTITIONERS

Cases 6.1 to 6.3 represent academic or policy research in the public domain. They are cases of formal research. It is useful also to refer to the potential of informal practitioner-based inquiry. Much workplace inquiry, for example, will be effective precisely because it is not publicly recognised as 'research'. It will take place as part of commitment to changing the workplace, or to learning as part of work (see chapters 10, 11). In the tradition of participatory action research (Hall & Kassam 1988; McTaggart 1991), it will be focused on working with others in a context on problems experienced by participants without the results necessarily going beyond this. There will be the possibility, as in any 'good' research, of learning about inquiry by debriefing the process. This is the essence of workplace action research, for example.

Let us say a public-sector manager is working in an organisation undergoing corporatisation, and has taken up a kind of 'management philosophy' based on open communication, personally committed individuals, and a process of 'robust debate among peers' about the key values of the new culture. The only problem is that this new philosophy has been dictated by the chief executive. The manager makes this her focus and considers how she can involve her peers in exploring their perceptions of culture change, and whether it might be possible to become more conscious of the restructuring process in order to act more effectively within it.

There is no explicit or theorised research method as such, nor a published report of the research. But the manager does collect and analyse data. The information-rich environment of the corporate workplace provides many opportunities to collect, share and reflect on perceptions of restructuring. The manager makes opportunities for workers to analyse and reflect on the value conflicts being thrown up by debate about changes sweeping the organisation and, with others, makes decisions about what actions will be taken. She sees how her managerial work can involve a process of inquiry wherein knowledge is generated in workshops and meetings, and mutual understanding about change processes is enhanced. She sees how action research can help her and others to 'ride the tiger' of restructuring in the workplace and gain more control over organisational change.

In this case, the research process is not applied to subjects, willing or unwilling, to generate knowledge that exists outside their comprehension and control.

Conclusion

In this chapter little has been said of the significant contemporary impact on educational research of feminist and poststructuralist approaches (e.g. Weedon 1987; Lather 1991a, b; Fonow & Cook 1991) and postmodernist thought (Usher & Edwards 1994; Usher et al. 1997). These theories challenge the notion that there are clearly identifable research frameworks, and suggest a diversity of theoretical and value assumptions and research methods (e.g. Lather 1991a, b). There has been enough said here about the confusion engendered by paradigm theory to suggest that the term might have outlived its usefulness, particularly when it has been employed in a countercritical way to reassert the authority of the behavioural science position in the guise of such unhelpful terms as 'post-positivism'.

Whatever the limitations of some accounts of paradigm, it is difficult to escape the conclusion that research knowledge is 'perspectival' rather than absolute. Knowledge is always generated within a perspective or research tradition and a particular set of assumptions about what is problematic, what is researchable, what counts as 'evidence' and so on. Thus this chapter has equated understanding research not to knowledge of research methods or techniques, but to examining how methods frame or 'construct' knowledge (Usher 1996).

The argument has emphasised the diversity of research practice in adult education and training, suggesting that this diversity reflects the nature of the field. Researchers differ in the perspectives they take on the field and its problems, according to their assumptions about such factors as the importance of formal courses provided by institutions, the kinds of policy forces driving research, and the nature of the context in which they work. This chapter has limited discussion to three competing research traditions which exemplify research in the field: *empirical-analytic research*, in the form of participation studies, will probably continue to dominate *policy research*, if only because of the demand of the contemporary state for 'hard evidence' of the value of adult education; *interpretive research*, centred on the exploration of learner perspectives, will also continue to advocate the study of the subjective meanings of adult learning. The challenge for research, however, is to transcend the limitations of this opposition between institution and learner.

The chapter also argues that research needs to do more justice to context than it has in the past. Diversity of context makes adult education distinctive; therefore, research must develop better ways to understand how learner and setting interact to produce 'adult learning'. Neither an institutional perspective (the focus of participation studies) nor a learner perspective (the focus of adult learning theory) can give an adequate frame of reference for understanding this interaction. New models for research will need to be found for this task, and they will need to engage more with the social and political forces that are determining the agendas for policy and practice in adult education and training.

FURTHER READING

Bredo, E. & Feinberg, W. (eds) 1982 *Knowledge and Values in Social and Educational Research*. Philadelphia: Temple.
Burrell, G. & Morgan, G. 1986 *Sociological Paradigms and Organisational Analysis, 2nd edn*. London: Heinemann.
Carr, W. & Kemmis, S. 1986 *Becoming Critical: Education, Knowledge and Action Research*. Geelong: Deakin University Press.
Kerlinger, F. 1994 *Foundations of Behavioural Research, 4th edn*. New York: Rinehart and Winston.
Reason, P. & Rowan, J. (eds) 1981 *Human Inquiry: A Sourcebook of New Paradigm Research*. Chichester: Wiley.
Robinson, S. 1993 *Problem-Based Methodology*.
Usher, R., Bryant, I. & Johnston, R. 1997 *Adult Education and the Postmodern Challenge* (*revd edn* of Usher & Bryant's 1989 book, *The Captive Triangle: Adult Education as Theory, Practice and Research*), London: Routledge.
Willis, P. & Neville, B. (eds) 1997 *Qualitative Research Practice in Adult Education*. Adelaide: Centre for Research in Education and Work, University of South Australia.

7

Policy formation in adult education and training

Griff Foley, Alastair Crombie, Geof Hawke
& Roger Morris

We begin this chapter with a discussion of the political and economic context of contemporary adult education policy, paying particular attention to the impact of the restructuring of economy and state that has occurred over the past 30 years and the ideologies and discourses that have accompanied that restructuring. Then we examine two recent developments in adult education policy: the emergence of a particular conception of vocational education, and the general direction for adult education policy articulated at a recent UN congress. We discuss the tension between the state's focus on educational outcomes and the creation of an educational market on the one hand, and the access and equity function of adult education on the other. We conclude by making suggestions about how the latter function may be promoted.

THE RESTRUCTURING OF THE POLITICAL ECONOMY AND ADULT EDUCATION

Globally, the conventional wisdom is that we are living in a post-Fordist, postmodernist, postsocialist and, some would argue, postindustrial age. The essential elements of this thesis are:

- A system of mass production and consumption, called 'Fordism' after the founder of assembly-line production and also known as 'welfare capitalism', was dominant in Western industrialised countries from the 1920s to the 70s. In these years Fordism delivered economic growth, high wages, high levels of consumption, and social security to the majority of people in those countries.

- Since the 1970s Fordism has been in crisis, for a variety of reasons, including: saturation of consumer markets in the developed countries; the emergence of mass production in cheaper labour areas, and the consequent 'deindustrialisation' of Western economies; the collapse of the Bretton Woods financial system in the 1970s; and the emergence of 'stagflation' (simultaneous inflation and economic stagnation).

- The general response to the crisis in Fordism has been for countries to try to stimulate export production by reducing government expenditure, reducing real wages, providing incentives for private investment, production and consumption, devaluing currencies, reducing government regulation of business activity, and encouraging foreign investment. While conservatives have sought to break the power of organised labour, and social democrats have adopted a more consensual approach to industrial relations, Western governments have all aimed to create technologically advanced, low labour-cost, export-oriented, internationally competitive economies.

- There has been remarkably little dissent from this policy prescription. Even among socialists the choice has usually been posed as being between an intensified Fordism (i.e. mass production intensified by computer technology), and 'flexible specialisation', involving technologically sophisticated production by skilled workers for niche markets. In the flexible specialisation scenario, it is maintained that the contradictions of Fordism have led to its demise and its replacement by a production once more controlled by the producers—albeit a much smaller group, an elite of skilled workers and technician-managers. The argument is that Western countries have no real choice: they either take the flexible specialisation path or they face continuing deindustrialisation, declining living standards, and economic vulnerability. They become 'banana republics'. (For discussion of Fordism and the post-Fordist thesis, see Harvey 1989: 121–97; Pollert 1991; Hyman 1991; Mathews 1989a, b; Hampson 1991.)

- In the post-Fordist problematic, education is to contribute to flexible specialisation by focusing on vocational training. Education systems, it is argued, should concentrate on developing people's competencies—their skills, knowledge and values—to enable them to move across jobs, from one sector of the economy to the other, and even from one country to another. Curricula should be redesigned along competency-based lines, enabling the recognition of existing competence as well as the more effective articulation of different levels of education and training. Education is seen as one component of a comprehensive approach to workplace restructuring, one which includes changes in industrial relations, technology and workplace organisation. The aim is a highly skilled, mobile workforce which will help to make industry internationally competitive. (For an exposition of this thesis, see Gonczi 1993: 9–78.)

While the validity of the post-Fordist thesis continues to be fiercely debated (see Brenner 1998 for a recent extended critique), it has had and continues to have a profound impact on education policy. The role of education and learning in a restructuring capitalism needs to be analysed at both macro and micro levels, at the level of policy formation, and at the point of practice in particular sites. This is an enormous task, and only a few indicative points can be made here.

At the macro level, the changing role of the state has shaped the direction of educational policy. The globalisation of production has transformed the welfare state into the 'competitive state'. The perceived need of governments to keep their economies internationally competitive has resulted in 'the state itself having to act more and more like a market player' (Cerny 1990: 230, cited in Yeatman 1993: 5). Internally, the function of the state changes from the delivery of public services (perceived as the universal rights of citizens) to the fostering of private sector production and the management of a continually contracting public sector. As Yeatman has noted, this transformation in the role of the state has a number of effects. First, bureaucrats become economic managers rather than service deliverers and client advocates. Second, the 'shared collegial culture' and the hierarchical seniority system of the welfare state bureaucracy is supplanted by an individualistic, competitive and careerist style of work imported from the private sector. Third, the relatively open competition of interest groups for public resources which characterised the welfare state has been replaced by a more remote and opaque style of decision making. Fourth, public services are more closely 'targeted'. 'Essentially what happens is that [the services] are cut back in relation to claims on them, which means that the quality of service declines, and those who can afford to "choose" opt out of the public system and pay for a private service'; a process of 'recommodification' develops, as public services are privatised and put back into the market (Yeatman 1993: 5–7).

These changes operate across countries. But there are important differences between the role of the state under conservative and social democratic regimes. Hard-line economic rationalist governments simply want to reduce the role of the state as much as possible. Social democratic governments retain some commitment, however compromised, to social justice goals. They attempt to 'create a more efficient and effective public sector by appropriating private sector models of management', and they rely heavily on tripartite activity (by government, business and trade unions) in policy formation (Knight et al. 1991: 13). This 'corporate managerialist' style of state action affords working people some protection against the worst excesses of a reorganising capitalism. However, by setting up a closed, hierarchical, tripartite style of decision making,[1] and by appropriating much of the economic rationalist ground, social democratic governments tend to demobilise trade unions, as well as encouraging conservative political parties, and capital, to move further to the right (see Rees et al. 1993: 15–102; Horne 1992; Pusey 1991; Ewer et al. 1991; Knight et al. 1991: 15–16).

The competitive state, of conservative or social democratic stripe, seeks to transform education from a citizen's right into an instrument of economic policy. A revived human capital theory conceives people as instruments of production, 'as objects to whom value, for both the individual and society, is added through education and training' (Lingard 1991: 30). The state develops a more comprehensive and controlling approach to education policy making. For example, in Australia in the 1980s, a series of government initiatives attempted to construct a comprehensive system of post-school education closely linked to production. An expanded university system with closer links to business was to focus on economically useful research and professional education. An expanded and better-funded technical and further education sector was to provide vocational training for the rest of the primary labour force (paraprofessions, technicians, tradespeople, white-collar workers). A vocationalised community adult education, a growing proportion of it provided by private agencies (many of these linked to church-based charities), was to provide labour market training for the secondary labour force and the unemployed, at the same time attempting to fulfil its traditional 'access' function. The most radical conception was of a comprehensive system of workplace reform, which linked workplace education to changes in work organisation, and which required employers to devote a percentage of payroll to employee training. Case 7.1 examines one aspect of these educational changes, vocational education policy.

CASE 7.1 A POLICY FOR VOCATIONAL EDUCATION

For over a century the major providers of vocational education in Australia were post-school institutions called TAFE (technical and further education) colleges. During the 1980s a federal Labor government legislated into being a 'national training market', in which private providers could compete with TAFE colleges. At the same time all state governments, which have administrative responsibility for TAFE systems, set in train organisational restructurings intended to prepare colleges to compete in the open training market. A National Training Authority was set up to oversee the distribution of funds and to 'assure the quality' of the emerging new vocational education system.

This system was still being established when in 1996 a conservative government was elected, which introduced a more radical version of the training market. The overarching policy structure is called the 'National Training Framework', and introduces a new mechanism for recognising providers of vocational education courses. Its linchpin is the Australian Recognition Framework (ARF), a system of agreements and guidelines adopted by state and federal governments and which cover arrangements for mutual recognition of courses, programs and qualifications, as well as the recognition of providers. The ARF does not recognise 'providers' as such, rather it expands the domain of coverage of an already existing system of Registered Training Organisations (RTOs) to cover a wide range of training services, including provision, assessment and curriculum development. These organisations are licensed to provide vocational education within a six-level accreditation system called the Australian Qualifications Framework (AQF).

There are two types of provider. RTO are registered to deliver specified—generally lower-level—qualifications. Their compliance with the terms of their registration is both internally and externally audited: that is, they are required to have established internal monitoring processes and will also be subject to occasional audit by an external body. 'Quality-endorsed RTOs' are registered to develop and deliver courses at all AQF levels, and are able to 'manage the scope of their recognition', develop and approve the issue of qualifications (subject to some nation-ally agreed guidelines) and, in some cases, can delegate some of their powers to others. This means that within the scope of their approval they may offer any course they want to. Achievement of this status is dependent on achieving an externally endorsed quality certification such as ISO 9000.

In some states at least, compliance auditing of both levels of provider is likely to become the responsibility of industry bodies, not governments. How this will occur is not yet clear, but one model that has been discussed is an approved industry body to offer—at a suitable cost—training for individuals or organisations who want to be recognised as industry auditors. Providers would then be required to engage a recognised auditor to monitor their compliance on some predetermined schedule. Initially, state recognition authorities were expected to phase out any role in this regard, but it now seems certain that they will maintain, at least, an overall supervisory position.

Also central to the new framework are 'training pack-ages'. These contain three compulsory components: competency standards, assessment guidelines, and qualifi-cations related to various packages of competency standards. There are also three optional components: learning structures (an as yet ill-defined concept), teach-ing/learning resource materials, and professional development plans/materials. Responsibility for developing and maintaining these packages will rest primarily with national industry advisory bodies.

Within the new framework funding is conceived as demand- or customer-driven rather than supplier- or provider-driven. Public funds are directed to individual training providers on the basis of 'user choice'. Clients negotiate training appropriate to their needs with providers and state training authorities, then release the appropriate funds to the provider.

This new framework for vocational education takes the notion of a state-legislated training market to its logical conclusion, with radical effect. A system based on large state vocational education providers is replaced by one comprising multiple competing providers. Adult learners are redefined as customers of these competing providers.

> The concepts of curriculum and course are replaced by the notion of generic training packages, which can be adapted to the needs of specific customers.

The framework in Case 7.1 typifies changes occurring globally in education. Such arrangements are presented as rational and fair and are difficult to challenge, for how can one argue against the principle of user choice? Yet clearly a key issue is how education equity can be maintained or extended in such a system. How do the poor, women, workers, indigenous people, the disabled effectively express their demand for adult education?

ADULT EDUCATION INTO THE NEXT MILLENNIUM

REALISING THE GOAL OF UNIVERSAL LIFELONG LEARNING

Every 12 years UNESCO convenes a world congress on adult education. These congresses provide a convenient point to assess the current state and possible future direction of adult education. As with previous congresses, the one held at Hamburg in 1997 concluded with a Declaration on Adult Learning, which set out goals for the next decade. Central to the Hamburg declaration is a call for lifelong learning for all adults and the creation of a 'learning society' (UNESCO 1997b: paras 1–10). Discussion at the congress illustrated the difficulties of achieving this goal.

Participation in adult education is a major indicator of how close we are to realising the goal of lifelong learning. Participation has been growing steadily across the world over the past 25 years, especially in work-related programs in industrialised countries and in literacy courses and campaigns in developing countries. But there are still substantial segments of populations not being reached—in particular, women, workers and indigenous people. In developing countries there are still a billion people defined as illiterate and hundreds of millions of people without a full elementary education. Even in an affluent country like Britain, in the early 1990s 25 per cent of adults reported that they had not participated in any further education or training courses since completing their formal education, which itself tended to have been of short duration. Any serious strategy for bringing into existence a universal approach to lifelong learning would have to look more closely at the composition and needs of these groups and develop ways in which they might be brought to formal education. One strategy might be to offer 'learning entitlements' to those who have had the *least* formal education—starting perhaps with the poorest 5 per cent—and monitoring the take-up and its effects (UNESCO 1997a, paras 5–8; Evans 1993: 8).

In a previous era it could have been hoped that the 'universalisation' of adult education would follow the same logic and pattern by which primary, secondary and most recently tertiary education have been made available to the whole population. Seeing the merits of lifelong learning, and aspiring to the ideal of creating a 'learning society', government might have deemed it appropriate, if not obligatory, to supply the resources to build a generic adult education service, to ensure that all adults had access to good-quality learning opportunities throughout their lives. Such a service would take its place in the community alongside schools, colleges and universities, and be funded by government on a similar rationale to the funding and provision of a public library service.

As illustrated by the changes to vocational education discussed in Case 7.1, such a vision derives from a superseded conception of government. This has been replaced by a shift that transcends party politics and the flux of the business cycle, although the pace and direction of transformation are affected by both these influences. The changing logic is exemplified in government assistance for the unemployed in many developed countries. For example, in Australia until the mid-1970s, 'unemployment benefit' was paid as an entitlement, as a form of social insurance to all those who could not obtain work. In the 1980s this 'passive' approach was progressively supplanted by a range of 'active' labour market programs, targeted to specific subgroups of the unemployed and based on the pursuit of specific, assessable outcomes. In the 1990s under a conservative government this approach has in turn been replaced by a system of individual case management, competitively tendered for by private providers and designed to 'progress' individuals towards 'job readiness' and possession of specific 'marketable competencies'. The obligations as well as entitlements of the case-managed are spelt out, and progress towards achievement of the designated outcomes is carefully monitored. Again we see the public provision of adult education directed at particular disadvantaged groups being replaced by an employer-driven system that individualises adult learners and defines them as human capital.

PROMOTING EQUITY

Clearly, it is difficult to promote educational equity within a policy environment that is likely in the foreseeable future to be characterised by the following features.

- There is unlikely to be a return to funding of institutions. This approach, which focuses on *input*, is being abandoned in favour of fixed contracts, which are put out to tender to produce specified *output* for customers or consumers.
- There is a strong bias in favour of competition in the provision of services that have hitherto been government monopolies. With some safeguards for disadvantaged groups, such as specific contracts for the supply of services to the weak and vulnerable, more and more areas of human and community services will become subject to some form of competition among providers.
- Assisted by modern computing and telecommunications technology, government services (more often delivered by non-government organisations) will be more finely tuned and monitored—to increase the probability that individuals get a specified service and that resources are not 'wasted' on those without need or entitlement.
- There will be more attention paid to the related questions of who benefits and who pays. The welfare state, it is now judged, erred in the direction of full public funding, from tax revenue, of government services such as health care and education. The state will now seek to regulate demand (e.g. for health care services, water supply) and improve overall 'fairness' by identifying beneficiaries and calibrating a contribution from them.

CONCLUSION

Policy making is about building in bias. Effective policy persistently influences or constrains the actions and decisions of planners, service deliverers and politicians in a particular direction—that which is most likely to realise the policy objectives. The bias most adult educators would want to see built into governmental and institutional decision making is one which would have the effect of consistently improving access to systematic, good-quality learning opportunities for a growing proportion of adults, so as to enable them to realise their full potential—as human beings, as citizens, and as workers. This might most appropriately be expressed in terms of a national policy and strategy for the development over time of a system of lifelong learning, whereby education and training opportunity becomes available on realistic terms throughout the lifespan.

For such a policy to be realised, the bias would have to be

built into income support arrangements and the organisation of work, as well as into the educational and training systems. There would need to be a recognition of the extent to which the structures and mechanisms to support a system of lifelong learning already exist. Opportunities for formal, non-formal and informal learning are already abundant, but the various elements are not well linked, conceptually or in practice. A stocktaking of the present situation might well find that lifelong learning is already at least a partial reality for the best-educated fifth or quarter of adults, including large numbers of women and some men who move between child-rearing, paid employment, and various community roles. The challenge would then be to extend such patterns of working and learning to the remaining three-quarters of the adult population. It would then need to be recognised that the emerging national system of vocational education and training, discussed in this chapter, has lifelong learning as one of its policy objectives, and that a substantial part of its attention and resources is already being applied to upgrading the skills and knowledge of the workforce in a systematic way. The task then would be to foreground this goal and in its pursuit to articulate formal vocational education, labour market access programs, non-formal work-based learning and community-based general adult education into a system that really did contribute to realising UNESCO's goal of universal lifelong learning.

NOTE

1   Former Labor Prime Minister Keating encapsulated this style in responding to a call by a leading trade unionist for the Australian Senate to amend the 1993/94 Budget. Keating, while acknowledging the right of the unionist to express his organisation's view, suggested that 'the best way to deal with the Government in the Accord [tripartite government/union/business policy-making process] is to deal with it persuasively. And that is, talk to us in private and not in public' (*The Australian* 28/8/93).

FURTHER READING

Adult Education and Development 1997 Special issue on the UNESCO Fifth International Conference on Adult Education, Hamburg, no. 49.
Brenner, R. 1998 'The economics of global turbulence: a special report on the global economy, 1950–1998', *New Left Review*, 229, May/June.
Foley, G. 1999 *Learning in Social Action: A Contribution to Understanding Internal Learning* 2nd edn, Chapter 6 'Adult Education and Capitalist Reorganisation' London: Zed Books.

8

Flexible learning for adults
Richard Edwards & Katherine Nicoll

In many industrialised nations, education and training institutions traditionally focusing on on-campus face-to-face provision are reformulating and diversifying modes of delivery and the content of course offerings. Within this environment previously peripheral forms of learning are brought to the fore. These are variously named 'distance', 'open', 'multi-mode' and 'flexible' learning. In national and international policy documents greater flexibility is increasingly said to be a precondition for lifelong learning (Kennedy 1997; West 1998). Often the discourse of flexible learning merges with the languages of technologisation, marketisation and managerialism, all of which contribute to 'flexibility' in their different ways.

The significance and consequences of a broad move within education and training towards 'flexible learning' are beginning to be subjected to critical scrutiny (e.g. Raffe 1996; Kirkpatrick 1997; Edwards 1997). Outside the more critical discussions, the tendency is to present flexible learning unproblematically, as a new technology for the delivery of learning which improves overall access to the system and 'choice' for the individual within it. Here flexible learning is positioned simply as 'better' rather than as anything that may change the process, content or outcomes of learning, or have significant effects on society.

In this chapter we view flexible learning as a specific site for the play of what might be called a 'governing metaphor' (Yeatman 1994) for the times, the notion of flexibility. Issues of access and equity are aligned with efficiency and effectiveness and subsumed within the metaphor of flexibility. Access and equity are held to be promoted most efficiently through curriculum and institutional flexibility, in particular through the deployment of new information and communications technologies. With this comes changed working practices and recognition of a growing number of learning settings. Flexibility then is taken up in ways which attempt to conceal its significance and effects and 'normalise' it as having particular meaning. It then becomes known as something about which there needs to be no further discussion. The notion of 'flexibility' thus comes to drive changes in education and training in particular directions, as though they were the only possible ones. In this way the 'facts' of flexibility are fixed (Nicoll 1998). Flexible learning becomes part of a rhetorical strategy through which attempted change is governed, wherein 'inflexibility' and 'flexibility' are invested respectively with negative and positive values, the latter constituted as the 'solution' to the 'problem' of the former. Evidence conflicting with this perspective, including evidence on its cost-effectiveness, is strategically ignored, rubbished or displaced.

This chapter explores moves towards flexible learning as a particular example of a wider strategy of governing (i.e. directing the activities of inidividuals or groups: Foucault 1983, cited in Gore 1993: 52) within which the pedagogical and political are related aspects. The chapter is in four parts. First, we examine the emergence of flexibility as a powerful metaphorical resource to be deployed by governments and others in support of specific forms of change. Second, we outline some of the implications of the deployment of flexibility within sites of learning. Third, we explore the implications of these approaches for learner identity. In conclusion, we suggest briefly some of the ways in which the meanings invested in flexible learning can be and are contested, as the workings of governing metaphors are never unidirectional nor complete. Here we are responding at least in part to Raffe's (1996: 24) view that

> flexibility [in education] itself has a number of possible meanings: flexibility as a competence or characteristic acquired through education; curricular flexibility; flexibility of delivery; or flexibility of pathways. There is thus a need for conceptual analysis; but there is also a need for empirical research.

While this chapter focuses on the conceptual, we advocate further empirical research.

EMERGING FLEXIBILITY

The academic interest in flexibility has largely developed in the analysis of and prescriptions for changes in the economy and workplace. Often it is associated with debates about Fordism, neo-Fordism and post-Fordism. As we have seen, flexibility was promulgated as a response to the economic problems of lack of growth and inflation in many countries in the 1970s. It found its strongest expression in the neoliberal economic policies of governments of the 1980s and 90s. Most often associated with the policies of Margaret Thatcher in the UK and Ronald Reagan in the USA, flexibility has been pursued by governments of many different political persuasions and supported by major regional and international economic organisations, such as the European Union and OECD.

There are three major explanations for this emphasis on flexibility: the neo-Smithian, the neo-Schumpeterian and the regulation school (Nielson 1991). In the first, it is the changing nature of markets and the moves from mass to niche markets which is central, resulting in a shift from Fordist mass production to what some term post-Fordist flexible specialisation. Webster (1995) identifies three flexibilities associated with post-Fordism—flexibility of employees, flexibility of production, and flexibility of consumption. In the second explanation, the technological and institutional flexibility made possible by information and communications technologies are said to result in innovation and productivity gains. The third explanation draws on neo-Marxist economics to posit a contemporary shift in the regime of capital accumulation (Harvey 1989: 147).

Over the past two decades the development of flexibility has been seen as central to transforming organisations and making them more competitive. If national economies are to function in an increasingly integrated global market, it is argued that they have to be more flexible, and this requires also organisations and individuals to become more flexible. Pedagogically this has been pursued through policies that place increasing emphasis on lifelong and flexible learning. Politically this has been pursued through deregulation and the legislative transformation of labour relations. The multiskilled, flexible worker has been promoted as paradigmatic of the economically successful organisation, moving from task to task, team working, problem solving, and learning as they so do. Alongside and as part of this flexibility has been downsizing, a casualisation of much employment, changes in the age and gender structure of the labour force, the development of notions of core and periphery workforce, and the growth of insecurity and inequality (Edwards 1997).

Organisations have pursued their own flexibility through a

range of strategies—numerical flexibility, functional flexibility, distancing strategies, pay flexibility (Atkinson & Meager 1990)—and in so doing have attempted to develop new workplace identities of the 'enterprising self' (du Gay 1996). On certain readings, the rigidities and regularities of the Fordist production line have been displaced by the post-Fordist 'learning organisation'. However, some argue that this is more myth than reality (Avis 1996), with Taylorist approaches to management continuing and resulting in the organisational form often termed 'neo-Fordism' (see chapter 7). At both social and institutional levels, strategies to promote flexibility tend to create insecurity, which itself can either be ignored or regulated.

Flexibility therefore is not a single phenomenon but is differentiated according to nation, sector, institution and management strategy. As the discussions of flexibility have migrated out of the realms of economics into other areas, such as industrial sociology, cultural studies, management, education and training, and as the influence of economics has been exerted increasingly on other domains, so the emphases and issues themselves have shifted. In many senses the theoretical positions have become more complex. Early notions of the post-Fordist artisan have given way to more cautious assessments, for there are a range of possible meanings and practices embedded in the pursuit of flexibility as a strategy for economic innovation and renewal.

Indeed, the pedagogic assumptions and management approaches of specific notions of flexibility influence the possibilities for innovation within organisations. Johnston and Lunvall (1991) talk of reactive and active forms of flexibility. If flexibility is constructed as an adaptive process, the notion of learning associated with it is stimulus response. People and organisations are positioned as reactive to externally imposed conditions. By contrast, if flexibility is constructed as an active process of learning, people can see greater possibilities for innovation.

This suggests two ideal types of flexible organisation. First, there is the adaptive type, developing flexibility in response to changing markets, where innovation is pursued through competition. This promotes insecurity, which is left unregulated or managed. Management may be delayered but remains hierarchical and Taylorist in its approach, a situation of low trust. Second, there is a more creative type of flexible organisation which seeks to develop and position itself within markets, where innovation is pursued through cooperation. Here flexibility and insecurity are regulated and managed as a single phenomenon. Each ideal type may be said to be a 'learning organisation', but each has differing pedagogical underpinnings: the first based on stimulus response, the second developmental, with the degree of development circumscribed by the extent of participation in the decision-making processes of the organisation by the different stakeholders. 'Flexibility' therefore does not imply inevitably a specific set of practices, and can itself be contested.

Most of the examination of flexibility has been in the profit-making areas of the economy. However, flexibility has been demanded also of non-profit and public sector organisations, including education and training organisations, to enhance efficiency and effectiveness. New public management approaches have been adopted, positioning the state as purchaser rather than provider of services. There has been more emphasis on management and responsiveness to customers. What then is the impact of flexibility on the provision of learning opportunities for adults?

FLEXIBLE LEARNING/LEARNING FLEXIBILITY

Simply put, the impact is double. On the one hand, the role of education and training is to service the flexibility required to support economic competitiveness and lifelong learning. On the other, institutions themselves become subject to differing regimes of flexibility (Edwards 1993; Wilmot & McLean 1994; Taylor 1997)—adaptive and/or creative. In education, as in other sectors, most attention has been given to the former. Moves to become more flexible tend to be posited simply as an instrumental response to changed circumstances which are enabled by the deployment of information and communications technologies (ICT).

Jessop (1991: 101) identifies a number of possible consequences of flexibility for education and training:

> there will be process innovation through distance learning systems backed up by telecommunications, video and computer equipment; and through the use of computers in secondary and tertiary education. And organisationally, there will be new educational packages for community education and the educationally disadvantaged; plus educational packages combined with entertainment for home use.

Organisational flexibility thereby provides the possibilities for innovation and the development of greater flexibility in learning in terms of what is made available, by whom, to whom, and in what forms.

Such developments raise many questions, the answers to which require much research and may vary according to one's workplace and role within it. How does flexible learning service and serve economic competitiveness, and in what ways? Is the flexibility to which institutions are subject supporting flexible learning, and in what ways? Do certain forms of flexibility repattern forms of exclusion? Is flexibility a situation to be achieved, or an ongoing process of innovation? What are the effects and consequences—pedagogic, social, economic and political—of developing flexibility through the use of ICT? We outline here briefly a few points for consideration arising from moves towards flexible learning.

The contribution of ICT to different pedagogic strategies, including those associated with flexible learning, is undeniable. Indeed the deployment of ICT for some may be paradigmatic of flexibility, thereby ignoring other forms of flexibility that do not require technological mediation. These technologies are argued to have a number of effects—including, for instance: the compression of space and time associated with processes of globalisation; the culturalisation and de-differentiation of public and private, work and civil society, national and international boundaries; the growth in importance of culture and lifestyle practices in the aestheticisation of life and the cultivation of identity; and increased employment of symbolic analysis and analysts within the workforce (Giddens 1990; Reich 1993; Morley & Robins 1995). Despite this, little has yet been said about the implications of these technologies for conceptions and practices of learning, apart from the necessity to ensure people have the skills to use them in employment and for some forms of computer and media literacy. Sometimes the assumption seems to be that these different media can be 'read' as if they were books rather than acknowledging the different forms of participation and practices they engender.

The growing range of technologies available and their deployment through flexible learning (e.g. computer-mediated communication, videoconferencing, multimedia) mean that there is a multiplication of signs, texts and discourses that adults encounter. This does not result simply in the requirement for different skills to use technologies, but entails different possibilities for making sense and interpreting that which is available. The new ICTs also require different learning strategies. The development of ICT provides for 'an increasing multiplicity and integration of significant modes of meaning making, where the textual is also related to the visual, the audio, the spatial, the behavioural' (New London Group 1995: 3). Here, 'knowledge can be understood as a form of meaning-making' (McLaren & Hammer 1995: 172). However, such concerns and issues rarely emerge in the dominant instrumental discussion of how to make learning more flexible. In a sense, provision may become flexible, but the nature and outcomes of the learning remain unquestioned.

The deployment of ICT within 'conventional' institutions means that learning is no longer constrained within their physical boundaries. This extends possibilities for access at the same time as offering potential for new exclusions. The more general proliferation of ICT also means that opportunities to learn are available through a wider range of sources than simply traditional providers of education and training. The effects are paradoxical. Traditional forms of pedagogy and the authority of education and training institutions in some ways may be subverted by the more general spread of electronically mediated networks of entertainment and learning, even as flexible learning provides the potential for extending the authority of those institutions. Who controls learning—and what constitutes a curriculum and a learning text—becomes problematic, something which can result in institutional and professional crises of authority and identity.

It is therefore important closely to examine discursive and other practices associated with certain forms of flexible learning. There are various ways of approaching this. We draw on Foucault's (1977) analysis of the mechanisms of observation, normalising judgment and the examination which he identified as central to the development of the disciplines of the human sciences and the emergence of certain institutions—prisons, asylums, schools—in modern nation-states. For Foucault, the emergence of these disciplining institutions was co-extensive with the development of certain disciplinary knowledge formulated through the mechanisms outlined above. Either explicitly or implicitly, these mechanisms are central to pedagogical practices and mark particular forms of pedagogy.

Traditionally in institutionalised education, mechanisms of observation were exemplified clearly in the placing of bodies within the classroom, most commonly seated in rows with the teacher facing them at the front of the class. Students are observed, however, in other ways. Individuals are inscribed within 'a field of surveillance [which] also situates them in a network of writing; it engages them in a whole mass of documents that capture and fix them' (Foucault 1977: 189). Here reports, performance appraisals, marks of attainment, the timetable and schedule of learning, lists of work to be completed and criteria for assessment, are all mechanisms of observation which attempt to discipline both students and teachers to act in particular ways. Mechanisms of normalisation operate as judgments over statements of truth and correctness are decided. True or correct knowledge or performance is decided traditionally by the teacher or trainer. These mechanisms of normalising judgment can be seen to operate in curriculum selection, in feedback to students on answers to questions and assignments, in guidance given on how best to learn, and so forth. The practices of observation and normalising judgment are brought together in the act of examination. Through examination students are made available for scrutiny, comparison and judgment, as objects. As subjects, they 'learn' the truth about themselves, as to whether they are afforded a particular rank: of 'educated', 'competent' or 'professional'.

These mechanisms are central to traditional forms of education and training and are reformulated and, in some senses, extended in flexible learning (Nicoll & Edwards 1997). For example, observation may not be continuous or direct as it is in face-to-face teaching, through the placing of bodies where they can be viewed from a particular position within the four walls of a classroom. In flexible learning observation may be reformulated so that it is intermittent and indirect: through telephone, letter and e-mail communication, tele- and videoconferencing, and so forth. The observation may be indirect through the texts from which students learn, wherein self-direction, self-assessment or self-policing may move to the fore. In addition, the power of normalising judgment may no longer be exerted on the student mainly, or solely, by the teacher or trainer. In flexible learning normalising power may become embedded within a variety of relations external to the institution—through, for example, the utilisation of learning mentors and workplace supervisors. Normalising power therefore may become more dispersed through flexible learning. This is also the case for examination. As the formal sites of learning are extended into the workplace and, through the use of written and other forms of teaching media, onto the public transport systems and into homes, disciplinary practices are stretched out across the social formation but are not the monopoly of the institutions of the nation-state. Flexible learning may thus be said both to reduce the disciplinary power of particular institutional practices and to extend and reconfigure forms of learning and governance—in some ways both literally and metaphorically 'keeping learners in their places'.

The latter is the case particularly in relation to the reorderings of space and time which are possible through approaches that do not rely on the regular face-to-face meeting in the classroom. As the relationship between learning and face-to-face interaction is broken in the development of many approaches to flexible learning, most notably those associated with open and distance learning, so the necessity for people to attend specific places for learning at specific times is undermined. Here the 'place' of the learner—the learning setting—rather than that of the provider, is foregrounded. Geographical dispersal and the compression of space-time through the use and speed of ICT can be said to enhance flexible learning's contribution to flexible accumulation. Learners and providers no longer need to be in the same place, or even nation-state, but are increasingly available on a global scale to each other through the various forms of media. Forms of flexible learning act as dispersal strategies, the extent of this process partly dependent on the media through which the learning is made available. The sending of printed materials through the post brings about a specific temporal relationship between places, one which is transformed through, for instance, the use of computer networking. Flexibility enables learning to take place in settings closer to other aspects of the learner's life. As workplaces become dispersed, so do the opportunities to learn. What then are the consequences of developments in flexible learning for students?

FLEXIBLE (L)EARNERS?

Flexible learning can be said to transform the possibilities for educational communities of practice (Lave & Wenger 1991) and, with that, what it means to be a 'student'. Here we sugest a schematic typology through which the impact of shifts towards flexibile learning on student identity can be explored.

Considering the notion of the student first, there is a clear role and identity. If we are a student, we are part of something—we belong within an institution. That sense of belonging is important in establishing a sense of identity. It provides a certain status, which is important to ourselves and in negotiating boundaries with others. This is partly dependent on the value given to education and training and different forms of these within a culture. Nonetheless, being a student provides a boundary against which other demands can be defended. It is a 'serious' role, which, although capable of being a threat to our sense of self, our relations with families and friends, nonetheless provides the grounds for affirming a particular identity. This has been important for adults whose participation in formal education and training is dependent partially on their ability to organise their learning, to defend a space for learning, around other demands (Morrison 1992).

This notion of the student is very much linked to certain conceptions of education and training in which a canon of knowledge, skills and understanding are transmitted to the participants. It is a serious and disciplined process of development and deepening, in which the relative institutional stability is reflected in the relative stability of the canon and its ordering, and, with that, a certain stability in the identity of the student. In many ways this conception of education and training continues and extends the monastic tradition of initiation, order and stability, replacing the religious elite and vocation with the secular elite of the modern nation-state, also often with a strong sense of vocation. Assumptions of the student as a full-time young participant have been challenged only relatively recently, with trends towards growing adult participation and part-time and modular study increasingly associated with flexible learning. It is therefore a view of education slowly disappearing from the post-school sphere in the contemporary period, with the emergence of lifelong learning as a central goal. With it goes the relative stability of education and training institutions, the canon and the boundedness of student identity.

As the range of opportunities for learning have grown, partly through flexible learning, so the very notion of what constitutes an education and/or training is reconstituted. Increasingly, the latter are packaged, commodified, consumable, their sources more diverse and more open. In the process, the notion of a canon to be imparted is itself undermined as modularisation, new delivery mechanisms and consumer 'choice' are given greater play. The sense of trust invested in educational institutions to impart the canon to students is undermined, as individuals are given greater opportunity to negotiate their own ways flexibly through the range of learning opportunities available to them, to invest their own meanings in the learning process, and to negotiate the relationship between learning and other activities (Atkinson 1996). As a result, the bounded sense of identity associated with being a student is challenged. The focus shifts from being a member of an institution to being an individualised and flexible learner. The choices available and the conditions under which they are exercised thereby create the conditions for less certainty and a more unstable sense of identity (Shah 1994).

It is no accident therefore that, as there have been developments in flexible learning, so the discourses surrounding and framing them have also changed. Part of that change has been a shift from notions of the student to notions of the learner. There is no clear boundary to the notion of the learner. While it recognises rightly the fact that people learn not only from formal institutions but also in various and diverse life settings, it also suggests a diffuseness about what constitutes learning. As learners we are not part of something, we are individuals flexibly negotiating the complexity and ambivalence of the contemporary period. In other words, inscribed in the very notion of the learner is the shift in emphasis, wherein greater responsibility is being placed back on the individual. The sense of being as thing, of being a student, is displaced by and overlayed with a sense of being as activity, of becoming, of learning and being a flexible learner (West 1998).

There are important gender dimensions to such developments. Marginson (1993: 76) suggests that it is 'important to look closely at the essentialised forms of human behaviour that are valued (and produced) by the [neo-liberal] economic model'. For him, the economically rational individual is dominantly constituted as male, self-centred, passive (determined by external forces), self-responsible although incapable of self-determining action. However, the deployment of flexibility as a governing metaphor has occurred alongside greater overall female participation in the workforce and education and training. This increase in participation has not necessarily produced or been the product of greater equity. For instance, Hart (1992) claims that flexibility has always been required by women. She suggests this flexibility is also sought now from the generic worker. Thus, there may be greater complexity in current trends than is suggested by Marginson. While flexible learning may open up opportunities for participation by women, this participation can remain differentiated, a position that may be exacerbated by the use of ICT, given current access to and use of the latter. In examining the impact of flexible learning, therefore, it is not simply a question of what is happening, but also to whom. Flexible learners are increasingly women, even as men are themselves reconstituted by the practices in play to become more flexible themselves.

Shifting notions of students and learners, their relationship to wider economic and cultural trends and the meanings invested in them can be witnessed therefore within educational discourses as a whole. Discourses of education and training emphasise the transmission of the canon. Within this, the student has a clear and bounded identity as part of the institution. By contrast, certain discourses of flexible learning have a different concern for the learner and learning, not as part of the institution but as a consumer of learning opportunities. When flexible learning is aligned with neoliberal economics, marketing lifestyle choices may become a key to institutional success, rather than the simple rites of initiation and exclusion. Lyotard (1993) adds to this picture the notion of a worker who is separated increasingly from the meaning of work, and the relationship of this work to pay received. For him, modern capitalism provides a seductive 'compensation' to the worker in the promise of a rising standard of living through growing freedom to consume. He suggests that systems of governance thus constitute the needs for goods which bring about that consumption: '[t]hat is to say that capitalism tries to incorporate the dynamic of needs ever more strictly within its global economic dynamic' (Lyotard 1993: 271). Within this dynamic, knowledge, skills and understanding themselves become increasingly a commodity for consumption, one which is now required by the individual to maintain his/her position within the workforce. In this situation neoliberal economics may be bound together powerfully with those of 'flexible learning', where the dynamic is one of growing incitement to consume learning and learn to consume, in order to maintain earnings, to continue to consume and work. Flexible learning becomes synonymous with flexible earning, with questions as to the opportunities and flexibilities available and possible for those excluded from the charmed circle.

CONCLUSION: FLEXIBILITY IN FLEXIBLE LEARNING

Increasingly, education and training institutions draw on the discourses and practices of the marketplace and neo- and post-Fordist strategies to enable them to service a range of market niches. Similarly, traditionally 'non-educational' settings, such as workplaces, adopt the discourses and practices of the educator. As the sense of bounded identity is ruptured therefore, so are the boundaries between, for instance, education, training, business, entertainment, leisure. New and different forms of teaching and learning are developed, the relative values of which are themselves contested.

The nature and extent of the processes outlined above need to be examined both in relation to the economy as a whole and more particularly in relation to practices of flexible learning. There is also the need to address the ambivalent consequences of such developments for, as we said at the start, there is no single meaning of flexible learning. In their argument for a form of productive diversity, for instance, Cope and Kalantzis (1997) suggest that multiplicity, devolution, negotiation and pluralism should be placed alongside flexibility as governing metaphors. Here the aim is for organisations not to compete against each other to provide the same goods and services, which simply drives down price; rather, organisations should provide distinctive goods and services for different individuals and groups, for which there will be demand precisely because of their distinctiveness. Both these trends can be witnessed in the contemporary economy, but the former is probably stronger than the latter in education and training.

Cope and Kalantzis' argument is suggestive rather than convincing. But they certainly indicate the possibilities that exist for contesting the meanings inscribed in governing metaphors. In the case of flexibility, possibilities exist for a range of practices to be developed: to embed adaptive and creative pedagogies; to keep people in their place and provide the possibility for being in different places or even more mobile; to build forms of social as well as human capital; to be more isolated or engage and interact with a more diverse set of people and perspectives. In different organisations and different parts of the organisation, flexibility and flexible learning may be governing metaphors but they may signify different things. The notion of flexible and creative learners with certain degrees of autonomy in how they define and achieve their goals, individually and as part of different communities of practice, with the capacity to engage with others in new ways, is suggestive of a critical dimension to learning which adaptive forms of flexibility may deny. Either flexibility and flexible learning can be invested with a variety of meanings or different governing metaphors will have to be developed. With them will emerge different pedagogies and different politics.

FURTHER READING

Avis, J. 1996 'The myth of the post-fordist society', in J. Avis, M. Bloomer, G. Esland, D. Gleeson & P. Hodkinson (eds), *Knowledge and Nationhood*. London: Cassell.

Cope, B. & Kalantzis, M. 1997 *Productive Diversity: A New Australian Model for Work and Management*. Annandale: Pluto Press.

du Gay, P. 1996 *Consumption and Identity at Work*. London: Sage.

Edwards, R. 1997 *Changing Places? Flexibility, Lifelong Learning and a Learning Society*. London: Routledge.

Hart, M. 1992 *Working and Educating for Life: Feminist and International Perspectives*. London: Routledge.

Kirkpatrick, D. 1997 'Becoming flexible: contested territory', *Studies in Continuing Education*, 19(2), pp. 160–73.

9

Reading the discourses of adult basic education teaching
Alison Lee & Rosie Wickert

Adult basic education (ABE), as a relatively new field of practice, has nevertheless formed a distinctive identity for itself. In a field where there is little research and little published literature, teacher-practitioners espouse a set of deeply held beliefs and principles about adult literacy teaching which appears to have varied little across institutional and geographical sites and across recent time (e.g. Nelson & Dymock 1986; Grant 1986; Hammond et al. 1992; McConnell & Treloar 1993). Teachers, it would appear, derive these beliefs in often informal ways, from colleagues, from in-service courses, from documents, from conferences and tutor-training processes. This chapter asks: What do these beliefs and principles mean? Where have they come from? What is their status? What relationships do they bear to practice? In particular, how do these principles relate to the contemporary policy context within which adult literacy teaching is located?

In questioning claims made about ABE, we are concerned to open the field to scrutiny—to expose some of its espoused principles about its practices to critical examination. It is necessary to take a critical perspective on documents that publicly represent the field of adult basic education. It seems clear that without such a critical perspective, which seeks to locate such statements within the history of their inception and derivation, they come to be constituted simply as public 'truths'. Our work in this chapter is to investigate some characteristic sets of these foundational statements to show how they are made up of different and sometimes even inconsistent and contradictory principles. Our argument is that, in order to intervene in and assume some control of the future of their field, teachers must develop an explicit under-

140

standing of the complexities and inconsistencies that constitute the field.

This chapter begins with a brief account of the place of adult basic education within the current 'training reform agenda' (see chapter 6) as a backdrop for our analysis of what adult literacy, in particular, historically claimed itself to be. Following that, we assert the importance of techniques of discourse analysis for contemporary social analysis in any field. Then we identify several of the dominant discourses that have gone to constructing the field of ABE and its practices: those of humanistic psychology, of progressive liberalism and of adult individualism, and, more recently (in a relationship of apparent tension and contradiction to these 'foundational' discourses), the discourse of economic rationalism.

POSITIONING THE ADULT LITERACY TEACHER IN 'NEW TIMES'

An examination of the operations of discourse in the changing positioning of the ABE teacher in the 1990s needs to begin with a consideration of the significant shifts in the way in which ABE is located in relation to its contemporary social context.

As traditional primary and secondary industries have declined, alongside a rapid growth in service industries and the information-based industry sector, new forms of work organisation have emerged. The 'new' workplace is claimed to be characterised by a much flatter organisational structure, with greater responsibility devolved to the point of production or the point of service. The language of workplace reform constructs the worker as a team member, with productive work becoming dependent on participation and joint decision making (Gee et al. 1996). The effective functioning of such a workplace must, to a significant extent, depend on the spoken and written language skills of its workforce. Funding for adult literacy and basic education programs has been increasingly harnessed to the language and literacy demands of the workplace reform agenda, through government labour market and employment assistance funding and program arrangements, and an emphasis on work-related learning outcomes.

In this context, adult basic education teachers are no longer construed as marginal to the main business of education. They are also no longer seen as being largely involved in welfare and social justice issues. They are now seen to be central to the human-capital thesis underpinning the training reform agendas sponsored by the 'competitive state' (see chapter 6).

The consequences of these kinds of policy shifts for adult literacy and basic education workers include a growing regulation of their work by bureaucratic management practices. The operation of what has been termed 'corporate federalism' is the manifestation of growing centralist control through the development of national policies and strategies and the consequent establishment of national initiatives, such as curriculum and reporting frameworks (Taylor et al. 1997). Ironically, as responsibility is devolved by having budgets managed closer and closer to the point of service or delivery, the actual regulation and the guidelines attendant on those budgets are more tightly controlled than ever.

For many ABE workers, one of the consequences of this shift in the positioning of their work is a sense of being coopted or colonised by these changes and of having to serve the requirements of funding bodies, often in apparent contradiction to the needs of students. It is a testimony to the power of the discourses of the new public-sector management that there now appears to be widespread compliance with its practices in spite of this sense of being taken over by the demands of the unfamiliar discourses of corporate managerialism and economic rationalism. Moreover, the training reform agenda itself consists of a bundle of different discourses, displaying a mix of traditionally progressive and conservative elements. We now begin to explore how poststructuralism and discourse analysis can provide the tools for analysis of how the field of ABE has been 'discursively constructed'.

DISCOURSE AND DISCOURSE ANALYSIS

Discourse is a term which has several different meanings in 20th-century scholarship. In the sense in which we use it here, however, the term discourse is strongly grounded in the theoretical and political movement known as poststructuralism, and most closely connected to the work of the social analyst Michel Foucault. Foucault was concerned to explore the local and specific relations of power. Instead of accepting a simple structure of domination that worked within the polarity of labour and capital, however, Foucault investigated ways in which individuals participated in multiple institutional practices, which positioned them differently in different relations of power or subordination—as women, for example, or as adults, as parents or as teachers. Power was understood not as a monolithic entity but as always existing with respect to these positions, in relation to their 'others'—men, children, offspring, students.

Accompanying this insistence on the local, specific and multiple nature of power relations was an understanding of the central role of language in the construction of the social meanings constituting these relationships. Foucault conceived discourse as a term that refers to systematic sets of meanings which circulate around the practices of particular institutions. These discourses are both enabling and constraining. On the one hand they enable meanings to be exchanged in specific sites, which make those sites recognisable as instances of a particular social relationship— for example, teacher–student. On the other hand, they constrain the meanings which can be made as a form of regulation of the terms and boundaries of that relationship (see Gee 1990).

For example, the discourse of the institution of formal education allows certain meanings but not others to be 'properly' exchanged between teachers and students. This means in turn that the relationships or positions available to teachers and students are governed by that institution and, more particularly, constrained by the limits set by that discourse. In 20th-century social history, some discourses have taken on a dominating role across a variety of institutions, determining the kinds of meanings and truths that can and cannot be developed. One of the most powerful of these has been psychology, which has so pervaded institutions such as education, the law and medicine that psychological conceptions of social relationships have often passed into 'commonsense' or universal understandings about the way things are, rather than being seen as discursive constructions with particular kinds of effects.

In order for ABE and its associated field, adult education, to enable different positions for teachers and learners to be possible, different discourses have had to be mobilised which name and position participants and practices differently. These have included discourses developed in part in opposition to state-sponsored formal education, and have historically included humanistic psychology's discourses of adult learning and experiential learning, as well as critical theory's discourses of liberation and conscientisation.

THE DISCURSIVE CONSTRUCTION OF ADULT LITERACY TEACHING

There has to this point been no substantial history written of ABE teaching. Indeed, there has been little systematic analysis of the field. As a consequence, ABE teachers have few places to go in order to contextualise their own practice. The few publications which span the 1980s, during the time of the establishment and major growth phase of adult basic education, did not penetrate deeply the history or sociology of the field. In many ways, for these workers coming into adult basic education, the field simply *was*. The principles governing its practices were truths that were perhaps self-evident or, at the least, incontrovertible 'foundations' of educational principle.

What was going on during the 1980s was an organisation of the field into a professional body. This was the work of small numbers of teachers and program managers who realised the importance of articulating some statements of principle that would serve to define the field of practice. These statements of principle provide a useful window onto the discursive framework in which ABE teaching was constructed during its first decade of self-identification and substantial growth. This is not to assert that teachers actually knew or know these texts in any explicit or detailed way; the relationship between texts and actual teachers is more complex than that. It is possible to suggest, however, that, like ABE teaching itself, for many these statements have had the status of truth, a 'foundational' status, separate from the history of their production.

That such statements of principle have discursively entered and shaped the field is evident in the ways that teachers consistently respond to the question: *What principles underpin your practice as an ABE teacher?* Although teachers and tutors cannot usually refer to any specific texts, brainstorming activities have typically produced lists of principles such as the following:[1]

- student-centred and student-directed learning;
- curriculum based on student needs;
- concern with student as a whole person;
- use student experience as a resource for teaching;
- negotiate learning with student;
- relevant and purposeful learning activities;
- learning which develops student independence;
- reflection;
- student as active participant;
- open access and flexible provision;
- small-group learning.

Here we look beyond the mere ubiquity of such statements to question not only their presence but also their effects in the constitution of the field. Where have they come from? What is their status? What meanings of the 'person', the 'adult', the 'learner' are being constructed? What is the 'pedagogy' that is being projected? And, importantly, how relevant and adequate are these principles to the demands of current practices and contexts of ABE practice? In what follows we examine excerpts taken from some of the foundational texts informing these positions. Our choice is not determined by any claim of representativeness or status; rather, the excerpts are chosen because of their illustrative value. Also, it should be noted, we do not draw on actual teaching materials. We examine how the language of the selected texts constructs particular meanings about the field. Further, we examine some of the meanings that are not available in these constructions. That is, we examine the discourses being mobilised within these texts, seeing how they allow certain meanings and not others. The readings we produce do not tell 'the truth' about the texts but are partial, in two senses: first, like all readings, they are incomplete, in the sense that they pay selective attention to particular elements of the texts; second, they are written from the perspective of our individual and shared discursive histories. Texts always exceed any reading that might be made of them. There are always other readings to be made.

THE PRIMACY OF THE INDIVIDUAL

A prevalent feature in these texts is a discourse of individualism. The first point in the first published set of principles for adult literacy provision reads (ALIO 1983):

> The individual student's perceptions, needs, aspirations, and learning style should determine the type of tuition s/he receives, rather than any pre-conceived notions of ideal educational content and delivery. This includes respect for the student's right to share in decision-making about his/her educational future.

Here the learner is constructed as an individual, first and foremost. It is this individual, or rather his or her 'perceptions', 'needs', 'aspirations' etc., which should determine the curriculum and the pedagogy. These perceptions, needs, aspirations emanating from the individual are constructed in a binary opposition with what are pejoratively termed preconceived notions about content and delivery. These are presumed to be notions held by a teacher, though there is no direct mention of a teacher in this statement. What teaching is meant to be is also implicit. The implied position available to the teacher in this formulation appears to be a passive one, of not imposing institutional barriers on students' realising their needs, like a natural unfolding. Such a formulation appears to preclude the possibility on the part of the teacher of expert knowledge, either about curriculum or about pedagogy.

THE QUESTION OF POWER

Supporting and extending the casting of the teacher and the learner as 'individuals' is the following statement (ALIO 1983):

> The use of labels as classifying devices in adult literacy work should be rejected . . . The giving of a label implies power and superiority on the part of the one who labels over the one so labelled; this power has led in many cases to the individual student being condemned to a tuition stream lacking in challenge or completely inappropriate to his/her needs and aspirations.

The implicit theory of power in operation here is a negative one. It is placed against the opposing position, also implicit, that the 'principled', desired relationship between teacher and learner is somehow outside power relationships. If power is equated with 'superiority', then power can only mean domination by the powerful of the powerless. This also means that power is defined largely in individual terms within the pedagogic encounter, and does not include an analysis of the larger social context in which each is located. Further, this power is represented as not really 'superior' in the sense of higher-status knowledge or judgment, as what is said to occur in many cases as an outcome is the 'condemnation' of a student to an inappropriate tuition stream.

It is important to stress here that our analysis does not imply that this statement is 'wrong'—nor that the kinds of outcomes being described here do not occur, or that they are not a problem. The point being made is that this construction is not a sufficiently complex one, adequate to the complexities of the actual pedagogic situation. Absent from these early statements of principle is an acknowledgment of the actual power differential in the relationship between the teacher and the learner, with particular respect to Foucault's notion of power/knowledge (Foucault 1972). This power is elided in the assertion of the common humanity and adulthood of both parties. Nowhere is there an account of the actual effects of the teacher's having certain competences and knowledge that the student does not have and may want to have. In placing the student's own 'perceptions' in prime position, it is implied that all 'perceptions' are equal in the sense that they are integral to the individual. The fact that the power/knowledge connection implies that power can have a *productive* effect, in enabling certain things to be said and done, is not mentioned.

This example is also interesting as an exemplary instance of the power of discourse. Discourses are not 'just' about language; through naming and positioning people in particular ways, they have material effects. Here the power to name, to 'label', conferred on the teacher brings about profound effects in the positioning, and hence the experience, of the student. The discourse being so strenuously rejected here is that of a tradition within cognitive psychology, which has constructed itself as a 'science' through methodologies of testing and measurement and enjoyed dominance in educational circles in the decades prior to the 1980s. What is being posited in its place in this example is a humanist discourse, asserting the primacy of individuals to 'know' themselves and their needs and aspirations as a 'natural' feature of their personhood.

TEACHER–LEARNER

One development of the humanist educational discourse leads to the notion of the interchangeability of the teacher and the learner, a position which continued to be republished in successive statements until it disappeared from the principles and recommendations of the Australian Council for Adult Literacy (ACAL) in 1989:

> The one invariable component in effective adult literacy teaching is positive personal relationships. This implies that, as in all truly adult interactions, the roles of teacher and learner will be frequently interchangeable and that both will gain some personal satisfaction from the relationship.

There is a great deal going on here in the construction of a discourse about teaching and learning. What appears to be posited in terms of positions for teachers and learners is again their common humanity and their common adulthood; assumed here, though not explicitly stated, is that this means an equivalence or reciprocity, if not an actual equality between the teacher and learner. There is an invocation of a 'truly adult interaction', implying some 'naturalness' about the pedagogic encounter which does not take into account the institutional nature of the contract between them. Teacher–learner interactions are 'adult', in the sense that they resemble ordinary adult conversation. Implied here is also a refusal of social difference, as if 'truly adult' interactions involve a refusal or transcendence of social hierarchy. Teaching here is constructed as conversation and exchange between equals, where the implicit notion of equality does not allow a difference between participants in terms of Bourdieu's (1977) notion of 'cultural capital'. Further, this discourse of 'adulthood' works almost to refuse the viability of the terms 'teacher' and 'learner', constructed as they are in relation to each other in terms of one being the 'opposite' of the other. Of course, adulthood is constructed here in opposition to childhood, and the positional hierarchy between teacher and learner being refused is that occurring within the dominant discourses and practices of school education.

It is the apparent refusal of the necessary asymmetry between the positions of teacher and learner and the status of what they know that conceals the actual relationship between them. If power can be seen only as repressive, then the productive power of knowledge must also implicitly be refused. One of the effects of requiring that the teacher abdicate her role as a certain kind of knower is that the teacher is left without a clear sense of what her work and her expertise consist of. She must conceal or repress her own knowledge in order for the 'good personal relationship' to be possible.

LIBERALISM/HUMAN RIGHTS

Much of the above commentary situates these statements of principle firmly and clearly within an educational discourse of liberal progressivism. This, often constructed in opposition to more hierarchical and authoritarian pedagogical relationships, including those created through the discourse of measurement psychology, sets up the individual in centre stage, thereby asserting the possibility of a genuinely student-centred practice. This is achieved by a refusal to acknowledge or attend to the social differences between teacher and learner that are inscribed within their different institutional positions (Bernstein 1971; Walkerdine 1984). The breaking down of the hierarchical distinction between the positions of teacher and learner is made possible through the discourse of what we might term 'adultism'. Within 'adultism' it is possible to imagine a space where power/hierarchical differences break down and true symmetry is possible, in opposition to the child–adult hierarchy within which teaching–learning relationships are traditionally constructed.

The prevailing liberalism of these texts can be seen in the overarching discourses within which they are framed: those of human rights, of the sovereignty of the individual, and of equal opportunity. By 1989 the tenor of the documents had shifted substantially into a kind of 'human rights' discourse. In the 1989 ACAL statements of principles and recommendations, the most recent articulation of principle by this professional body, three of the first four principles are statements of rights.

These texts show traces of themes in the literature of the

associated field of adult education. What is noteworthy in the ABE texts, however, is that certain of the available discourses of adult education are substantially missing. One major alternative, or even competing, discourse to the more individualist forms of liberalism has been the Marxist-inspired discourse of emancipation. Of particular influence in this sphere has been the work of Paulo Freire. Within this discourse, the educational project is a project for social change through political action, community development and the 'conscientisation' of citizens. This latter term involves a revolutionary imperative whereby education for literacy is aimed at freeing the oppressed from the shackles of capitalist (and sometimes patriarchal) oppression. In this discourse, the adult basic education learner is constructed as one who has been oppressed by the institutions of the capitalist state, of which education is seen as a major arm. The teacher is constructed as one who is committed to such a project of education for social change through the conscientisation of learners.

We came to the task of assembling and analysing the successive statements of principle of adult literacy teaching with an expectation that they would contain traces of liberationist discourses. The absence of such material is striking and warrants further investigation. Whatever the reasons, the absence of social analysis or a political project for education for social change determines the prevailing positions available for the adult basic education teacher, welfare provider or defender of human rights, or the sovereignty of the individual (Wickert 1993). The student is constructed as one who might either be helped to achieve her or his own human potential (the dominant personal growth discourse) or be brought to understand her or his own citizenship (liberal education for citizenship). We do not mean to suggest here that there is no evidence of teaching practice informed by a radical position (e.g. Bee 1989), rather that the texts articulating foundational principles do not.

CULTURAL DIVERSITY, ACCESS AND EQUITY, AND STATE INTERVENTION

The early dominance of liberal individualism and progressivism persists throughout the successive reformulations of statements of principle, though with some discursive shifts in two particular directions. Also, one of the most striking absences, already briefly alluded to, from the statements through the 1980s is that of social difference. The first shift, then, marks a growing engagement with questions of the social context in which ABE teaching and learning take place, while the second can be understood as a response to the growing intervention in the field by the state, via policy and funding developments.

In the case of the first shift, there is much attention paid to questions of the social—of the integral role adult basic education plays in community development and thus to the role of education for social change of some kind, rather than mere personal growth for individuals (e.g. Nelson & Dymock 1986; NSWALC 1988; ACAL 1989). Further, with the lead-up to the National Language and Literacy Policy bringing together the hitherto institutionally separate domains of adult ESL and of ABE, issues of the social—including cultural—difference emerge in the texts. For example the *Literacy Strategy for the People of New South Wales* (NSW Government 1990) shifted a long way from the 'individual differences' emphasis of earlier formulations. In that text there is a notion of a stratified society and of education for diversity, but still no evocation of struggle.

The second major discursive shift is in response to the growing intervention of the state in ABE provision, particularly its attempts to link education and work more closely. Earlier we outlined something of that intervention and the new discursive climate within which adult literacy teaching is located. Here, we refer to the report *An Emerging National Curriculum* (NSW TAFE 1992).

This document was one of the first reports to emerge following the announcement of the 1991 National Language and Literacy Policy, which attempted to place various initiatives together under the bureaucratic gaze and harness them to the emerging national training reform agenda. The report documents the outcomes of a national mapping exercise of adult literacy curricula. Many tensions exist in this text, such as those between diversity and national consistency, including common terminology; personal goals and national standards; the competing claims of 'critical enquiry' and 'competency-based training'; outcomes in terms of 'attitudes' and 'active' and 'informed' citizenship, and outcome measurement in terms of 'performance indicators' of 'student progression'; flexibility and responsiveness; and compliance with structured and comprehensive national curriculum (Beazley 1997).

The point to be made is the way in which such texts bear the traces of multiple and often competing and contradictory discourses. In this sense, texts are like archaeological sites within which history and change can be read. Texts demonstrate to an analytic reader that they are best read as accretions of the discourses that have been mobilised to construct the field through its history. There are no instances of texts that are 'pure' realisations of a single discourse, but neither is it possible to see history as simple progress and development, either in the sense of adding to past positions or supplanting past discourses with the new. Texts such as those we have looked at here grow in complexity as the field grows, setting up tensions in terms of the practices they purport to describe. Only by making these tensions explicit, we argue, can 'stakeholders' be in a position to participate in what Anna Yeatman (1990) calls the 'politics of discourse'.

CONCLUSION

How relevant are the discourses historically mobilised by ABE teachers to current ABE practice? Do they help practitioners deal with the current demands? For example, do they provide the tools to enable ABE practitioners to respond adequately to the pressures on them to be accountable for student learning? Do they provide for principled and acceptable ways of reporting on student progress? Are the underpinning principles sufficiently discursively complex to allow inappropriate demands to be contested and to enable more appropriate responses to be constructed?

ABE teachers have, on the whole, been slow to enter into debate with the government version of ABE teaching as constructed through the discourses of human capital and economic rationalism. Their experiences of ABE learners make it clear that there are complex reasons why these learners are not occupying more powerful social and economic positions. The discourses most commonly available to teachers for explaining that experience range from individualist psychological notions such as 'lack of confidence' and 'poor self-esteem' to critiques within the adult education literature of mainstream schooling. Whatever the analysis, adult literacy teachers appear to find it difficult to 'buy' the human capital thesis and the construction of the adult learner as primarily a 'worker' in this era of long-term unemployment (Wickert & Baynham 1994).

In this chapter we offer these initial readings to provide some tools for dialogue and debate, for making greater sense of the material emanating from government, and for naming the disquiet that may accompany the readings of such texts. Instead of simply surfacing feelings, poststructuralist text analysis enables the reader to surface the operation of discourses. We have selected from a few historically significant and public documents and have begun to explore the potential of poststructuralist methods of discourse analysis, to demonstrate how ways of talking about the field of ABE have been constructed, how complex these 'ways of talking' are, and how they constantly shift and change. As the field of ABE continues to be built within increasingly bureaucratic structures, powerful forms of analysis are essential to enable productive critical debate.

NOTE

1 Data were consistently gathered in workshops with ABE teachers over a number of years.

FURTHER READING

Beazley, H. 1997 'Inventing individual identity in the Australian language and literacy policy', *Literacy and Numeracy Studies*, 7(1), pp. 46–62.
Brown, M. (ed.) 1994 *Literacies and the Workplace: A Collection of Original Essays*. Geelong: Deakin University Press.
Gee, J.P. 1990 *Social Linguistics and Literacies: Ideology in Discourses*. London: Falmer Press.
Lee, A. & Poynton, C. 1988 *Discourse and Text*. Sydney: Allen & Unwin.
Weedon, C. 1987 *Feminist Practice and Post-Structuralist Theory*. Oxford: Basil Blackwell.

PART III
WORKPLACE CHANGE AND LEARNING

Introduction to Part III

Part III of this book examines various aspects of a central contemporary issue, the relationship between workplace change, adult learning and training.

Chapter 10 explores the concept of the 'learning organisation'. The current interest in organisational learning is attributed to a number of factors, including the internationalisation of production, the rapidity of change in production processes, the growing lack of distinction between organisations and their environments, and the growing importance of knowledge to the process of adding value. It is argued that the 'learning organisation' is an idealised goal rather than an attainable reality. Nevertheless, a workplace can become more like a learning organisation if three things occur: if learning is fostered through critical questioning; if workers and managers learn how to learn; and if learning needs are taken into account in all aspects of an organisation's functioning, from production processes to information management. Organisational learning emphasises the learning potential of everyday work activities. Structured classroom-based training courses still have their place in a learning organisation, but only as one of many learning opportunities that are available as individuals and groups work and learn concurrently.

In recent years probably the only constant in adult education and training has been continuous change. Chapter 11 focuses on the 'how' of change—on how adult educators and trainers can more effectively implement change, wherever they happen to be working. The chapter begins with a brief discussion of why change is so all-pervasive and what this means for adult educators. Readers are then invited to reflect on their past experience of educational change and to compare their experience with a summary of research on change dynamics. In doing this, a number of popular change management myths are exposed. This is followed by an overview of the key factors that usually trigger a change effort and influence the way it turns out. Key sources of educational change are identified, the main types of change are noted, the way in which the scope and size of the change play a part is illustrated, and the central roles played by motivation, values and evaluation are outlined. The chapter concludes by proposing a framework for understanding and acting on educational change.

Chapter 12 discusses competence, another central concept in the effort to link education to workplace reform. The chapter begins with a critique of the approach known as 'competency-based training' (CBT), which emerged in the USA in the 1950s and has been adopted extensively in vocational education in other countries. It is argued that CBT equates competence to technical task skills, that it is fixated on the measurement of a narrow range of competencies, that it restricts workplace creativity by positing single acceptable ways in which work outcomes can be achieved, that it objectifies and reifies performance, and that it privileges individual learning and discourages group learning. These flaws in CBT are attributed to its positivist assumption that knowledge and skills can be reduced to their component parts and then taught to learners.

In opposition to the positivist view of competence enshrined in CBT, chapter 12 offers an 'integrative' conception. This view of competence takes account of all aspects of work performance, places equal emphasis on learning outcomes and underpinning attributes of performance, encourages the development of generic rather than atomised competencies, allows for multiple acceptable outcomes in learning and work, takes account of contextual factors in the definition of competence, and proposes a practitioner-oriented evidential approach to the articulation of competency standards and the demonstration of competence. This view of competence is based on the interpretive assumption that in the culture of practice practitioners socially construct the meaning of their work. It sits comfortably with learner-centred educational approaches like peer learning, contract learning, self-assessment and problem-based learning. The chapter ends with a discussion of the critique of competence. Critics argue that even the integrative approach to competence fails to take sufficient account of the ways in which power relations shape all aspects of life and learning. (This critique is developed further in chapters 4, 7 and 10.)

Chapter 13 examines six approaches to cross-cultural training in the workplace. The first of these, the ethno-specific approach, introduces learners to the practices and values of particular cultures and trains learners in ways of overcoming communication barriers across cultures. The second approach, which is associated with equal employment and antidiscrimination initiatives, looks at issues of access and equity in culturally and linguistically diverse workplaces. The third approach provides social and historical information about different migrant groups, assuming that such information will improve cross-cultural understanding. The fourth, linguistic, approach concentrates on improving trainees' understanding of, and capacity to conduct, written and spoken communication across cultures. The fifth approach helps learners to become more aware of psychological and interpersonal barriers to cross-cultural communication. The sixth approach seeks to harness cultural diversity to the goals of improving workplace productivity and international economic competitiveness. The chapter concludes with a table designed to help readers select the cross-cultural training approach most suited to their needs.

10

Organisational learning: basic concepts

Laurie Field

Learning organisations have been talked about for the past few decades, but during the 1990s, interest soared. This chapter[1] begins by examining factors that are contributing to the sudden upsurge of interest in organisational learning. It then looks at what a learning organisation is, and highlights the importance of learning through critical questioning. Moves to improve organisational learning have profound implications for an enterprise's human resource development effort, and these are discussed at the end of the chapter.

WHY THE SUDDEN INTEREST IN ORGANISATIONAL LEARNING?

The main factors contributing to the interest many enterprises are taking in organisational learning are:

- environmental turbulence;
- new forms of organisation;
- knowledge as a primary resource;
- multidimensional change;
- more permeable, fuzzy boundaries;
- reduced time frames;
- internationalisation.

In this section, we look briefly at each factor.

ENVIRONMENTAL TURBULENCE

In an influential paper of the 1960s Emery and Trist introduced the idea of environmental turbulence. In their words, in a turbulent environment 'the ground is in motion' (1965: 20). Since the 1960s the operating environments of many enterprises have become even more turbulent. One implication is that there is more and more information to be processed, and this creates a pressure for rapid learning.

NEW FORMS OF ORGANISATION

During the past decade, the concept of 'organisation' is itself having to be modified to encompass new forms such as consortia, joint ventures, flexible manufacturing networks, business incubators and strategic alliances (Dempster & Rooney 1991). According to Limerick and Cunnington, arrangements like these have profound implications for organisational learning: 'Our analysis suggests that companies have to become action-learning organisations. What is needed is a new kind of organisational learning paradigm' (1993: 220).

KNOWLEDGE AS A PRIMARY RESOURCE

According to Drucker (1993: 38), enterprises' success will increasingly depend on the capacity to extend knowledge and apply it effectively. In part, this transition results from the growing importance of service and information industries, and the decline of manufacturing in established industrial countries. But even within manufacturing itself, there is growing awareness that the vast majority of employees—involved in areas like sales, marketing, and purchasing—are primarily involved in service jobs and rely on information as their key resource. As Quinn (1992: 257) has observed, unlike mechanical systems, which run best when left undisturbed, intellect grows most when continually challenged.

According to Quinn, in the emerging knowledge-based enterprise, problem solving, challenge and intellectual capacity underlie effectiveness. The catalyst for developing these characteristics is the capacity of individuals and the organisation as a whole to learn.

MULTIDIMENSIONAL CHANGE

Enterprises try to improve quality, productivity or profit in a variety of ways. Some invest large sums in new software or equipment. Others concentrate on employee involvement and reward systems. Still others focus on documentation and 'total quality management'. Initiatives like these cannot be taken in isolation. An enterprise constitutes a subtle, complex system, and change in one area often affects (and is affected by) change in many other areas. Successful enterprises are those which integrate approaches to employee relations, work organisation, skills, technology and information management in order to be productive, cost-effective or profitable over a period of time. To take an integrated approach, people in an enterprise need knowledge that overrides narrow specialties. They also need to feel secure enough to share their expertise (rather than hoarding it) and to risk making mistakes as they learn. Organisational learning is concerned both with how to manage multidimensional change and with the learning opportunities that such changes create.

MORE PERMEABLE, FUZZY BOUNDARIES

Within many enterprises, the boundaries between inside and outside are becoming increasingly blurred and fuzzy. In retailing and manufacturing, just-in-time practices are effective only if there is a close relationship with suppliers. Public sector agencies are becoming more responsive and less walled-off. In the construction industry, the level of expertise needed to win contracts may be attainable only if long-term strategic alliances are established with subcontractors. Benchmarking within and between enterprises, visits to other sites and intercompany collaboration also span the boundary between enterprise and environment, and pave the way for two-way information flow.

The same type of change is occurring within many enterprises at work-group level. Divisions are becoming less distinct as layers of management are reduced, demarcations become less pronounced, and communication channels such as e-mail and the intranet are used to facilitate collaboration and sharing. As boundaries become fuzzier and more permeable, it is far easier for knowledge to flow, and this creates enormous potential for learning.

REDUCED TIME FRAMES

Part of the pressure to improve organisational learning comes from individuals and groups having to work within ever-reduced time frames. In a world economy, enterprises are having to do things faster in order to access emerging markets and to become competent in new areas. Many enterprises are having to absorb new concepts (including the concept of 'learning organisation'), to integrate new forms of software and hardware, and to take advantage of new products, services and market conditions.

INTERNATIONALISATION

In the past few decades many formerly national economies have had to learn to compete in fast-changing world markets. As a consequence, enterprises are having to become much more concerned about constant improvement and innovation in the interests of satisfying customers and delivering consistent high quality (Lawler 1994).

In a deregulated commercial environment, it is relatively easy to transfer innovations in the form of patents, software and equipment. But one cannot transport the skills necessary to take advantage of these innovations (Thurow 1992). While skills are not the only consideration (many factors, including industry policy and trading practices, contribute as much to an enterprise's competitive advantage as skills), the difficulty of getting employees with the right mix and level of skills when and where they are needed is a major one. To develop a more skilled workforce, it is essential to manage organisational learning effectively.

What is a learning organisation?

The combined effect of factors like these is creating enormous pressure to improve organisational performance and learning. Some commentators (e.g. Garratt 1990; Pedler et al. 1991; Garvin 1993; Lessem 1993) discuss learning organisations as if they were tangible entities, and are often very idealistic.

Part of this idealism is that the organisational learning literature tends to assume that learning is always a positive and beneficial activity. Of course, this need not be so. In poor work environments, employees can learn that cynicism is justified, that commitment should be avoided, that risk-taking leads to blame, that mistakes should be denied. In an organisation where learning is encouraged and where there are deliberate attempts to open things up (e.g. by reducing barriers between work units and introducing more transparent channels for information exchange), employees are likely to learn more about organisational realities, and to become better able to regulate their own work. Similarly, with the introduction of technical systems that foster 'intellective skills' (Zuboff 1988), employees will be able to apply these newly acquired skills to understand present organisational dynamics more clearly and to formulate and promote more acceptable alternatives.

Under these circumstances, empowered workers are quite capable of undermining management wishes, deliberately underutilising company technology and avoiding work pressures.

For example, in one organisation where the introduction of e-mail was studied (Romm et al. 1996), employees quickly learnt to use the new communication medium for political manipulation, with the result that personal relationships were strained and management power was undermined. (For other examples with similar outcomes, see Schwartz 1987 and Thomas 1993.)

Given these realities, one needs to be aware that when commentators such as Karpin (1995) talk about managers 'creating conditions conducive to learning', they have in mind a particular type of learning—namely, learning which results in employees acquiring new knowledge and insights, sharing it with others, and applying the results to the benefit of the enterprise.

My view is that a learning organisation is an idealised goal. Nevertheless, becoming more like a learning organisation is an important, worthwhile goal, particularly for enterprises facing turbulent environments. Internationally, a growing number of enterprises are committed to becoming more like learning organisations, and have derived considerable benefit from their efforts to translate the rhetoric of organisational learning into reality.

One major obstacle to doing this is that organisational learning is related to many different aspects of enterprise functioning, including information management, skill formation, culture, history, job security, work organisation, and technological systems. There is no simple blueprint that will improve learning across this wide range of interconnected areas.

Moreover, it can be difficult to get practical assistance from the literature of organisational learning, because so many different disciplines are represented, each with their own particular emphasis. Even the first book about organisational learning—Argyris and Schon (1978)—could identify six different ways of understanding organisational learning, each based on a particular field of study: social psychology, management theory, sociology, information theory, anthropology, and political theory. In the 20 years since this book appeared, not only have investigators from each of these disciplines continued to write about organisational learning, but exponents of many other areas as well—computer sciences, adult learning, organisational psychodynamics, industrial relations, biology, strategic planning—have entered the field and contributed to the rapidly expanding literature. The result is a rich mix, but one from which it is hard to extract the essence.

In my view, the essence is that in a learning organisation:

- there is a capacity for double-loop learning;
- there is ongoing attention to learning how to learn; and

- key areas of organisational functioning (in particular, employee relations, work organisation, skills formation, and technology/ information systems) support learning.

Each of these aspects needs to be explained more fully.

COMPONENT 1. THERE IS A CAPACITY FOR DOUBLE-LOOP LEARNING

Learning takes place in every enterprise, regardless of whether or not it is like a learning organisation. But the type, quality and benefits of learning vary greatly from one enterprise to another.

Three different types of learning can be identified—haphazard learning, goal-based learning, and double-loop learning, with a continuum from haphazard learning to double-loop learning (see Figure 10.1). As organisational learning improves, the capacity for double-loop learning becomes more fully established.

In an enterprise where *haphazard learning* is the norm, the first step to improving organisational learning is to ensure that work groups and divisions have goals (targets, plans, strategies and objectives) and that there are mechanisms for delivering timely, appropriate feedback about progress towards those goals. Guidance, in the form of software design, prompts and help devices, procedures, schedules and guidelines can also support rapid learning. Attention to organisational memory (including any method of capturing and retaining the lessons of organisational experience) also provides a foundation for goal-based learning.

Goal-based learning is important, and many enterprises (particularly small businesses) could greatly improve what they do if they got as far as establishing operational goals and feedback mechanisms. Strategic planning and quality assurance are examples of attempts to clarify goals and agree on processes, and then to learn by monitoring progress.

Obviously, such an unchanging work environment is not the norm. Learning in the context of well-defined outcomes is a necessary but not sufficient basis for becoming more like a learning organisation. In goal-based learning, the focus is progress relative to established goals.

In the organisations for which many of us work, goals and the whole frame of reference keep changing, because of the sorts of pressure discussed earlier in this chapter. Furthermore, people at work are continually learning from their own personal and social environments—unplanned incidents, their family lives, the media, social contacts, and so on (Foley 1999). Both factors— enterprises and people, the pressures on each and the dynamics of each—mean that even if goals, feedback mechanisms and work

Figure 10.1   The learning continuum

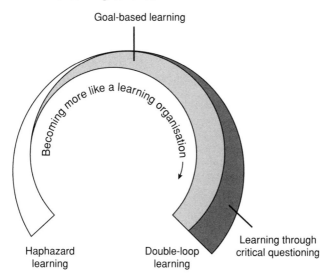

Goal-based learning

Becoming more like a learning organisation ⌐

Haphazard
learning

Double-loop
learning

Learning through
critical questioning

processes are appropriate when established, they can quickly become outmoded.

Instead of being able to take for granted the way things are done, managers and employees need to be able to question critically what they are doing to ensure that goals and processes are optimal. That means approaching problems from different angles, introducing ideas from other contexts, and experimenting with new approaches. For enterprises that have to contend with change—and that means most enterprises—goal-based learning needs to be supplemented by learning through critical questioning. Because two feedback loops are involved, Argyris and Schon (1978: 22) call this composite learning process 'double-loop learning'. In other words:

Double-loop learning = Goal-based learning + Learning through critical questioning

Fostering the capacity for *double-loop learning* is central to any attempts to become more like a learning organisation.

COMPONENT 2. THERE IS ONGOING ATTENTION TO LEARNING HOW TO LEARN

To develop a capacity for learning through critical questioning, enterprises need to learn how to learn. The idea of learning to learn can be traced back to Bateson (1973), who labelled it 'deutero' learning (from the Greek *deuteros*, meaning second). Argyris and Schon (1978: 27) were the first to draw attention to the importance of learning to learn as a component of organisational learning.

Learning to learn encompasses processes that have been discussed extensively in the literature of adult learning, under headings like 'action research' (Carr & Kemmis 1986), 'the reflective practitioner' (Schon 1987), 'critical thinking' (Brookfield 1989), 'critical reflection' (Mezirow et al. 1990), 'self-directed learning' (Candy 1991), and 'learning from experience' (Boud et al. 1993). Essentially, learning to learn involves becoming aware of one's own assumptions and thinking processes, developing approaches to explore new avenues, trying those out, seeing what happens, and using the results as a basis for further experimentation. The first step—critically scrutinising one's own assumptions and processes—is particularly important. As Bill Ford (1989: 56) has commented:

> There is an urgent need for people to understand their traditional 'mind-sets'. These are often based on many years of experiential learning. People need new frameworks to unlock their visions of the past and develop new, more dynamic mind-sets, based on developing their understanding of their contemporary and future environments.

Learning to learn involves looking freshly at enterprise functioning and learning from what you discover. As I have detailed elsewhere (Field 1998), doing so is not at all easy. Both managers and employees may be reluctant to learn. By fostering learning, managers risk loss of control and consequent blame. By facilitating critical questioning, they also risk exposing their own (and more senior managers') mistakes. Similarly, employees may be reluctant to contribute to organisational learning involving critical questioning—for a variety of reasons, relating to their skills and capacities, past experiences with learning, rewards and job security, and relationships with managers. Efforts to improve learning (and learning how to learn) need to be complemented by minimising hostility, blame and threats of loss of control as well.

COMPONENT 3. KEY ASPECTS OF ORGANISATIONAL FUNCTIONING SUPPORT LEARNING

To translate the ideas we have been looking at into reality, key aspects of the enterprise need to change so that they better support learning. In terms of organisational learning, the most important areas of enterprise functioning are:

*   employee relations, including employees' security, rewards and recognition;
*   work organisation, including the various forms that an organisation can take, the links with other enterprises and agencies, and the role of supervisors;
*   skills, training and learning, including training courses and a whole range of other approaches to skill formation;
*   technology and information management.

In any organisation, each of these areas can support or hinder learning. Of course, learning is not the main objective for most enterprises; profit, quality, productivity or service are. But if an enterprise wants to become more like a learning organisation, the four areas listed above need to be taken into account. The remainder of this chapter looks at how the role of 'training' needs to shift in order to support organisational learning.

'TRAINING' AND 'LEARNING' IN A LEARNING ORGANISATION

As organisational learning becomes established, the difference between 'training' and 'learning' is increasingly evident (Marsick 1988). Learning potentially occurs all the time, although some individuals are more open to learning than others and some environments support learning better than others. Training, on the other hand, is about delivering content. One designs and conducts training. You can train someone, but you cannot 'learn' them. Training implies a flow of information from a supplier (often a trainer) to a receiver (trainee).

Training is generally expected to relate to specific training needs. The assumption is that as workplace requirements change, a gap will show up between enterprise needs and available skills. Training is the mechanism by which employees receive the skills they need to catch up. As such, it is a narrow concept. To improve organisational learning, this narrow concept of training needs to be replaced by a more open, learner-centred view, which recognises that working and learning are inextricably linked.

To understand and apply this broader way of looking at learning, it is necessary to rethink basic assumptions about training. In moving towards a learning organisation, the emphasis needs to change from:

*   competency-based training to people-centred learning;
*   passive, uninvolved trainees to active, involved learners;

- training leave to learning time;
- training courses to learning opportunities.

We now look at each of these conceptual shifts.

FROM COMPETENCY-BASED TRAINING TO PEOPLE-CENTRED LEARNING

There is currently a great deal of interest in competency-based training. It is not hard to see why it is attractive to some groups, including government agencies, unions, industry associations and standards bodies. Competency-based training makes it easier for employees who previously have had no post-school credentials to see the things they have learnt at work formally recognised. It highlights the need to plan outcomes when conducting formal, classroom-based training. And, because it involves measured outcomes, competency-based training makes it easier to gauge cost-effectiveness.

On the other hand, from the point of view of organisational learning, competency-based training can be more of a hindrance than a help. As it is currently being implemented in many industries, competency-based training tends to overemphasise the routine, visible aspects of work and to neglect 'under-the-surface' skills (Field 1990: 30–5), like problem solving and information handling.

Moreover, the process of identifying and then assessing competence can get bogged down in excessively wordy detail. In some industries, the literacy demands of the competency standards far exceed the literacy skills of the people doing the work. When converted into the jargon of competence, it can be hard to recognise what one does amid all the abstractions.

Determining competency standards is as much a political as an educational process (Jackson 1989). Scrutinising what people do challenges established boundaries and relativities. The process inevitably leads to compromises that blur differences. The net result may be development of a long, overly general competency profile that tries to accommodate everyone's requirements but in fact does not end up satisfying anyone's needs.

Some government and union officials would argue that the frustration enterprises may experience in trying to fit into a national or industry-wide competency-based training framework is a small price to pay for transportability of qualifications and national consistency. Those involved in managing organisational learning within individual enterprises, however, often have a different perspective. For them, the new training framework can seem rigid and unwieldy (Ashenden 1991).

At worst, competency-based training merely perpetuates the old club-like employee relations arrangements that lost some ground during award restructuring and the introduction of enterprise agreements in the early 1990s. Traditionally, employee relations in many countries have been characterised by artificial segregation of skills and jobs, rigid rules, a specialised technical terminology and highly centralised power. It is unfortunate that, not long after this approach has declined, it is being replaced by a similarly constituted competency-based training club!

FROM PASSIVE, UNINVOLVED TRAINEES TO ACTIVE INVOLVED LEARNERS

Brazilian educationalist Paulo Freire (1972a) was strongly critical of what he termed the 'banking' approach to education. This is the belief that education is a process in which learners are passive and empty (like empty bank accounts), and that the educator's job is to fill them up with knowledge (like making a bank deposit).

The 'banking' view of education greatly underestimates people's natural tendency to learn actively in the context of what they already know. In terms of Freire's banking analogy, a better way to view learners would be as active investors who already have existing 'funds' (i.e. knowledge) which they are interested in expanding. It is more appropriate to see learners in this way than as passive receptacles for other people's knowledge.

A study conducted in 1985 by Carroll and Mack illustrates just how actively people learn. The two investigators observed a number of office workers as they tried to learn to use a word processor for the first time. The only aid provided was the standard manual. The learners were asked to think aloud as they went, and this information was recorded. One thing was common to all the learners—they simply struck out into the unknown and tried to learn by doing, even if they had little or no information to go on (1985: 17):

> Our learners relentlessly wanted to learn by trying things out rather than by reading how to do them. In part, this was impatience. They were reluctant to read a lot of explanation or get bogged down following meticulous directions. But it also devolved from mismatched goals. Learners wanted to discover how to do specific things at particular times, and this did not always accord with the sequence in which topics were treated in the manual.

In many organisations, it is not just manuals and software that put employees in a passive position but training programs as well.

The pressure during the 1990s for well-planned, cost-effective structured training often resulted in training programs that echoed Freire's banking analogy. To improve organisational learning, computer software, the physical work environment (including the design of work stations and office furniture and fittings) and task allocation all need to be designed to support active learning in the workplace.

FROM TRAINING LEAVE TO LEARNING TIME

For training programs to be worthwhile, there needs to be more than just time off to attend. But making adequate provision for structured courses like this is only one aspect of learning in the workplace. As Ford (1991: 64) comments:

> The old industrial agenda of asking for training leave—out and away from the workplace—cannot match the potential rewards of creating learning time within the actual working project. By developing continual learning in the workplace, the concept of continuous improvement by all members of the team can be encouraged. This promotes both structured and unstructured learning.

Employees need regular time to learn, particularly during periods of changing technology, the introduction of new services or products, and new work arrangements. Learning involves being creative and taking risks. Inevitably, this means that sometimes learners will try out unfruitful approaches or make mistakes. Time to get a project back on track and to rectify mistakes is all part of learning time. If learning time is to be well-used, people in a work area need to appreciate that thinking and learning are legitimate ways of spending time. Without the tolerance of co-workers and the sanction of management, learning time may well be dismissed as wasted time.

FROM TRAINING COURSES TO LEARNING OPPORTUNITIES

Support for learning in many medium-sized to large enterprises is often restricted to structured classroom-based training programs designed and delivered by specialist trainers.

It is not too hard to understand why there has long been this emphasis on structured classroom training. By defining training in this way, it is hoped that:

- the information provided is standardised;
- outcomes can be measured;
- training sessions are professionally delivered by trainers with good presentation skills;

- trainers can justify their existence by showing how many people they have trained.

But, in practice, the disadvantages of such a restricted view often outweigh the advantages. First, training can end up isolated from the enterprise's needs. Trainers who work in this kind of environment complain that management rarely involves them when changes are being planned. And because specialist trainers are often not involved in the enterprise's main activities, their expertise and credibility is reduced.

Second, after a training course is conducted and trainees have been filled up with knowledge (to use Freire's analogy), no-one can be sure that they will use it when they go back to work.

Third, structured classroom-based training is often intimidating for employees with limited English language or literacy skills and for those who are uncomfortable with being passive for extended periods.

Fourth, structured classroom-based training is simply not appropriate for some employees, particularly those who work in small businesses on a casual or part-time basis. Not only are many employers in sectors like retailing unwilling to pay for training, but employees themselves may find it hard to attend because of family or other commitments.

Artificial separation of the training function from the rest of work may start off as a decision about organisational structure, but it ends up inhibiting the enterprise's efforts to improve organisational learning. How, then, do you start to bring training and working closer together? Several strategies have been used with considerable success. One is to look for opportunities to replace training courses with *action-oriented learning* projects. In such a project the group undertakes tasks of interest, with the assistance of a facilitator. The group seeks to balance goal-based learning (and thus needs to attend to its goals, feedback mechanisms, sources of guidance, and memory) and ongoing critical questioning.

A second strategy is to involve employees in the *development of learning systems* (e.g. the help section of a new software installation) or paper-based materials to support learning. When employees are responsible for systems and materials development, the learning starts as soon as the project gets underway. In contrast, when outside experts develop such systems and materials, the learning does not begin until people sit down to be 'trained' or to begin work.

A third strategy is to introduce the idea of *learning contracts* (Knowles 1980). A learning contract is an agreement about learning goals and how these are to be pursued. In one financial organisation, for example, learning contracts are negotiated every six months between employees and people with particular expertise (other employees, supervisors, managers, information technology specialists), who agreed to act as mentors. A range of computer-based resources are provided to support learning. The new emphasis on negotiated rather than prescribed training is having a major impact on the financial organisation's human resource development strategy. The organisation no longer employs specialist trainers, although there are several human resource development consultants attached to specific work areas. Formal, structured courses are rarely provided except when they directly relate to business priorities. When offered, such courses are normally run by managers or by technically expert employees, not by professional trainers.

CONCLUSION

This chapter has argued that becoming more like a learning organisation involves three areas in particular—learning through critical questioning; learning how to learn; and taking learning into account in decisions about key areas of organisational functioning (in particular, employee relations, work organisation, skills formation, and technology/information systems). As the transition occurs, new concepts of training and learning begin to emerge. In place of traditional, classroom-based approaches to training, the focus shifts to the learning potential of everyday work activities. From the new perspective, employees are recognised as active participants in the learning process, and a whole range of workplace experiences—participation in decision making, developing learning resources, teamwork, undertaking new assignments, mentoring, even dealing with controversy and crises—are seen as opportunities for learning.

When the workplace is viewed in this way, it is obvious that human resource practitioners alone cannot have sole responsibility for employee development. Instead of concentrating on delivering training, those responsible for managing organisational learning need to concentrate on increasing everyone's capacity to learn and to facilitate the learning of others. Structured classroom-based training courses still have their place, but only as one of many learning opportunities that are available as individuals and groups work and learn concurrently.

NOTE

1   This chapter is adapted from Field & Ford (1995).

FURTHER READING

Argyris, C. & Schön, D. 1978 *Organizational Learning: A Theory of Action Perspective*. Reading, MA: Addison-Wesley.

Brooks, A. 1994 'Power and the production of knowledge: collective team learning in work organizations'. *Human Resource Development Quarterly*, 5(3), pp. 213–33.

Coopey, K. 1996 'Crucial gaps in "the learning organization": power, politics and ideology'. In K. Starkey (ed.), *How organizations learn*. London: Thompson Business Press.

de Geus, A. 1997 *The Living Company: Growth, Learning and Longevity in Business*. London: Nicholas Brealey.

Easterby-Smith, M. 1997 'Disciplines of organizational learning: contributions and critiques'. *Human Relations*, 50(9), pp. 1085–113.

Field, L. 1998 'The challenge of empowered learning'. *Asia Pacific Journal of Human Resources*, 36(1), pp. 72–85.

Field, L. & Ford, B. 1995 *Managing Organisational Learning: From Rhetoric to Reality*. Melbourne: Longman.

Kim, D.H. 1993 'The link between individual learning and organizational learning. *Sloan Management Review*, 35(1), pp. 37–50.

Miner, A.S. & Mezias, S.J. 1996 'Ugly duckling no more: pasts and futures of organizational learning research'. *Organization Science*, 7(1), pp. 88–99.

11

Understanding and achieving successful change in adult education

Geoff Scott

This chapter shifts your focus from the 'what' of change in adult education and training to the 'how'—that is, to the processes of change and the implementation and management of planned change. While the chapter was written primarily for practitioners working in educational institutions[1] (e.g. vocational education, community-based education, higher education), its insight applies equally well to other educational settings (e.g. corporate training, workplace learning) and to organisational change more generally.

It has been included in the book for the following reasons. First, change is all around us. The need for both individuals and organisations to engage in continuous adaptation, enhancement and innovation is relentless. Yet such processes are typically poorly managed. Second, the pressure for change is growing. In a context in which adult education is coming under increasing scrutiny, in which it is facing significant cuts, in which technological change is speeding up, and in which there are heightened levels of local and overseas competition, we cannot rest on our laurels. In many instances a capability to manage change quickly and effectively is becoming essential to the survival of organisations and the maintenance of jobs.

Third, failed change does cost, economically and psychologically. When enthusiastic workers and managers commit to a change project and that project fails, they carry the scars of that experience with them. Fourth, books on change have become increasingly popular in recent years. It is reported that some 800 were published in the USA alone in the first half of the 1990s.[2] However, many of these are peddling 'change management snake oil'. What they advocate rests on flimsy research foundations. Some offer magic formulas which, when followed, achieve little. Others describe the change process but offer little by way of practical advice. In general there is a need to identify and question the change management myths that are currently being put about.

Finally, the chapter aims to help readers to 'see the forest for the trees', to identify, label and explore the links between all the components that make up the change management puzzle. For example, it is important to become clear on how individual and organisational change are linked, how change is a complex learning and unlearning process rather than an event, and how, at the heart of change, are people, their values, beliefs, motives and relationships. What follows has been developed specifically to fill the above needs.

In the first section of the chapter you will be asked to reflect on your past experiences of organisational or educational change, and from this to identify your views on how it works. You will then be invited to compare your conclusions with a summary of research on change dynamics. This will expose a number of popular change management myths.

The next section gives an overview of the key factors that usually trigger a change effort and influence the way it turns out. Key sources of change are identified, the main types of change are noted, the way in which the scope and size of the change play a part is illustrated, and the central roles played by motivation, values and evaluation are outlined.

The fourth section outlines an overall picture of how the change process in education operates. This conceptual framework[3] underpins the book *Change Matters* (Scott 1999), which explores each component of the framework in more detail.

THE DYNAMICS OF CHANGE

EDUCATORS' CHANGE ANALOGIES

One of the most useful ways to develop a quick, overall feel for what practitioners' day-to-day experiences of change in education and training entails is to invent a personal analogy that describes it.[4]

Your change management analogy

Consider the analogies in Table 11.1. They are some of the more common ones developed by practitioners in a wide range of teaching and management roles in education over the years. Compare these with your own analogies.

Table 11.1   Educators' Change Analogies[5]

When I am involved in change I feel like I am a:
- Guide
- Coach
- Director of a play
- Chef in a restaurant
- Potter
- A surfboard rider on the waves of change
- Person negotiating a swamp
- Skipper on an ocean-going yacht
- World War II general
- Person having a baby
- Swimmer in a tidal pool
- Mechanic trying to fix a car while it is going 100 km/h
- White-water rafter
- Father confessor
- Juggler balancing spinning plates on the end of sticks
- Person in an Escher drawing

The analogies in the above group were given by educational managers; those below were given by teachers and trainers.

- Crew member
- Member of a chorus line
- Fellow traveller
- Person learning to cook for myself
- Collector
- Creature in metamorphosis
- Piece of clay being moulded
- Person all at sea
- Bouncing ball
- Person on an icy slide
- Person going up a down escalator

Research on the dynamics of change

The change analogies presented in Table 11.1 point to many of the key findings from research on the nature of the change process in education (Fullan 1991, 1993; Scott 1990, 1996). They reveal, for example, that the change process in adult education: is uncertain; operates in phases; is cyclical, not linear; comprises a mix of factors; is reciprocal; requires educators who can 'read and match'.

Is uncertain. Things never go completely as predicted. There will always be that unexpected twist or surprise. No educational change, whether program innovation or workplace improvement, ever unfolds exactly as planned. The greater the scope and degree of change, the greater the uncertainty.

Operates in phases. There is a time when a need for change is identified, a time when people start work on figuring out how

Figure 11.1   The cyclical change process

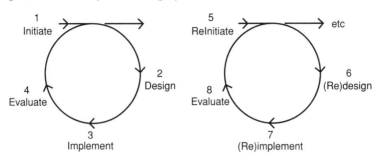

best to handle it, a time when they start to implement their plan, and a time when they seek to consolidate their change.

Is cyclical, not linear. Although the change process does involve different phases, it is wrong to assume that these unfold in a 'one-off', linear fashion. No educational change is ever fixed or permanent. The local and external context in which education takes place is too volatile. Because of this the change process is best seen as operating in a cyclical fashion, as in Figure 11.1.

Comprises a mix of factors beyond and within one's control. Any change effort always involves a mix of factors: those beyond the individual's control (e.g. in the yacht analogy, the ocean) and those within one's influence (e.g. how much sail to carry or what course to chart).

Is reciprocal. What happens at one point of time will influence how things turn out at a later point. For example, a negative experience early on in a change project helps individuals shape their reactions to it later on. The change process is reciprocal in another way: each new change effort both influences and is influenced by the milieu in which it is attempted.

Requires educators who can 'read and match'.[6] Given the number of factors involved in any change effort and the fact that each of these factors is itself constantly shifting, what one does will always depend on being able to 'read' what is going on in each unique situation and 'match' the most appropriate response. That is, what is done must always be contingent[7] on what the unique circumstances of each case dictate is feasible, appropriate and desirable.

177

Change management myths

Many of the change management books currently on the market[8] fail to take account of the factors discussed above. A number of myths keep cropping up.[9]

The knight-on-a-white-charger myth. All that is necessary is to appoint a dynamic, reform-oriented leader to assure successful change.

The consensual myth. A proposed change will work only if everyone it affects has approved of it. Therefore, a 'bottom-up' approach to change always works.

The linear myth. Change proceeds in a fixed, one-off, linear fashion from initiation, through development and implementation, on into institutionalisation.

The brute logic myth. Change is achieved by brute logic; provided the proponent's argument for a change is compelling, those it affects will automatically adopt it.

The change event myth. Change is an event, like the launch of a new policy or curriculum, rather than being a long iterative learning (and unlearning) process for all those concerned.

The silver bullet myth. There is a set procedure which, if followed, will guarantee successful change.

The one-size-fits-all myth. All that is necessary is to develop a standardised, 'teacher-proof' curriculum or procedure and users will implement it fully and exactly as intended in every location across the system.

The either/ or myth. Change management involves having to make rigid choices between, for example, taking a 'top-down' or a 'bottom-up' approach, giving clear direction or allowing a large degree of flexibility, adopting an organisation-wide or a local emphasis, focusing on enhancement or innovation.

THE KEY INGREDIENTS IN THE EDUCATIONAL CHANGE PROCESS

The change process is complex because so many ingredients are often at play simultaneously. It is important to develop an overview of these in order to lessen the feeling that one is always going to be a victim of mysterious forces. Labelling these ingredients and understanding the many ways in which they interact provides a starting point for effective change management in education. What emerges provides a series of checkpoints that can be used to make sure a potentially relevant influence has not been overlooked as the change process unfolds.

A WIDE RANGE OF SOURCES AND INFLUENCES

Each change situation is shaped by a unique mix of external, system and local factors. In some cases external or even system factors have far less influence than local ones (e.g. the teacher who decides to introduce a new learning resource into an existing class). In others, external and system factors are far more significant (e.g. a system-wide introduction of computer-assisted learning). External influences like changes in technology, the economy, work or social values can, through government policy and funding guidelines, play an important part in shaping the overall change agenda for education. System influences, like the structure and decision-making process of a large education department, can also help or hinder the management of continuous innovation and enhancement. At a local level the culture, climate and quality of leadership in the workplace, along with the nature and expectations of the student body, the standard of equipment and available facilities, will also play a part.

Table 11.2 summarises some of the major conditions, procedures and individuals that can trigger an educational change and influence the way it turns out. As Table 11.2 suggests, change is always a mix of broader forces and individuals' interaction with them. People, individually or in combination, shape these broader forces and factors to influence the way in which a change effort turns out. Depending on the type and size of a change, politicians, senior bureaucrats, captains of industry, unions, professional groups, key committees, institutional leaders, local managers, teachers, students and the general community may all play a part. The way in which these people relate to each other, the culture, morale and the standard operating approach of the institution they populate will all influence the outcomes of the change process.

Table 11.2 also demonstrates that, whereas some educational improvements or innovations may be entered into voluntarily by a local unit or institution, many may be forced on educators by an outside funding body. This is because education is always at the behest of the government or other external funding groups. Many of the major changes in education and training over the past years have come from the interaction between a change

Table 11.2 Change sources and influences

External conditions	Procedures	Key players
1. Societal trends	Change management	Politicians & Advisers
2. Relationships between key bodies (especially in funding areas)	Administrative	Accreditation bodies
3. Resource position of clients/ students	Communication	Employers
4. Clients' learning requirements	Decision making	Granting bodies
5. Government policy		Unions Professional bodies Parent organisations (in the school sector) Lobby groups
Organisation conditions	Procedures	Key players
1. Social conditions (Culture & climate)	Change management	CEO & senior staff
2. Prior change experiences	Administrative	Central admin staff
3. Structure	Communication	Council/governing body
4. Financial position	Decision making	System wide liaison
5. Policy requirements	Staff selection & support	Union representatives, staff/ project managers
6. Appropriateness & clarity of mission	Dissemination of good practice	
7. Record systems		

forced by a new government and the attempts of the local system and institutions to accommodate it.

DIFFERENT TYPES OF CHANGE

In education there are two major types of change: changes in learning programs and changes in the milieu in which these are developed, delivered and supported. Table 11.3 summarises some of the main aspects of learning programs that can be changed.

Table 11.4 summarises some of the major ways in which the operating milieu of education can be changed.

There is a close relationship between Table 11.3 and Table 11.4. Learning program innovations will usually require some adjustment to their operating milieu if they are to be supported effectively. For example, one of the reasons why many intrinsically worthwhile and well-shaped learning program innovations founder is because administrative and support personnel are either unaware of or unwilling to make the necessary adjustments in what they do to support the innovation's smooth implementation.

Table 11.3   Aspects of learning programs that can be changed

- Learning objectives and content
- Teaching and learning strategies
- Learning resources
- The sequencing of learning
- Learning procedures
- Learning locations and modes of learning
- Approaches to learner recruitment and participation
- Approaches to evaluation and enhancement
- Administration
- Timing and flexibility of learning
- Fee structures

Table 11.4   Aspects of operating milieu that can be changed

- Culture and climate
- Staff selection and support
- Leadership
- Approach to identifying and disseminating good practice
- Systems of communication
- Administrative focus and procedures
- Structure
- Approaches to monitoring and enhancing organisational operation
- Documentation and statistic keeping
- Planning and decision making
- Resource distribution

CHANGES OF DIFFERENT SCOPE, SIZE AND CONDITION

The scope and size of educational change efforts can vary dramatically. Some educational changes are enhancements of existing practices, whereas others are innovations (something quite new).

For example, some learning program innovations will entail a teacher simply enhancing one aspect of a teaching session, like a new way of using a learning resource. Others can be far more ambitious—involving, for instance, many teachers in a complete course restructure. Similarly, some educational changes might affect only one location (e.g. one school, college, training unit or university) whereas others may have system-wide implications. Some changes have already been tried, 'debugged' and enhanced in one location and provided educators in other locations with a sound working model as a starting point. Others are untested and ground-breaking, and the staff involved find themselves entering completely uncharted territory.

This great variability in the size, scope and condition of educational changes explains in part why the process is so complex, and how 'silver bullet' approaches to change management can never work.

MOTIVATION: THE HUMAN DIMENSION OF CHANGE

An understanding of what motivates individuals to engage in and stick with a change effort is central to ensuring that a desired change is successfully implemented and sustained. There are three key influences on educators' motivation to get involved in and stick with a change effort that must be taken into account.

Individual influences
The role individuals play in adult education will, in part, shape their interest in and expectations of a particular change. Senior managers are held accountable for different things and have different roles from teachers or learners, and these things help shape their expectations and the 'success indicators' given priority by them in each change effort. The influence of role on the individual's perception of 'efficacy' (capacity for influence) in the change process has already been noted in discussing educators' change analogies (Table 11.1).

Degree of job security can influence commitment to change. In a period of increased redundancies in some sectors of education, there are likely to be different levels of commitment to change from those obtaining in periods of full employment.

The individual's reasons for seeking to work in the field of adult education can also play a part. For example, some people see work as only a minor component in a complex and varied life; others see it as central. Family and other obligations can shape people's reactions when change is in the air. Similarly, people's assumptions about the purpose of adult education vary widely, and influence the way in which they react to different change proposals.

Stage of career can be an influence too. People new to education have different things on their mind from those who have been in the job for many years. This partially explains why fledgling adult educators often talk of white-water rafting or being on an icy slide, whereas their more experienced colleagues prefer to use analogies like swamp negotiation.

The individual's commitment to a specific change is always influenced positively if the local manager and senior staff publicly anoint the change, noting that work on it is a priority for them and that funds to support the effort are being committed to its success.

When a change idea is first mentioned, but also as it is

developed, implemented and monitored, each of the individuals involved in it will be continuously asking questions like the following:

- Is this relevant? That is, does this look as if it will meet with a positive response from my students, employers and other interested players? Is it something they want?
- Is this desirable? That is, does this development align with my goals for education—with what I believe constitutes valuable education?
- Is what is being proposed clear? That is, do I understand what I will have to do differently in order to make the proposed change work in practice? Am I getting consistent messages about this innovation?
- Is all of this feasible? That is, considering the apparent size and scope of what is involved, do I have time to get or stay involved in this development given all my other commitments? Does it look as if we have the resources to make this work? What will we be getting rid of in my workload to make room for this innovation?

If the answers to such questions are predominantly negative, the individual's motivation to persevere with the change effort will fade.

How the change process itself is handled
It is perfectly possible for individuals to start off with a positive response to the above questions and, because the change process itself is poorly handled, for their enthusiasm for the particular change to wane.

For example, there are many instances of initially promising change projects, where the team members involved met endlessly and aimlessly discussing what to do and finally became so exhausted that they had no energy left to put anything new into practice. Well-meaning people asked to lead a change effort can quickly dampen motivation if they ignore the lessons concerning effective start-up strategies and support for implementation now available. As implementation proceeds, the motivation of those who are to make the change work in practice will soon fall away if they are left unsupported, if inevitable implementation glitches are brushed aside by managers, if anticipated resources fail to turn up on time and so on. Similarly, a too-quick or too judgmental evaluation should be avoided.

Overall, if people find that the costs to them continue to be outweighed by the benefits, they are more likely to persevere with a change effort. Otherwise they will disengage.

Influence of the local operating milieu

It is possible for people to be initially motivated to tackle a given change and yet to find that, due to a counterproductive or unsupportive workplace, staff enthusiasm for the change fades as the change process gets underway.

For example, in research reviewed and undertaken by Ball (1987) and Scott (1990), numerous cases were identified where the efforts of an enthusiastic local change group were white-anted by other 'rival' groups in the local workplace; where the local head was uninterested in their efforts; where the culture was conservative, blaming and negative; where there was little positive recognition and reward for successful change; and where the local operating processes were so inefficient that the change effort stalled. Every workplace has its own psychological history, and this partly explains current levels of interest in improvement and innovation.

It is so important when studying the change process not just to look at how best to develop, implement and monitor a learning program innovation, but to concurrently understand how best to develop a workplace milieu conducive to continuous quality improvement and innovation. The exact way in which motivation and change in education are linked is still comparatively unstudied, especially in areas of postsecondary education like training, community education and higher education.[10]

EVALUATION

Evaluation is 'the process by which individuals make judgments of worth about an innovation, a process, procedure, project or strategy'.[11] It is the driving force of the change process. It is through ongoing evaluation that people determine whether a proposed change is still, from their perspective, feasible, relevant, desirable or clear. It is through evaluation that people make judgments about whether or not the change process is being well-handled or whether the milieu in which the change is being attempted is sufficiently supportive to warrant putting effort into making it happen. Every person involved in a change effort is continuously gathering evidence with which to make judgments about such matters. Their judgments determine how they react. If, for example, individuals conclude that a particular change is no longer feasible or that it is being poorly managed and supported, their motivation to stick with it can fall away. If they come to the opposite conclusion, their commitment to persevere with the process is enhanced.

It is important to remember that such a process is not, as

emphasised above, a one-off matter: it is ongoing. Evaluation occurs when an idea for change is first proposed, it occurs as innovations are designed, and it continues to take place as these are being implemented. If tapped positively, ongoing evaluation is the key mechanism for ensuring that an initiative is subject to continuous quality improvement. And it is ongoing evaluation that is both influenced by and shapes motivation.

Evaluation is reciprocal. That is, evaluation at one point in time can dramatically influence behaviour at another. And the judgments made can be surprisingly durable: staff involved in a failed change project can remember this experience for years, often refusing to become involved in subsequent projects because of it.

It is naive in the extreme to assume, therefore, that the formal, documented processes of evaluation are sufficient. Instead it is usually the informal, ongoing, micropolitical side of evaluation that is most telling. In this hidden side of organisational life different, rival groups make judgments about each call for change, not necessarily by looking at the intrinsic merits of the idea but by making judgments about the people proposing it. When micropolitics are at play the change effort can stall simply because one subgroup concludes that, as the idea is being put forward by a subgroup regarded as being inept, untrustworthy or of the 'wrong' educational persuasion, it should be dismissed out of hand.

A FRAMEWORK FOR UNDERSTANDING AND WORKING WITH CHANGE IN ADULT EDUCATION

THE OVERALL PICTURE

Figure 11.2 summarises the discussion so far. External (D), organisational or local influences (B) can all play a role in triggering a change effort and in determining how it turns out. Changes are possible in an educational organisation's milieu (B) or in its learning programs (C). These changes can be enhancements (i.e. improvements in the quality of existing aspects of an organisation's milieu or learning programs), or they can be innovations (the introduction of something completely new).

Changes in learning programs will often generate a need to make adjustments in operating milieu. As a general rule, for change management to be effective and efficient in adult education, changes in (B) and (C) should be explicitly linked, with the initial focus being on continuous improvement and innovation in learning programs and the implications for enhancements or innovations

Figure 11.2   Change management framework for education

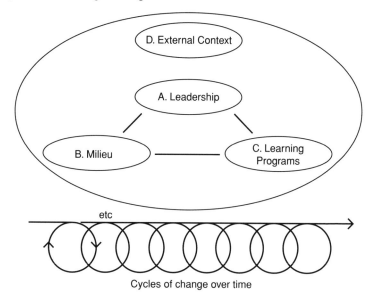

Cycles of change over time

in milieu arising out of these learning developments. Changes in the milieu that do not demonstrably add value to the quality of learning program design and delivery should be avoided. There is extensive research now available on what optimises the success of learning program innovations and enhancements in such an environment.

We also now know far more about what sort of organisational climate, culture, structure, approach to staffing, communication and decision making best supports learning program innovation, enhancement and delivery. A key tool, characteristic of the 'learning organisation', which can be used to continuously enhance workplace milieu is workplace action research.

Given the volatile and infinitely variable context in which education must operate, the aim should be to engage in an ongoing process of 'mutual adaptation',[12] a process in which the external context (D) or current experiences with learners may indicate a learning enhancement or innovation (C) and, from these developments, the changes in (B) necessary to support their efficient and effective implementation are identified. The approach must be cyclical, not linear, as constant movement in the local, organisational and external environment over time will necessitate continuous adjustment, enhancement or innovation in both learning programs and milieu. The ongoing challenge is, therefore, to figure out how best to maintain synergy between B, C and D. As there are always going to be more change possibilities than there is time to deliver them, priorities will have to be set, monitored and, when necessary, adjusted. To set priorities close consideration must be given to what is going to be most feasible, relevant, desirable and strategically significant.

From the outset, the driving force of change is people: their motives, histories, learned ways of behaving, perceptions and relationships. If an organisation or unit is populated by people who are disaffected, who feel uninvolved, unappreciated, unsupported or are unwilling to embrace change, then even the most committed leaders will have difficulty gaining their commitment for educational reform.

The change management approach which has been found to best account for the complexity outlined in this chapter and summarised above involves not taking an either/or position but combining apparently paradoxical tactics. These include the adoption of:

- top-down and bottom-up strategies;
- an internal and an external focus;
- pan-institutional developments and uniquely local ones;
- clear direction and flexibility;
- stability and change;[13]
- enhancement and innovation;
- learning program changes and milieu enhancements;
- attention to learning program change and associated administrative/support system change;
- an emphasis on implementation support as well as development support;
- attention to resistors and enthusiasts.

Educational changes do not unfold spontaneously—they have to be led (A). Depending on the nature and scope of the change, different people may take on the role of change leader. For example, a staff member who is already expert in running interactive web-based learning may be the best person to lead a team whose job it is to spread the innovation across the organisation. For a policy innovation, a more senior staff member who is accountable for this work might be better-positioned to lead the development. There are effective change leaders and ineffective ones. What is clear is that the best leaders do not just possess the requisite skills and knowledge—they are particularly sensitive to people's motives, they understand the human, subjective side of change, and operate contingently by being able to 'read' and 'match'. Of particular significance is the recurring finding that the most effective leaders have a profile remarkably similar to the best teachers of adults. As the external context (D) in which educational services must operate is continuously changing, it is essential to look not only within the organisation for change ideas but outwards and forwards.

Conclusion

There are close links between this chapter and chapter 10. Change requires those involved learning to do something new and unlearning old ways of doing things at the same time. Learning involves a change in one or a mix of skills, knowledge, attitudes or way of thinking. Clearly, then, change and learning are different sides of the same coin. To manage ongoing change in adult education effectively we need not just individuals who understand and are adept at navigating its relentless demands but organisations that in their culture, structure and way of operating are well-positioned to support such people. This is why organisations that are effective at workplace research, provide staff with a wide range of learning opportunities relevant to their strategic development priorities, and are capable of continuous quality improvement and innovation are correctly characterised in chapter 10 as learning organisations.

NOTES

1 This chapter is an adaptation of the first chapter in the book *Change Matters: Understanding and Achieving Successful Change in Education and Training,* Allen & Unwin, 1999.
2 Price Waterhouse (1996).
3 'A conceptual framework explains, either graphically or in narrative form, the main dimensions to be studied—the key factors or variables—and the presumed relationships among them' (Miles & Humberman 1984: 28).
4 See the methodologies used by Hunt (1987), Russell (1987) and Russell et al. (1988) on the development and use of metaphors in education for further detail.
5 The analogies listed are among the more popular and revealing ones identified by practitioners in a series of workplace research projects in education and training (the method used is detailed in Scott 1990).
6 I am indebted to David Hunt (1987) from the Ontario Institute for Studies in Education for this concept.
7 Contingency theory simply says to be prepared to use different

strategies and tactics in different situations (Fullan 1982: 999). It acknowledges that there can be no one fixed approach to change that will work across all settings (Sivage 1982: 101–2) and that there is no one formula but rather that there are 'configurations of variables that, if manipulated, can be successful in one family of settings and not another'; (Miles & Huberman 1984b: 34).

8 The Price Waterhouse Change Management Team (1996) have identified 800 books on managing change published in the USA alone from 1989 to 1994.

9 See Binney & Williams (1995) for a more detailed discussion.

10 Moses (1995: 13–14) identifies two theories, commonly applied in other contexts which may be of relevance. They are:

(a) Maslow's theory of a hierarchy of needs. The idea here is that the willingness of an educator to become involved in change is determined by whether or not lower-order needs like job security, well-paid employment, a feeling of being part of a group, being appreciated and so on are first met.

(b) Hertzberg's 'two-factor theory'. Herzberg postulates that one set of factors are negative motivators or 'dissatisfiers'—being blocked, going unrewarded, not having one's talents recognised and so on. The other set of factors are positive motivators or 'satisfiers'. These include a sense of achievement, recognition, challenging work, autonomy, opportunities for growth, status and a sense of belonging.

11 This definition is derived from that used by McDonald & Bishop (1990: 12).

12 See Berman & McLaughlin (1977).

13 This notion is summed up nicely in the words of Octavia Paz: '*Wisdom lies in neither fixity nor in change but in the dialectic between the two*'.

FURTHER READING

Ball, S. 1987 *The Micropolitics of the School.* London: Methuen.

Binney, G. & Williams, C. 1995 *Leaning into the Future: Changing the Way People Change Organisations.* London: Brearley.

Fullan, M. 1991 *The New Meaning of Educational Change.* New York: Teachers College Press.

——1993 *Change Forces: Probing the Depths of Educational Reform.* London: Falmer Press.

Fullan, M. & Hargreaves, A. 1991 *What's Worth Fighting for: Working Together for Your School.* Toronto: Ontario Public School Teachers' Federation.

McLaughlin, M.W. 1976 'Implementation as mutual adaptation: change in classroom organisation'. *Teachers' College Record,* 78, pp. 339–51.

Morgan, G.M. 1986 *Images of Organisation.* Beverly Hills: Sage.

——1988 *Riding the Waves of Change: Managerial Competencies for a Turbulent World.* San Francisco: Jossey Bass.

Price Waterhouse Change Integration Team 1996 *The Paradox Principles:*

How High Performance Companies Manage Chaos, Complexity and Contradiction to Achieve Superior Results. Chicago: Irwin.

Schön, D. 1983 *The Reflective Practitioner.* New York: Basic Books.

——1987 *Educating the Reflective Practitioner.* San Francisco: Jossey Bass.

Scott, G. 1990 *The Change Process in a Teacher Education Institution.* EdD Thesis, Toronto: University of Toronto.

——1996 'The effective management and evaluation of flexible learning innovations in higher education'. *Innovations in Education and Training International,* 33(4) pp. 154–70.

——1999 *Change Matters: Understanding and Achieving Successful Change in Education and Training.* Sydney: Allen & Unwin.

12

Competency-based education
Clive Chappell, Andrew Gonczi & Paul Hager

The concept of competence continues to be contested in adult education. Given the contexts in which the concept is currently being used, this should come as no surprise: competence is now not only a central feature of education and training reforms in many countries—it is also crucial to government-initiated wider industrial reform agendas. Workplace competency standards, the benchmarks for workplace performance, are being used as a basis for determining enterprise agreements, wage rises, recruitment policies, staff development, and selection for promotion (see Dawkins 1989). In order to align educational goals and objectives more closely to the needs of a rapidly changing industrial land-scape, a 'new vocationalism' argues that educational content must be related to the knowledge and skills required in the workplaces of postindustrial societies (Burke 1989; Mathews 1989a). The suggestion is that this alignment can best be achieved by using the competency standards benchmarks developed by industries, organisations and professions to inform the content of education and training programs.

The reluctance of many educators to embrace the concept of competence can, in part, be attributed to the history of the competency-based training movement in vocational education, a history which fills many educators with considerable disquiet. Our intent in this chapter is to discuss the reasons for this concern, and to suggest a more educationally defensible notion of competence.

COMPETENCY-BASED TRAINING—A NARROW VIEW OF COMPETENCE

The use of competence in adult education has long been controversial. The model of competence that has been used most extensively in adult education was developed by the US defence forces in the 1950s. Competency-based training (CBT), as it came to be called, is based on the view that standardised training outcomes can be achieved by all learners if a thorough analysis of the behaviours demonstrated by any competent performer is undertaken and then transposed onto a set of standardised learning sequences.

With its origins in the training of people to develop technical competence, CBT as it developed took on a 'curriculum as technology' approach to learning. In this approach, curriculum is seen as a tool to achieve prespecified training goals, which will most effectively be achieved when the curriculum operates within a highly controlled learning environment (Blachford 1986). This curriculum development process is also known as the instructional systems model of curriculum development, and has been used extensively in vocational education settings. It has come under sustained criticism. It is said to take a technical instrumental view of work, ignoring the crucial position of human agency (Smith 1993). It is accused of trivialising work and ignoring the fundamental changes that have occurred in modern work organisation (Mathews 1989a; Field 1990). Methodologies used to surface work-related skills are said to miss crucial attributes required of workers when performing their work roles (Gonczi et al. 1990). It is accused of using a narrow, fundamentally flawed conception of competence.

The narrowness of the approach manifests itself in CBT curricula in a number of ways. First, the narrow definition in itself limits the content of the course. An overemphasis on technical task skills leads to the omission of general social, intellectual and emotional abilities (e.g. cooperation, communication and independent decision making) from the competency descriptions and the courses developed from those descriptions.

A second feature of the narrow definition is that it not only proposes that competence must be measurable but suggests that the quality of CBT courses should be judged on the basis of whether the 'competencies' outlined in the course are written in ways that make them measurable. Course designers are therefore *required* to write conditions and criteria into competency statements so that they can be measured. The problem with this position is that, though it is reasonably easy to produce these sorts of descriptions when the focus is limited to the relatively straightforward task skills needed in the workplace, attempts to produce descriptions of more complex work practices, commonly involving complicated interactions of various sets of knowledge, skills and abilities, generally fail. More complex work practices that pose difficulties for the narrow task approach to competence include skills relating to overall job planning and management, contingency management skills (what happens when things go wrong), and the interpersonal and other skills (e.g. negotiation) that are commonly needed to deal successfully with the wider environment in which the job is being carried out. In short, it seems unlikely that competencies developed and written using this approach could possibly capture the complexity of work.

A third feature of the narrow definition is its insistence that there are single acceptable outcomes and single paths to acceptable outcomes. In most workplace contexts there are a number of acceptable possible outcomes and ways in which work outcomes can be achieved. Moreover, the notion that there are only single acceptable outcomes in workplace practice ignores important aspects of competence, such as the creative and critical thinking that are needed when circumstances require novel or unusual strategies for the successful performance of the work. The narrow definition of competence overemphasises behaviour at the expense of this cognition. While recognising that knowledge, practical skills and attitudinal requirements are essential to successful performance, CBT reifies these attributes into behaviours by insisting that they be expressed as 'behavioural' objectives. Behavioural objectives are seen as the cornerstones of CBT, becoming the organising framework for the instructional design process (Davies 1973).

A fourth flaw in CBT is that it objectifies performance: it separates the subject (performer) from the object (performance). Objective performance as constituted by CBT is viewed as separate from, independent of and privileged over the subjective performer. Performance therefore is alienated from the work experiences of people: first, by the use of disintegrating behavioural objectives which atomise and make unrecognisable real work; second, through positing competence as separate from and independent of the individual worker.

Fifth, CBT also raises the individual learner above the learning group. The process of learning is seen as beginning and ending in the acquisition of prespecified task competencies. CBT in fact suggests that group learning is detrimental to individual learners.

It holds back 'quick learners', it wastes learners' time, or it forces teachers and trainers to aim at the average learner at the expense of the fast learner.

In sum, the reification of behaviours, objectification of performance, use of task-based analyses of 'competent work performance' and the privileging of the individual over the group are all integral features of a CBT system based on a narrow conception of competence.

CBT—A POSITIVIST PROJECT?

Positivism emerged as a way of seeing and explaining the world in 17th-century Europe. Galileo and Newton had begun the process of demystifying the universe, holding out the possibility that through science the future could be predicted and controlled. The concept of competence embedded in the practices of the CBT movement is consistent with a positivist world view. One of the tendencies of positivism is to privilege the parts of any system over the whole. This breaking down of a system, in the quest to know it, is a powerful feature of positivism. This reductionist analysis would insist that competent work is no more than the sum of the behaviours which make up the components of competent work. By precluding any suggestion of a *Gestalt* in work activity, the potential *integration* of the behaviours—and of the knowledge, skills, attitudes and abilities that underpin them—is not given a high priority in the learning process.

A further feature of positivism is that it asserts its authority over other explanatory paradigms by claiming human reason as its own. A rational human being is seen as one who stands outside of everyday life, unengaged, objective, one who accepts and employs the strict rules of reason. This ideal of objectivity is also a central feature of CBT, where the focus is on the measurement of directly observable performance against prespecified and objectively developed criteria. This reification of competent behaviour into the realm of the objective effectively precludes any questioning of its legitimacy by learners and prevents any negotiation of the content, processes or assessment of learning.

The tendency of CBT to elevate the technical over the interpersonal and the individual over the group can also be traced to the positivist paradigm. The machine is a powerful metaphor of positivism. Stemming from the work of Galileo and Newton, the world is conceived as a complex but ultimately knowable machine. Most if not all human problems, it was argued, could be explained in terms of technical breakdown in the individual 'machinery' of life, and technical or instrumental solutions to these breakdowns could be found. The technico-instrumental position became the *rational* way of seeing all problems. The individual was constituted as the agent who would identify, cause and solve the problems of the emergent technico-scientific world.

A positivist approach to teaching and training
An illustration of the narrow positivist approach to competence is provided by the recent debate over teacher testing in the USA. As a reaction to a widespread concern about the quality of teachers, almost every state has used one of a number of standardised tests to certify teachers. These tests are of multiple-choice format and typically test basic general and professional knowledge and basic skills such as communication skills. They are based on the proposition that teacher competence depends on a foundation of low-level skills and knowledge and that, moreover, these are sufficient indicators of teacher competence.

The teacher tests seem to ignore the mass of evidence stretching over decades that teacher quality depends on a combination of traits, capacities and knowledges which enable teachers to respond to the contexts in which they are working. The implication of this for teacher testing is clearly that certification tests need to take into account a variety of evidence, including actual teacher performance, student and parent views, and professional activities undertaken by the teacher.

This narrow view of competence was demonstrated in Australia in a number of early attempts to develop competency-based curricula in vocational education. One of the first national curriculum projects was that in the metal trades area. The modules emerging out of this project were based on a highly mechanistic, task-oriented, fragmented view of the occupations in the industry. They ignored the relationships between the tasks, the possibility that the sum of the occupation could be more than the individual tasks, the relationship between knowledge, skills and attitudes, or any theory about the nature of generic competencies and about the importance of context in competent performance. This early attempt has been replaced in more recent times by far more integrated holistic curricula (as we see in the next section). Nevertheless, these two examples do illustrate a danger of the competency movement—the attempt to devise simplistic, reductionist solutions to complex issues and problems.

COMPETENCE—A BROAD VIEW

The language currently used to explain competence in government-sponsored industrial and educational reforms in Australia seeks to distance itself from the narrow view which characterised the CBT movement. A literature review undertaken by the NSW Vocational Education and Training Accreditation Board revealed almost total support from commentators for a more broadly defined conception of competence (VETAB 1994). The National Training Board NSW (NTB 1990), early in the development of competency standards, endorsed 'a broad concept of competency in that all aspects of work performance, and not only narrow task skills, are included' (NTB 1993: 29). The reports also proposed sets of 'key competencies' generic to all forms of work. This position, however, while moving considerably from that held by the behaviourists in the CBT movement, continued to emphasise performance and outcomes over knowledge, cognition and the other attributes of effective performance. Such criticism encouraged the NTB to adjust their guidelines so that the knowledge and values base underpinning work could be addressed in the competency standards descriptions (NTB 1993: 34–6). Work undertaken by Gonczi, Hager and Oliver for the professions broadened the definition of competence further; they questioned the proposition that competence should concern itself exclusively with the description of outcomes. They proposed an integrated approach to competency description, which places outcomes and underpinning attributes of performance on an equal footing (Gonczi et al. 1990; Gonczi et al. 1994; Hager 1995; Hager & Beckett 1995; Hager & Gonczi 1996).

The exclusive emphasis on skills and outcomes in competency analysis proposed by the National Training Board in 1990 alienated large parts of the education sector. The NTB position was accused of totally ignoring the crucial importance of knowledge and understanding in the actions of human beings, whether in the workplace or elsewhere. The NTB was also accused of harbouring a technicist view of work closely aligned to an industrial production model of competence. Critics further argued that work involving a high degree of personal interaction and sensitivity to the needs of others cannot be judged entirely by outcomes. A patient who suicides, a dissatisfied customer or a disgruntled art critic cannot necessarily be attributable to the incompetent performance of the psychiatrist, shop assistant or artist. These criticisms led the community services industry to redefine performance and outcomes in terms of expectations of performance and demonstrable and/or defensible performance (NCSH ITAB 1993: 29).

The narrow instrumental conception of competence on which the previous CBT model was based has been rejected by almost all commentators. The broader view of competency-based learning does not confuse performance with competence, and argues that a large variety of attributes that underpin performance must be considered in any competency analysis. It rejects single acceptable outcomes as being indicative of competent performance, proposing that in most situations multivariable contexts inevitably lead to multivariable acceptable outcomes. It argues that the processes undertaken by the worker during work activity are often a more valid indicator of competence than the products or outcomes of work. It emphasises human agency and social interrelations in competency descriptions. It regards competence as developmental and elaborative rather than static and minimalist. It places great importance on groups of practitioners coming together and, through a process of debate and dialogue, developing competency descriptions of practice.

It does not, therefore, deny subjectivity in competency assessment, taking the view that competency assessment should be based on an evidence model of competence. An individual should be judged to be competent on the basis of evidence presented when compared with predetermined descriptions of practice previously agreed by practitioners through the process of inter-subjective dialogue. It is thus quite distinct from the measurement model preferred by CBT (Woodruffe 1990). It does not attempt to create the illusion of objectivity by developing a litany of precise, measurable outcome statements, each of which needs to be 'measured' before competence is determined. It views descriptions of competence as being open to renegotiation and change, not as objective truth statements standing outside and independent of the contested views of work found within the workplace.

As against the positivist leanings of the narrow CBT approach, this broad definition of competence is more consistent with another commonly accepted paradigm or world view—humanism.

COMPETENCE-BASED EDUCATION—A HUMANIST PROJECT?

Like positivism, the humanist tradition owes its existence, at least in part, to the evolution of the natural sciences. The view that science develops objective, immutable, universal truths has always been contested. Chaos theory and the work of Karl Popper (1968) and Thomas Kuhn (1970) suggest that the claims of science have always been conditional and relational. Sometimes referred to as the interpretive or hermeneutic paradigm, humanism regards the subject as critical to developing meaning and explanation, and rejects much of the positivist paradigm. It argues that an act of interpretation inevitably occurs in any investigation, and that these acts of interpretation must always get in the way of simple means–ends theories of action and attempts at objective investigation. In the interpretive framework, individuals are seen as the architects who construct meaning.

The humanist paradigm, like the positivist paradigm outlined earlier, is a major influence on the way the concept of competence is currently being reinterpreted and renegotiated by the various players. Characteristics of the broad view of competence are consistent with features of the humanist paradigm. Generally, those commentators who hold to the broad definition of competence regard participatory methodologies as important strategies in developing the descriptions of practice called competency standards. Among the different ways professions have gone about the business of describing practice, a common feature has been the use of competency analysis workshops, where practitioners have come together to develop negotiated and agreed descriptions of practice. The results of these workshops were in turn widely disseminated and discussed throughout the respective professions, leading to further refinement of the competency standards.

The shift of emphasis from positivism to humanism in adult vocational education and training can be traced to the recommendations made by the Australian Committee on Technical and Further Education (1974). Widely known as the Kangan report, it set the direction and philosophy of the vocational education sector, articulating a view that the vocational education sector should be mindful of the needs of individuals and be committed to access and equity for all learners. It called for vocational education to become broader in its focus—committed to the provision of second-chance education and the elimination of barriers to recurrent educational opportunities.

Despite the popularity of economic rationalism with governments during the 1990s, a large number of educationalists in adult vocational education continue to support and promote these humanist educational principles. Kinsman (1992) suggests that the Kangan tradition explains why teachers continue both to support and to adapt the concept of competence in adult vocational education. She argues that the concept of competence is attractive to those working within the humanist paradigm because of the variety of ways it supports access and equity. Making learning goals and assessment criteria explicit, the recognition and certification of competence independent of the pathway through which it was achieved, the development of more flexible educational entry and exit points, and the recognition by educational sectors of each other's contribution to learning—all of which are facilitated by the competency approach—are contributions to access and equity in adult vocational education.

IMPLEMENTING AN INTEGRATIVE APPROACH TO COMPETENCE

An example of how competency standards can be developed which are holistic and integrated can be found in the adult basic education branch of the teaching profession. Here the competencies were developed through a research methodology that used a variety of methods: expert workshops, observation of performance, and interviews with teachers.

Rather than being a long list of tasks which fragment the occupation and ignore the relationship between knowledge, skills and attitudes, competence here consists of only 23 elements. Complex combinations of attributes in performance criteria are brought together and are written at a reasonable level of generality, taking into account generic competencies. At the same time, there has been an attempt to give examples of what the competencies might look like in certain contexts.

The performance criterion—that part of the standard that says how one might judge whether the element can be satisfactorily completed—attempts to describe the combination of attributes needed to do this. It is written in such a way as to illustrate the difficulty of separating out the atoms of performance:

- A range of approaches to language learning and teaching is used that takes into account the knowledge of the individual student and the purpose of the task. Sensitivity to student need is demonstrated, as is adaptability to student language and learning development. The use of these approaches is explained and justified in terms of current approaches to language in social context.
- A series of cues or examples is supplied to show the kinds of evidence from which one might infer competence. For example:
  (a) refers to established and current theories of language and language learning in justifying teaching and learning strategies;
  (b) discusses with students the reasons for particular classroom practices where appropriate.

The Australian national curriculum for laboratory science technicians is another illustration of how the holistic/humanistic approach to competence can be applied. In addition to analysing tasks, the project analysed the generic competencies of laboratory technicians, including such things as problem solving, teamwork and adaptability. In the modules that have been developed, attention is paid in the content sections to all these attributes.

199

Appropriate delivery modes that exhibit the best adult learning principles have also been covered. Assessment methods are proposed that do not assess individual low-level skills but instead attempt to suggest methods that assess whole tasks using a variety of methods to gather evidence from a range of sources.

PROBLEM-BASED LEARNING

Competency-based approaches to adult learning are quite different from those used by the CBT movement. The content and processes of learning are integrated. Independent learning becomes a feature of the curriculum. Peer and group learning activities are included, as are collaborative learning and learning contracts; self-assessment becomes a central feature of the learning process. An example of this approach to learning, and one which has been used widely, is problem-based learning (PBL). The principal idea behind problem-based learning is: 'that the starting point for learning should be a problem, a query or a puzzle that the learner wishes to solve' (Boud & Felletti 1991). The problems posed in PBL courses are central to practice and, therefore, are said to avoid many of the difficulties found in more traditional vocational education programs. These difficulties include issues of relevance, learner experience, and those associated with the 'front-end' approach of many courses, whereby all the knowledge is provided first. Proponents of problem-based learning also argue that knowledge is never static and can never be totally accommodated in pre-employment programs. It therefore views the purpose of pre-employment courses as developing the skills to learn new knowledge quickly, effectively and independently. The problem-based approach is seen as a way of developing these skills.

Boud and Felletti also suggest that PBL serves two distinct purposes. The first concerns the practice and development of a number of generalisable competencies, including:

- adapting to and participating in change;
- dealing with problems;
- making reasoned decisions;
- reasoning critically and creatively;
- adopting a more holistic approach to work;
- practising empathy and collaborating in groups;
- identifying personal strengths and weaknesses;
- undertaking self-directed learning.

Boud and Felletti also suggest that PBL meets the conditions for effective adult learning by allowing learners to set and solve problems; by integrating the learning; and by encouraging cumulative learning, learning for understanding and learning through reflection.

Problem-based learning has been used mainly in the education and training of the professions. A number of schools of nursing, engineering, optometry, architecture, law and business have used this curriculum approach (see Boud & Felletti 1991; Boud 1985). It is somewhat ironic that those wanting to develop a broad model of competency-based education for tradespeople and people in other non-professional occupations that avoids the mistakes of the CBT movement may need to look to professional best practice within the university sector—the educational sector most opposed to the concept of competence.

COMPETENCE—A CRITICAL VIEW1

We would not like to give the impression that the debate about competence and its application in adult education is only between those who hold either positivist or humanist world views. A significant number of adult educators would argue that both the positivist and humanist paradigms ignore or downplay the significance of the social distribution of power. For critical theorists, any analysis must engage in an investigation of the power relations as constituted within society. They argue that without this analysis positivist and humanist explanations are incomplete. (For extended discussion of these points, see M. Collins 1991 and Hart 1992.)

Critics suggest that the concept of competence is founded within the positivist policy framework of economic rationalism, and that it has only been softened somewhat by the application of humanist analysis in the ensuing debate. They point out that the world view contained within the national training reform agenda appears to contradict the lived experiences of workers, learners and educators. Many commentators (Burke 1989; Evans 1988) describe a modern workplace far removed from that developed by Henry Ford. These commentators portray workers working together to solve problems, make decisions, work autonomously, think creatively and communicate effectively. Yet the reality for many workers falls far short of this ideal. Even where workplaces have been reorganised to achieve these outcomes, organisational structures and power relations place clear limits on the application of the sorts of abilities referred to above. Workers and managers often have opposing ideas about the meaning of and means of attaining 'efficiency', 'productivity' and 'knowledge', as well as about the nature of workplace learning. In competency standards development, the selection of methods and participants, together with managerial power in the organisation, will have a major influence on the final form the competency standards descriptions may take. (For discussion of these points, see Bengtsson 1993; Collins 1993; Billett 1993, 1994; Centre for Skill Formation Research and Development 1993.)

The competency debate in education has generated other contradictions and ambiguities. Universities generally have assumed that two types of education are needed—one designed to develop leadership within the professions and the other to develop followership in the 'non-professions'. In our culture, convention dictates that universities are the knowledge creation and development centres of society. In education this position has been regarded as self-evident. The vocational education and training sector is characterised as being one designed for knowledge-users as opposed to knowledge-producers (Centre for Continuing Education 1992: 26). However, the integrative approach to competence suggests that the workplace of the future has the potential to be a knowledge creation and development site (Mansfield & Mitchell 1996).

COMPETENCE—A POSTMODERN VIEW

This chapter has focused on exploring different interpretations of the concept of competence that are used to critique and inform its application in adult education settings. Postmodern perspectives add a further dimension to debates on the appearance of competency-based education (CBE) and training in contemporary adult learning.

As discussed earlier, a positivist orientation emphasises the technical aspects of work over any personal or social dimension, and takes a much narrower view of occupational competence than the humanist orientation. The humanist perspective emphasises the social, interpersonal and cognitive aspects of work in its conceptualisation of competence, highlighting the underpinning and often generic aspects of being competent in work. The critical perspective, while having little to say about which conception of competence should underpin CBE, suggests that the competency-based education and training movement is, itself, embedded within a particular set of existing economic, social and political power relations that are antiemancipatory and exploitative. From this perspective, competency-based descriptions of work cannot be divorced from the ways in which they are used to continue the exploitative nature of work as organised in market economies.

Despite the obvious differences between positivist, humanist and critical orientations to CBE, they all assume, albeit from different perspectives, that competency descriptions have the capacity to describe real work. This is the point of departure for postmodern perspectives on competency-based education and training.

Postmodernism sits uneasily under the title 'paradigm', because postmodernism stands as a diffuse collection of intellectual ideas, with a genealogy involving a variety of theories that pervade many disciplines and aesthetic endeavours. It consists of a number of different genres and perspectives and has a close affinity with its more theorised companion, poststructuralism. In the literature, postmodernism and poststructuralism overlap and are often subsumed by each other. Nevertheless, it is possible to distinguish three assumptions that, for the most part, appear to be common features in the literatures of poststructuralism and postmodernism.

First, there is an emphasis on the local in social relations. Postmodernism and poststructuralism privilege the local because they suggest that it is only at this level of social interaction that narratives come close to capturing the complexities of power relations. Situated discourses avoid the tendency to construct normative discourses, which purport to provide explanations that are applicable across social, cultural and historical location. In arguably the most famous aphorism of postmodernism, there is an incredulity to metanarratives. Postmodernism rejects the idea that there are universal truths with transcendental applicability, arguing that, while all discourses produce 'truths', the meaning of truth always remains uncertain. Meanings can never be clear because their constituent terms are textual representations, which are inexact and open to interpretation.

The second assumption of postmodernism is that the conceptual categories used to ground argument commonly involve using categories that are discrete and in opposition to each other. However, these categories are definitionally interdependent. Called 'deconstruction', this approach in social and educational research attempts to show that many categorical oppositions that are used in social and educational analysis (man/woman, capital/labour, theory/practice, manual/mental etc.) are socially constructed oppositions rather than natural and immutable. Their existence as conceptual categories are maintained through mutual dependency. In other words, one side of the dichotomy can have meaning only in the presence of its opposite.

203

The third assumption involves positing the idea that language does not reflect an existing reality but rather constructs a reality, thereby turning the commonsense notion of the relationship of language and the material world on its head (see also chapter 18). Rather than language being seen as representing the world as it is, language is conceptualised as creating the world. The construction of knowledge and reality, including descriptions of competence, is therefore regarded as a process of 'languaging'. Words have meaning only through their insertion within a particular classificatory system. Consequently, meaning is constructed through discursive practices and thus becomes implicated in questions of social power. Discourses set conditions on what kinds of meaning are legitimate, what kinds of talk can occur, who can speak and what can be said.

From this perspective, therefore, the discourses of competency-based education act as powerful devices that construct learning in particular ways. Competency standards are constructed as being generally applicable across the different contexts and situations in which learners and workers exist. They also construct learning in terms of predetermined outcomes that are either achieved or not achieved by learners. Learning that is different or occurs beyond these outcomes is unacknowledged in the discourses of competence. Finally, the discourses of CBE legitimise and privilege particular meanings for learning. All learning is constructed as instrumental and performative, closely associated with the requirements of work. Learning for other purposes increasingly becomes incorporated within the paradigm of CBE or finds itself marginalised and ignored. A new social reality for learning emerges—a reality constructed by the discourses of competency-based education.

CONCLUSION

The move to competency-based education has stimulated a major re-examination of fundamental features of the education and training system in the 21st century. As a result, many of the taken-for-granted ideas about education and training have become problematic. What is the relationship between the different sectors within education? What outcomes are common to each sector? What outcomes are unique to each sector? What is the difference between vocational and general education? What is knowledge?

NOTE

1   The contribution of Peter Willis to the development of this section is gratefully acknowledged.

FURTHER READING

Billett, S. 1993 'What's in a setting? Learning in the workplace', *Australian Journal of Adult and Community Education*, 33(1), pp. 4–13.
——1994 'Authenticity in workplace settings', in J. Stevenson (ed.) *Cognition at Work*. Adelaide: National Centre for Vocational Education Research, pp. 36–75
Centre for Skill Formation Research and Development 1993 *After Competence: The Future of Post-Compulsory Education and Training*. Brisbane: Griffith University.
Collins, C. (ed.) 1993 *Competencies: The Competencies Debate in Australian Education and Training*. Melbourne: Australian College of Education.
Collins, M. 1991 *Adult Education as Vocation: A Critical Role for the Adult Educator*. London: Routledge.
Gonczi, A., Hager, P. & Heywood, I. 1992 *A Guide to Development of Competency Standards for Professions*. Research Paper no. 7, Canberra: Australian Government Printing Service.

13

Cross-cultural training in the workplace

Daphne Brosnan, Hermine Scheeres & Diana Slade

The current emphasis on workplace restructuring and the institution of flattened hierarchies, work teams, multiskilling and so on means that serious attention is being paid to the management of cultural and linguistic diversity in the workplace. In this chapter we examine six different approaches to cross-cultural training in the workplace, outlining their strengths, weaknesses and educational outcomes, and the view of language and culture underpinning each approach. As a precursor to considering these pedagogies, we discuss what we understand by 'culture'.

DEFINING CULTURE

First, what is 'culture'? When this question is raised in an educational or training context, answers differ enormously. Similar variation is reflected in the academic literature. Kalantzis et al. (1992a) explore the multiple meanings and uses of the word 'culture'. They point out that it can be used in its narrowest sense, which is related to 'cultivation', as in bacterial culture, agriculture and horticulture; or it can be used to describe the arts, as in 'high culture'—to cultivate the mind—a concept that gave rise to ministries of the arts and culture. Or it can focus on 'folk culture'—that is, those things that people do in their social life; 'ethnic' culture is often thought of in this way, as a kind of folk culture. Finally, the most widespread use of the word 'culture' today is in the sense of a whole way of life, as synonymous with society. This meaning was developed during the rise of cultural anthropology in the late 19th and early 20th centuries, when anthropologists identified connections between politics, economics and culture. So we now have 'Australian culture', 'American culture', 'Japanese culture' and so on.

The complexity inherent in any notion or definition of culture is captured by a recent report, *Cultural Understandings as the Eighth Key Competency* (Queensland Department of Education 1994: 14), which refers to the relationship of culture, learning and the making of meaning:

> Culture arises through socialisation and learning; it is neither natural nor fixed. Culture entails multiple personal and social meanings, relationships, practices and values.
>
> There are no fixed boundaries to cultures, and cultures are always changing. Any individual lives in and between many different cultures: the culture of the workplace; the culture of educational institutions; culture as ethnic background; culture as aspiration, interest or inclination. In this sense, all our cultures have multiple layers, each layer in a complex and dynamic relation to the others.

Such a holistic understanding of culture enables workplace culture itself to be seen as an equally important concern to cross-cultural training as the many other cultures from which workers and clients come. It also helps us to see that culture and learning are interrelated.

SIX APPROACHES TO CROSS-CULTURAL TRAINING

The issue of cross-cultural communication and training is not specific to any one academic discipline: it is an area of investigation for a variety of disciplines, ranging from linguistics and communication studies to sociology, psychology and management studies. Cope et al. (1994) identified six principal approaches to cross-cultural communication and training:

- ethnospecific;
- EEO/antidiscrimination;
- sociohistorical;
- linguistic;
- psychological/interpersonal;
- productive diversity.

Such a classification is also a useful heuristic device, enabling educators to distinguish between various approaches to cross-cultural training and critically to evaluate and identify the theoretical premises these are based on. Such an understanding is a prerequisite to a principled and informed approach to cross-cultural training. The six approaches are discussed in Cope et al. (1994) in terms of the notion of culture employed, the view of language and communication embedded in the program or materials, the competencies and skills covered, the pedagogical orientation of the program, and the extent to which the training is incorporated into mainstream training or treated as a separate, one-off activity. Below, each of the six approaches to cross-cultural training are outlined, the strengths and weaknesses of each approach discussed, and the view of language and culture incorporated in each of the approaches identified.

ETHNOSPECIFIC APPROACH

Until the mid-1980s, cross-cultural training was predominantly identified with the training needs of professional people whose work would bring them into frequent contact with members of other cultures. This approach introduced trainees to a particular culture with which they were unfamiliar, and could thus broadly be defined as 'ethnospecific'.

Examples of this approach are Bird and Storz's programs (both unpublished), as well as the cross-cultural program for health professionals developed by the Multicultural Centre of Sydney College of Advanced Education (1984). Participants are introduced to specific cultural practices such as Japanese management styles and the differences between Anglo-Australian and Vietnamese understandings of legal concepts. The approach focuses on culture in terms of ethnic differences, thereby equating ethnicity and culture. It sees culture as something that is fixed and static, rather than as a dynamic process open to negotiation.

Language is not explicitly discussed in this approach. However, ways of overcoming possible communication barriers are suggested. These include:

- using interpreters effectively;
- speaking in plain English, and minimising the difficulties of technical language;
- discussing body language;
- emphasising the importance of active listening;
- discussing other communication issues subject to cultural variation.

Because this approach focuses on differences between groups, cultural groups are often described as if they were homogeneous, and differences within groups are ignored. Potential drawbacks are that it can lead to damaging group stereotypes, and to supporting the notion of outgroup members being all alike and undesirably different from the dominant group. The strength of this approach is that it draws participants' attention to specific cultural practices. Such knowledge can be useful in training contexts in which educators are working predominantly with people of one nationality.

EEO/ANTIDISCRIMINATION APPROACH

From the mid-1980s cross-cultural training has diversified, and approaches have arisen that recognise this reality, with some programs focusing on migration movements and the consequent issues of social justice and equity that arise. It is these concerns that underlie the EEO/antidiscrimination approach and the sociohistorical approach. Both of these are specialist training programs targeting specific groups of people.

The central concern of EEO/antidiscrimination training programs is that of access and equity in culturally and linguistically diverse workplaces and communities. Two recently developed training packages that approach cross-cultural communication training from this angle are the Human Rights and Equal Opportunity Commission's *Diversity Makes Good Business* (1993a) and the *Multicultural Access Training Kit: A Trainer's Manual* (1989), produced and published by the Canterbury-Bankstown Migrant Resource Centre.

The Human Rights package examines the concept of affirmative action in the context of legislation affecting the day-to-day operations of organisations. Accompanying this training package is a video entitled *Racial Discrimination in the Workplace*, which is designed to raise managers' awareness of how racist behaviour and discriminatory practices adversely affect productivity. The Migrant Resource Centre's kit is intended to assist the community sector in developing multiculturally sensitive services, and includes sessions on such subjects as developing multicultural policies, growing participation in service delivery, and management and personnel practices.

Both packages employ a sociological/anthropological definition of culture: that is, they see culture as a total way of life and do not simply equate it to ethnicity or nationality (thereby not limiting it to the practices and habits of one particular ethnic group). Culture is seen, rather, as encompassing all aspects of social life—gender, class, socioeconomic status, ethnic background, and workplace culture.

As language is often identified as a barrier to access and equity, there is an emphasis in these packages on providing information about:

- the use of translated material;
- language services, such as the telephone interpreter service, and language aids;
- language reference lists, and guidelines for writing translations and using interpreters;
- language issues such as the organisational reasons for the growth in written communication in the workplace;
- obstacles to effective intercultural communication, such as issues of stereotyping and accents.

The purpose of this approach is to provide tasks and activities focused on how to implement government policies and regulations. This approach to cross-cultural training assumes, therefore, that there are legal responsibilities that a person must abide by. This very focus can create tension—the fact that it is a legal obligation may give rise to resistance. Participants often see EEO/antidiscrimination policies as intrusions from outside rather than as something that can help them to develop internally relevant, positive measures to make the organisation work better. Effective training in this area involves bridging the gap between theory and practice, between the letter of the law and truly affirmative programs.

SOCIOHISTORICAL APPROACH

The sociohistorical approach is very closely linked to the history of migration. The distinctive features of this approach are that it identifies the demographic and social factors of diversity and provides a historical overview of multiculturalism. Two examples of this approach are Kalantzis et al.'s (1992a, b) materials developed for the NLLIA's Centre for Workplace Communication and Culture at the University of Technology, Sydney, and Issaris' materials developed for Qantas Airways (1991).

The emphasis in this approach is on the presentation of 'facts', acquaintance with which, it is assumed, will lead to an understanding of cultural and linguistic diversity. Kalantzis et al.'s programs begin with an examination of the concept of culture and explore questions of identity. For both these programs, the purpose of providing sociohistorical information is to argue for the necessity of cross-cultural policies and strategies in all workplaces.

The sociohistorical approach to cross-cultural training does not deal explicitly with language. However, it provides information about the logistics of language in the migration process. By providing such factual information the approach hopes to raise awareness of the difficulties that employees from predominantly oral societies may experience when they work in a literate society. Information is provided about services such as specialist language education and telephone interpreter services. The advantage of the sociohistorical approach is that it provides a clear picture of the origins and dimensions of cultural and linguistic diversity. A disadvantage of this approach is that participants can find these facts difficult to deal with and it may therefore not change their attitudes or workplace practices.

LINGUISTIC APPROACH

The linguistic approach to cross-cultural communication training focuses explicitly on language. Four examples of recently developed materials that exemplify this approach are Gumperz et al. (1991), King (1992), Dwyer (1991) and Willing (1992).

The linguistic approach argues that misunderstandings and breakdowns that occur in cross-cultural communication are to do not only with a lack of contextual or cultural knowledge but also with linguistic factors, such as different ways of structuring discourse and different intonations and stress patterns. According to Gumperz et al. (1991: 9):

> These breakdowns may be linguistic because there are linguistic skills involved in maintaining conversational continuity and in building up what sounds like a reasonable and polite argument. These skills are automatic, that is [they are] learned as part of a speaker's linguistic background and [are] subject to cross-cultural variation.

King's package (1992: vii) similarly takes language as its main focus, arguing that:

> An advantage of this language oriented approach is that attitudes, beliefs, values and assumptions can be examined by developing skills to, for example, analyse a written text such as a newspaper article, or to analyse a spoken interaction such as service encounter in a government office. Through analysing the language, assumptions (both general and specific) can be made explicit, and then the attitudes, beliefs, values etc. that rest on these assumptions can be critically analysed.

The Dwyer package argues that barriers to communication include pronunciation of English sounds, the grammar of English language, different perceptions of intended meaning, and gender role models. Willing's book is based on an analysis of language collected at different workplaces. His study includes a corpus of tape recordings of task-oriented interactions (mainly two-person) between white-collar professionals, involving at least one participant whose first

211

language is not English. Willing is concerned with identifying the causes of language difficulties, and strategies people may use to overcome such communicative difficulties; hence, as with the Gumperz model, his study focuses on language issues, examining in detail 'the practical means people use in order to keep their communication adjusted to each other's current states of knowledge and to deal with communicative difficulties' (1992: 1).

Although the focus of these materials is on language, they also emphasise the importance of dealing with cultural issues. King and Gumperz look in detail at cultural issues. Gumperz argues that there are three elements to culture: communicative style, assumptions and values based on shared experience, and power realised through the dominant culture. Both Gumperz et al. and King recognise the dynamism of culture—that it is not a fixed entity but rather something which helps people make sense of their experience and which is itself moulded by their experiences.

The advantage of the linguistic approach is that it sees language as central to cross-cultural communication. However, unless it also deals systematically with issues of culture, it runs the risk of becoming too narrow and too focused on non-English-speaking background (NESB) language difficulties and issues.

PSYCHOLOGICAL/INTERPERSONAL APPROACHES

The psychological/interpersonal approach to cross-cultural training began in the USA in the 1980s. Two examples of this approach are Kogod (1991) and Bennett (1991). Kogod's training program is intended for managers and supervisors, and has three modules: interpersonal relationships, relationships at work, and learning to manage diversity. Bennett's approach is typified by his introductory activity, which emphasises that 'we each have cultural biases, perceptual gates and we can get hooked by our tints'. His training package includes an interactive video disc used as an aid in 'understanding other cultures, and allowing the exploration of the relationships of cultural values to customs and behaviour through vignettes'.

This approach views culture as a shared design for living based on the values and practices of a society, and therefore as a set of values, beliefs, attitudes and customs. The focus is on the individual. An attempt to understand another's beliefs and behaviours in terms of that person's culture is promoted through self-exploration of one's own values, beliefs and attitudes. By experiencing/reliving their own and others' life experiences, participants, it is argued, are able to see alternative ways of behaviour. Negotiation based on respect for cultural differences is central to this approach. Language is therefore addressed through activities involving negotiation of meaning, active listening, mediation and non-verbal behaviour. This approach does not deal with detailed language features, such as those covered by the linguistic approach.

One of the disadvantages of this approach is its emphasis on the individual, which gives the impression that the social dynamics of prejudice and racism are matters of individual failure. Culture is therefore seen as being concerned with personal feelings and attitudes. On the other hand, awareness is potentially raised by participants' identifying and working through their own stereotypes as well as developing pride in their own cultural backgrounds.

PRODUCTIVE DIVERSITY APPROACH

As noted in chapter 7, since the early 1970s many countries have been attempting to internationalise their economies. One of the central aspects of this program is microeconomic reform and the restructuring of workplaces. The productive diversity approach argues that communication and culture are at the heart of these changes. It mentions that cultural and linguistic diversity now needs to be seen as a resource to be developed and built on, and not just as a reality to be tolerated. Therefore, the approach sees cross-cultural training as an integral part of mainstream training, looking not just at non-native language speakers but at all workers and managers. As this is a recent development, there are as yet few materials available. However, two often-used sets of materials are: the Office of Multicultural Affairs' publication *Value in Diversity* (1992), and the Human Rights and Equal Opportunity Commission's report *Diversity Makes Good Business* (1993b).

The productive diversity approach to cross-cultural training illustrates by practical strategy formulation and the presentation of case studies of best practice how diversity might be used as a productive resource. This approach can be incorporated into mainstream management training programs. It illustrates to participants the ways in which diversity is a crucial management and training issue, arguing against the approaches to managing diversity that 'consider themselves to be about minorities or "ethnics"—how to bring those on the margins into the mainstream of a work culture' (Cope et al. 1994). As such, the productive diversity approach argues against the notion of a single work culture to which people should more or less assimilate. Rather, it regards work itself as a cultural activity. As Cope et al. (1994) argue:

> This is in contrast to, for example, ethno-specific approaches to diversity which tend to emphasise culture as an event outside work (domestic, ancestral, ethnic and so on, an external influence to work). It is also in contrast to some EEO/anti-discrimination approaches to cross-cultural training which emphasise system and regulation.

The productive diversity model underpins the Human Rights and Equal Opportunity Commission's *Diversity Makes Good Business* (1993b). The central idea of this training program is that valuing diversity is an important part of team-building in workplaces. Such an approach, it is argued, not only ensures the contribution of all involved, but draws on a diversity of points of view, styles of communication, ways of working and interests. This makes for more effective and more innovative teams than monocultural ones. The Office of Multicultural Affairs resource kit has as its theme 'valuing diversity rather than confronting difference'. It looks at managing diversity in such areas as strategic and operational planning, communication, managing change, managing safety, client/customer service, innovative thinking, counselling, improving productivity and quality improvement.

The productive diversity approach adopts a broad definition of culture, encompassing many of the features of the other approaches but focusing on the culture of the workplace. The culture of the workplace, shared by all who work there, is contrasted with the cultural differences people bring to that workplace. As Cope et al. (1994) explain:

> The training is not about abstract ideas of culture or about particular cultural groups but about the negotiation and interplay of many cultures together. It explains to participants the way in which the central tenets of recent management theories and the practice of restructuring—management by culture, total quality management, multi-skilling, award restructuring, and so on—are themselves transformed when diversity is viewed as a productive resource. In addition it reassures participants that a productive diversity model is not only achievable, but workable in very practical ways.

This training approach, then, focuses on the importance of managing cultural and linguistic difference leading to efficiency, productivity, competitiveness and profitability. The approach can be integrated into all facets of mainstream training. The content of the program focuses on case studies and people's own work and life experiences, allowing for reflection and comparison.

However, because of the strong focus on workplace culture, there is a tendency in the productive diversity approach to neglect the role of language and communication in both management and work.

CONCLUSION

This chapter has outlined six approaches to cross-cultural education and training.[1] Each of the approaches is seen to have both advantages and disadvantages, and it is argued that each may be effectively employed in specific contexts. As language and culture are inextricably linked, in that one cannot be dealt with systematically without reference to the other, all of the approaches would be strengthened by a closer analysis of this relationship.

If cultural and linguistic diversity is to be seen as an asset, cross-cultural training needs to be integrated with mainstream education and training and offered across all levels of the workplace. Some key questions to guide educators and trainers in the selection of activities and experiences drawn from the different approaches are listed in Table 13.1.

Table 13.1   Key questions for selection of cross-cultural activities

Ethno-specific

- Does your organisation either have to deal with specific groups here in Australia, or is it in contact with other countries? Describe your experience (the context and the type of contact).
- Does the staff have adequate factual understanding of the different cultural practices involved? If yes, what practices are they?
- If no, where can you find out this sort of information in order to integrate it into education and training?
- Taking into account the possible limitations of this approach, such as stereotyping, how might this information be integrated into education and training?

EEO/anti-discrimination

- Are all employees and management adequately aware of the internal regulations and public legislation relating to discrimination, equal employment opportunities and affirmative actions policy?
- If not, taking into account the possible limitations of this approach, such as resistance to regulations, how might appropriate information be integrated in to education and training?

Socio-historical

- Does management have an adequate understanding of the social and demographic background of the organisation's employees and clientele?

- If yes, what are the facts? If no, where can you find out this sort of information?
- Taking into account the possible limitations of this approach, such as labelling people, how might you integrate this information into education and training?

Linguistic

- Is management aware of the variety of language that is appropriate to effective communication in a culturally diverse workplace?
- How do you identify oral and written language demands now placed on all employees?
- Taking into account the possible limitations of this approach, such as neglecting the broader organisational, cultural and social issues, how can you integrate these language demands into education and training?

Psychological/interpersonal

- Is there evidence of poor interpersonal relations in the organisation and are these poor relationships related to ethnic/cultural differences?
- Can you identify and describe incidents that exemplify these poor interpersonal relationships (the context, the parties concerned, the ethnic/cultural issues involved)?
- Taking into account the possible limitations of this approach, such as laying the blame on individuals, how might these issues be integrated into education and training?

Productivity diversity approach

- Are the managers and team leaders in the organisation aware of the importance of managing cultural and linguistic differences?
- Are you aware of best practices in the organisation as they relate to cultural and linguistic diversity?
- Best practice in terms of an integral model includes systems and structures that allow for differences in interacting in groups and within the organisation and community. This would be reflected in broader job descriptions that inform recruitment, selection and promotion criteria and procedures; a variety of communication channels to facilitate the flow and exchange of information; opportunities for individuals to express their knowledge and opinions; and opportunities for collaborative work where partners or team members with different experiences and skills work together on tasks.
- If yes, how would you describe them?
- How might these best practices be integrated into education and training?

NOTE

1   Peter Willis points out that it is useful for adult educators to also be aware of two related bodies of Australian literature. One of these deals with cross-cultural training in Aboriginal contexts, and the other with anticolonial and antiracist adult education, much of the latter having been developed at the Institute of Aboriginal Development in Alice Springs and at Tranby College in Sydney, both independent indigenous educational institutions. Important work has also been done on cross-cultural critical incident training by Dan Plooij and Gordon O'Brien of Flinders University (O'Brien & Plooij, 1973a, b; O'Brien et al. 1973). The *National Directory of Cross Cultural*

Training, published in 1994 (Office of Multicultural Affairs 1994), has a section on cultural awareness education in Aboriginal contexts, and in South Australia Chip Morgan has trained Aboriginal people to run cultural awareness courses for government and business organisations (Morgan 1994, 1995).

FURTHER READING

Clyne, M. 1991 'Australia's language policies: are we going backwards?' *Australian Review of Applied Linguistics,* series S, no. 8, pp. 3–22.

Collins, J. 1991 *Migrant Hands in a Distant Land.* Sydney: Pluto Press.

Cope, B., Castles, S. & Kalantzis, M. 1991 *Immigration, Ethnic Conflicts and Social Cohesion.* Canberra: Bureau of Immigration Research.

Cope, B., Pawls, A., Slade, D., Brosnan, D. & Neil, D. 1994 *Local Diversity, Global Connections.* Canberra: Office of Multicultural Affairs.

Cope, B. & Kalantzis, M. 1997 *Productive Diversity: A New Australian Model for Work and Management.* Sydney: Pluto Press.

Ozolins, U. 1993 *The Politics of Language in Australia.* Cambridge: Cambridge University Press.

PART IV
CONTEMPORARY ISSUES

Introduction to Part IV

This section of the book examines four aspects of the theory and practice of contemporary adult education and training: experience-based learning, women's learning and education, Aboriginal adult education, and the relationship of adult education and social action.

Experience-based learning (EBL) is the subject of chapter 14. The defining characteristics of EBL are: involvement in learning of the whole person, recognition and active use of learners' life experience and learning, generated by reflection on experience, the use of experiential learning, activities, negotiated learning, skilful facilitation of learning and appropriate assessment of learning. Insight into EBL can be found in the writings of such philosophers as Aristotle, Locke and Mill. Contemporary influences on EBL include the US philosopher John Dewey, who saw that experience is educational, but not automatically so; the Italian educator Maria Montessori, who devised a form of education that encourages children to construct their own understanding of the world; the German educator Kurt Hahn, who established the 'Outward Bound' school of adventure training; and the English educator A.S. Neill, who emphasised the importance of freedom and the unconscious in education. Other important influences on EBL have been the psychologists Jean Piaget, Carl Rogers and Abraham Maslow, who pointed to the importance for learning of, respectively, stages of cognitive development, non-judgmental facilitation, and the recognition of the personal needs of learners. Also important to EBL have been the literature of lifelong education, feminist and antiracist writing, and the educational thoughts of Mao Tse-tung and Paulo Freire, which focus on the connections between political action, social transformation and learning. Influential models of EBL include that of Boud and Pascoe, which emphasises the importance in EBL of learner control, involvement of self, and correspondence of learning and 'real' environment; the experiential learning cycle of David Kolb; Weil and McGill's categorisation of the contexts of EBL; and Boud and Walker's model of stages of reflection. Applications of EBL occur in a variety of settings, including therapy, professional education, HIV/AIDS education and workplace education. The recognition of prior learning in workplace education is potentially a major means of gaining educational equity and access for workers. EBL raises important ethical issues for educators, two of which are discussed in this chapter: the ethics of facilitation, and the impact of mandatory participation.

Chapter 15 provides an overview of issues related to women's learning. Barriers to women's access (e.g. lack of child care, geographical isolation, disadvantage generated by class and race) are discussed, as are programs in schools and adult education designed to improve educational access for women, the important role of neighbourhood houses in providing a space in which women can learn, and issues related to women's access to workplace training. It is argued that the definition of what constitutes work, and the relationship of work and education, both need to be rethought. The second part of chapter 15 examines various aspects of women's experience as learners: the ways in which dominant curricula and pedagogies ignore and distort women's experience; the variety of feminist pedagogies which have emerged in recent years; the dynamics of mixed-gender classrooms; the stages of women's development as learners; and the advantages and drawbacks of women-only courses.

Chapter 16 examines the relationship of indigenous Australians to adult education. The chapter begins with a critique of the notion that Aboriginal culture and Aboriginal adult education are homogeneous. It is argued that there are diverse indigenous cultures and a variety of forms of indigenous education and learning, and that these are in increasingly vigorous contestation with white culture and education. Historically, the state has attempted to control indigenous people through a variety of means, including adult education. Indigenous people have fought to improve both the quantity and quality of adult education provision. The considerable gains made in the provision of both institutional and community-based adult education during the past 20 years have generated new complexities, two of which are examined in the second part of the chapter. First, analysis of government policy documents a new paternalism, which is still preoccupied with cultural questions and which diverts attention from deep-seated structural problems in adult education and other spheres. Second, an extended analysis of university programs identifies a 'quality-compromised' education, one which requires a lower level of performance from students, which sets up a spiral of failure and resentment, and which continues the marginalisation of indigenous graduates. It is argued that the sources of this form of education lie in a mixture of economic, professional and emotional factors, including educators' fear and ambition, the hunger of universities for student numbers, and the way the state funds indigenous education. The way out of this morass is for educators to honestly examine their role in maintaining this quality-compromised education and then to have the courage to take what will often be unpopular ameliorative action.

Chapter 17 explores the relationship of adult education and social action. It begins by identifying two distinguishing features of adult education in social action: it is collective, and it involves struggle against constraining forces and for greater autonomy. Four categories of adult education in social action are then discussed: learning that is incidental to action, informal yet deliberate learning, non-formal education which is organised yet sporadic, and systematic formal education. Various histories of adult education in social action are outlined: working-class adult education, folk high schools, popular education in the majority world, and education and learning linked to indigenous people's anticolonial struggles. The nature of social control is then examined, particular attention being paid to the process of ideological hegemony—control of people through ideas. Some of the ways in which education and learning can counter this control are then discussed, including teaching activist skills, teaching critical thinking, and learning in and through social action. The crucial role of analysis of power relations, social structures and economic processes in learning and education for social action is then canvassed. The chapter ends with a discussion of the role of the adult educator in learning for social action, particular attention being paid to the ethical issues generated by educators' interventions.

14

Experience-based learning
Lee Andresen, David Boud & Ruth Cohen

The distinguishing feature of experience-based learning[1] (or experiential learning[1]) is that the experience of the learner occupies central place in all considerations of teaching and learning. This experience may comprise earlier events in the life of the learner, current life events, or those arising from the learner's participation in activities implemented by teachers and facilitators. A key element of experience-based learning (henceforth referred to as EBL) is that learners analyse their experience by reflecting, evaluating and reconstructing it (sometimes individually, sometimes collectively, sometimes both) in order to draw meaning from it in the light of prior experience. This review of their experience may lead to further action.

All learning necessarily involves experience of some sort, prior and/or current, although scrutiny of many contemporary teaching and training practices might lead one to think otherwise. Much of the impetus for EBL has been a reaction to an approach to learning that is overly didactic, teacher-controlled, and involves a discipline-constrained transmission of knowledge. It supports a more participative, learner-centred approach, which places an emphasis on direct engagement, rich learning events and the construction of meaning by learners. EBL is of particular interest to adult educators because it encompasses formal learning, informal learning, non-formal learning, lifelong learning, incidental learning and workplace learning.

EBL is based on a set of assumptions about learning from experience. These have been identified by Boud et al. (1993) as:

- Experience is the foundation of, and the stimulus for, learning.

- Learners actively construct their own experience.
- Learning is a holistic process.
- Learning is socially and culturally constructed.
- Learning is influenced by the socioemotional context in which it occurs.

THE DEFINING CHARACTERISTICS OF EXPERIENCE-BASED LEARNING

EBL does not lend itself to being reduced to a set of strategies, methods, formulas or recipes. It is possible, however, to recognise within it some features that characterise and distinguish it from other approaches (Kolb 1984: 38):

> EBL appears to demand that three factors each be operating, at some level. These are:
> 1. Involvement of the whole person—intellect, feelings and senses. For example, in learning through role-plays and games, the process of playing or acting in these typically involves the intellect, some or other of the senses and a variety of feelings. Learning takes place through all of these.
> 2. Recognition and active use of all the learner's relevant life experiences and learning experiences. Where new learning can be related to personal experiences, the meaning thus derived is likely to be more effectively integrated into the learner's values and understanding.
> 3. Continued reflection upon earlier experiences in order to add to and transform them into deeper understanding. This process lasts as long as the learner lives and has access to memory. The quality of reflective thought brought by the learner is of greater significance to the eventual learning outcomes than the nature of the experience itself. 'Learning is the process whereby knowledge is created through the transformation of experience.'

However, EBL varies in practice according to three possibilities, which represent factors that may or not be applicable in a particular instance. These are:

1. *Intentionality of design.* Deliberately designed learning events are often referred to as 'structured' activities and include simulations, games, role-play, visualisations, focus group discussions, sociodrama and hypotheticals.
2. *Facilitation.* This is the involvement of some other person(s) (teachers, leaders, coaches, therapists). When such persons are involved, the outcomes may be influenced by the degree of skill with which they operate. EBL often assumes relatively

equal relationships between facilitator and learner, involves the possibility of negotiation, and gives the learner considerable control and autonomy.

3. *Assessment of learning outcomes.* In the event that assessment takes place, much depends on by what means, by whom, and for what purpose it is carried out. EBL is often as much concerned with the process as the outcomes of learning, and assessment procedures should accord with this. Assessment tasks congruent with EBL include individual or group projects, critical essays located in the learner's own experience, reading logs, learning journals, negotiated learning contracts, peer assessment and self-assessment. They might include a range of presentation modes other than writing, so as to enable the holism, context and complexity of the learning to be evidenced.

ESSENTIAL CRITERIA

EBL is not limited to being a mere 'method' or 'technique' or even a particular 'approach'; it is as wide and deep as education itself. Although there is no single way to identify the process of EBL, there are some criteria that need to be fulfilled if teaching and learning activities are to be labelled 'experience-based'.

The most important criterion we start with refers to the 'ends' of education—its goals, its purposes, what it is trying to achieve. We follow that with a number of criteria that refer to the 'means' of education—how we go about doing things to try to achieve those goals or ends.

First, the end . . .

• The ultimate goal of EBL involves learners' own appropriation of something that is to them personally significant or meaningful (sometimes spoken of in terms of the learning being 'true to the lived experience of learners').

Next, the means . . .

• EBL has a primary focus on the nature of learners' personal engagement with phenomena (sometimes described as being more or less directly in touch with the realities being studied).
• Debriefing and reflective thought are employed as essential stages (experience alone is not necessarily educative).
• There is acknowledgment of the premise that learning invariably involves the whole person (senses and feelings as well as intellect; affect and conation as well as cognition); and that this is associated with perceptions, awareness, sensibilities and

values being invoked, representing the full range of attributes of the functioning human being.

- There is recognition of what learners bring to the learning process (informal or formal recognition of prior learning).

- There is a particular ethical stance typically adopted towards learners by those who are their teachers, trainers, leaders or facilitators (involving such features as respect, validation, trust, openness and concern for the wellbeing of the learner, and both valuing and pursuing the self-directive potential of the learner).

It is our view that all these criteria are probably *conjointly necessary* before an educational event becomes properly called an experiential learning activity.

HISTORICAL ROOTS

The history of learning through experience follows the history of epistemology itself—the search for the basis of true knowledge. The terms experience and experiment are etymologically one.[2] In ancient Greek times Aristotle attacked the influential notion Plato had earlier advocated about the value of truth achieved by pure thought alone, uncontaminated by the world. Aristotle (in McKeon 1948: 689–90) argued instead that:

> All . . . by nature desire to know. An indication of this is the delight we take in our senses; for even apart from their usefulness they are beloved for themselves . . . With a view to action, experience seems in no respect inferior to art, and men of experience succeed even better than those who have theory without experience.

In the 17th century the English philosopher John Locke adopted a similar position. He asked the question, 'Whence has it all the materials of reason and knowledge?', to which he answered (Locke, in Cross & Woozely 1964: 89, 339):

> . . . in one word, from experience. In that all our knowledge is founded, and from that it ultimately derives itself . . . Experience here must teach me what reason cannot.

In the 19th century, John Stuart Mill wrote of the distinction between formal instruction and self-education, and stressed the virtues of learning a foreign language by living in the country where it is spoken rather than by studying it from books (Houle 1976: 27).

One of the twentieth century's most influential educational thinkers, John Dewey, took up the same theme when he wrote (1938: 25):

> I assume that amid all uncertainties there is one permanent frame of reference: namely the organic connection between education and personal experience.

Dewey continued this argument with 'all genuine education comes about through experience [but] . . . not all experiences are genuinely or equally educative'. Current thinking might amplify this, and suggest that the learning is likely to be recognised and applied only insofar as the learner actively reflects on the experience.

The experiential learning movement has evolved in an eclectic fashion, making its presence felt at all levels of education. Montessori, Hahn and Neill are all remembered as educators of children, but they have nonetheless greatly influenced our understanding of EBL for adults.

The Italian educator Maria Montessori's work can be understood as what we today call EBL. Her method involved imposing nothing, but creating an environment in which children learn to think by themselves, through the progressive mastery of their first-hand experiences (Kraft n.d.: 10). The tradition of infant schooling with the child as the discoverer constructing his or her own knowledge, and the importance of the environment in facilitating this development, has influenced many aspects of adolescent and adult education.

Kurt Hahn's establishment of the 'Outward Bound' movement in the UK during World War II can similarly be appreciated as a historically significant instance of EBL. Reacting against the formal, remote-from-life German education he had himself received, Hahn saw the experience of adventure itself as a critical educational activity for youth, having profound moral and even political significance. Today's wilderness and adventure-training traditions for groups as diverse as corporate managers and unemployed youth derive directly from this early work.

The progressive movement of the 1930s in US education is paralleled by the work of A.S. Neill at Summerhill School in the UK. Working from a Freudian position, Neill emphasised the importance of non-repressive environments in releasing the unconscious to develop self-motivated and self-directed students who would never lose the early joy of learning. Alternative schools in various parts of the world were greatly influenced by Neill's work and, through their example of what it is possible to achieve by giving students freedom to direct themselves, have in turn influenced mainstream school education.

More recently, our understanding of EBL has been influenced by developmental, cognitive and humanistic psychologies. Jean Piaget's research identified stages in the cognitive development of children (see chapter 3). Carl Rogers emphasised the role of the teacher as a non-judgmental facilitator whose unconditional positive regard is crucial in enabling students to develop an openness to experience (see chapter 3). Abraham Maslow suggested preconditions for effective learning which took account of the personal needs of learners and recognised the social context of learning.

Links between Third World development issues and EBL are also evident. UNESCO's Faure Report of 1972 was the first fully argued case for the principle of lifelong education, work and leisure. Faure's report envisaged students leaving and returning to studies without penalty at any time, the distinctions between in-school and out-of-school education being eliminated, and all education becoming self-education. These are principles situated at the heart of EBL.

A belief in the unity of knowing and doing is not the exclusive property of liberal Western, First World thinking. It was also central to the teachings of Mao Tse-tung, some of whose works vividly highlight the importance of this relationship (Mao 1968: 7, 8, 20):

> All genuine knowledge originates in direct experience . . . human knowledge can in no way be separated from practice . . . practice is higher than [theoretical] knowledge. Whoever wants to know a thing has no way except by coming into contact with it, that is, by living [practising] in its environment . . . practice, knowledge, again practice, and again knowledge . . . such is the dialectical-materialist theory of the unity of knowing and doing.

In a similar vein, the Brazilian educator Paulo Freire stressed the dialectic between action and reflection as the two inescapable aspects of any truly liberating education (1973: 66, 75–76):

> Liberation is a praxis: the action and reflection of men upon their world in order to transform it. When a word is deprived of its dimension of action, reflection automatically suffers as well; and the work is changed into idle chatter, into verbalism, into an alienated and alienating 'blah'. On the other hand, if action is emphasised exclusively, to the detriment of reflection, the word is converted into activism . . . Men are not built in silence, but in words, in work, in action-reflection.

David Kolb laid the foundations of much modern experiential

education theory; his *Experiential Learning* (1984) has become a foundational text in this area. His experiential learning cycle, greatly influenced by the earlier work of Kurt Lewin, has been widely reproduced and used (see chapter 3).

John Heron (1989, 1993) has written widely on the role of the facilitator, stressing the power relationships between facilitators and learners. Heron emphasises the importance of facilitators developing an ethical stance which takes account of the often hidden or overlooked manipulative processes that can be part of 'neutral' facilitation. Marilyn Peterson's *At Personal Risk* (1992) discusses boundary violations in professional–client relationships which are apposite to many of the issues raised by Heron.

More recently, feminist pedagogy has contributed to our understanding of what constitutes learning and how it may be acquired and facilitated. Work by writers such as Belenky et al. (1986) questioned the prevailing wisdom about how women learn and broadened our definition of educational activities to include autobiographical, intuitive and subjective strategies, encompassing co-counselling, learning pairs and small groups. Feminists have contributed to this redefinition. Dale Spender questioned the validity of many accepted truths and the gender-specific (male) evidence on which research findings are often predicated (Spender & Sarah 1980). Until recently, women's experience has been systematically neglected in research and writing in this field.

Attitude and value change is liable to be promoted if authentic experience is used to define and raise awareness of attitudes and values not previously recognised by the holder. Antiracist work to develop a more inclusive society has found that experiential methods can effect more pervasive change than didactic approaches, through addressing the experience of those who act in ways that consciously or unconsciously discriminate against others (Chambers & Pettman 1986; Pettman 1991).

MODELS

We discuss only a few of the many models that have been proposed.

In an early attempt to develop a model, Boud and Pascoe (1978) identified three factors they felt to be fundamental to experiential learning: degree of learner control, degree of correspondence of learning environment to real environment, and degree of involvement of self. They declared that significant presence of one dimension would be sufficient to name a program experiential.

David Kolb's development of the Lewinian experiential learning cycle (see Kolb 1984 and chapter 3) has touched the imagination of many educators as a useful way of explaining the process of experiential learning. The focus is on the felt experience, from which learning can be initiated, reviewed, challenged and reconsidered: 'Knowledge is continuously derived from and tested out in the experiences of the learner' (Kolb 1984: 27). This is in accord with Dewey's principle that (Dewey 1938: 35, in Kolb 1984: 27):

> the continuity of experience means that every experience both takes up something from those which have gone before and modifies in some way the quality of those which come after . . .

Kolb's view of learning as a continuous process grounded in experience is borne out by many feminist autobiographies (e.g. Steedman 1986), and by 'new paradigm' research (Reason & Rowan 1981; Reason 1988). Nod Miller (1993) researched her own learning, against the background of the literature review required in a doctoral dissertation. Her unfolding story is illustrative of what Kolb has identified as experiential learning—a holistic, integrative perspective on learning that combines experience, perception, cognition and action.

Susan Weil and Ian McGill (1989) developed a 'village' metaphor to categorise the varieties, and the diverse contexts, of EBL. The four 'villages' are not mutually exclusive, but interact and intersect with each other. Village 1 concerns itself with assessment and accreditation of experiential learning as a means of gaining access to educational institutions, employment and professional bodies. Village 2 sees experiential learning as catalysing change in education. Village 3 is concerned with learning from experience as the core of education for consciousness-raising, community action and social change. Village 4 takes as its focus personal growth and development to heighten self-awareness and group effectiveness.

One consistent feature in this literature is the central place of reflection. Boud and Walker (1990: 6180; see Boud et al. 1985) developed a model positing three stages of reflection associated with experiential learning activities (see Figure 14.1). The model draws attention to: (a) preparation for experiential events, where it is important to focus on the learner, the learning milieu and the skills and strategies employed in reflection; (b) reflection during an experiential activity, with its phases of noticing and intervening; and (c) reflection after the event, involving the individual in returning to experience, attending to feelings, and re-evaluating the experience.

Figure 14.1   Model for promoting learning from experience

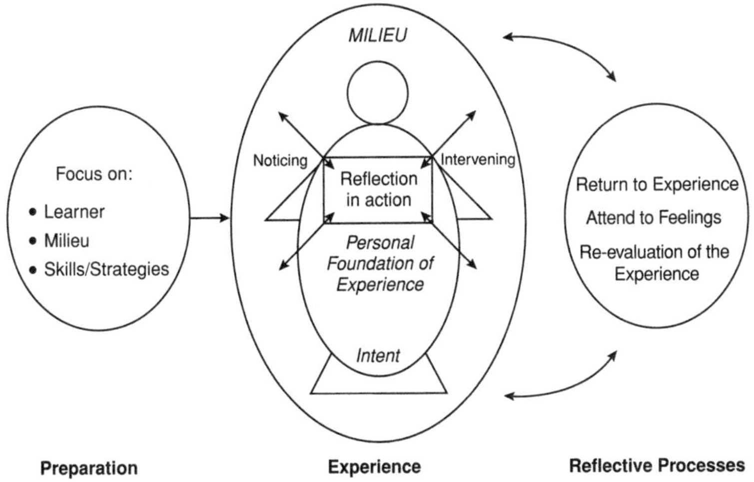

| Preparation | Experience | Reflective Processes |

THE CONTEMPORARY SCENE

EBL is actively pursued in a variety of contexts. Experiential methods have been particularly productive in the affective domain, where attitude recognition prior to change is imperative and where sensitivity and support on the part of the facilitator is essential. Reflection has been a powerful tool for enabling professionals to acknowledge their own positions and review the ethics and efficacy of their practice. Areas of application include personal growth, equal opportunity and affirmative action, HIV/AIDS education, and antiracist education.

The many forms of EBL used in vocational and professional education include internships, work placements, on-the-job training, excursions, adventure and wilderness trips, studios, laboratories, workshops, clinicals, practicums, case study approaches, action research, role-plays, hypotheticals, and simulations. Other more subtle, less easily recognisable methods include active learning in lectures, computer simulations, use of realistic models, video-based activities, group discussions and syndicate methods, autobiographical writing, problem-based learning, group work, use of reflective journals, and self-directed projects. Action research and action learning are workplace examples of experiential learning in operation.

Workplace implementation of EBL involves the conscious attempt to establish situations which provide learning in a real context or in one that is as close to some aspect of the real context as can be designed. A number of would-be 'learning organisations' feature active and experience-based approaches for induction, on-the-job training, evaluation and reform, with a focus on active involvement. There is a growing awareness that recognition of adult learning cannot be restricted to the learning that occurs in formal settings. The development of competency-based training and enterprise agreements, which take account of a range of useful skills and learning acquired in workplaces and other settings, has enhanced the importance currently being accorded to EBL.

Proponents of EBL have presented a challenge to higher education providers to broaden their perspective on what constitute appropriate standards for entry to university-level learning. The desire to more effectively harness workers' skills and knowledge, and the consequent change in notions of articulation between different levels of education, together with concerns expressed by students about the unproductive relearning of existing knowledge, have led to a major application of EBL in the recognition of prior learning (RPL). This approach is well-established in other countries, such as the USA, the UK, France and Sweden. In Australia, recent nationally agreed university guidelines define learning from experience very broadly, to include learning acquired from non-credentialled courses, from workplace learning and from life experience (Cohen et al. 1994).

The acknowledgment by government, educational providers and workplaces that RPL is an equity matter, as well as according with training reform agendas (see chapter 6), legitimises EBL beyond its informal and community roots. This enables the diversity of adult learning settings to be acknowledged and status given to equivalent learning outcomes beyond formal, credentialled instruction. The process of developing learning portfolios, development of assessment methods relevant to the purpose and context of learning, acknowledgment of the learning adults bring from their life and work contexts to new learning situations, and the equity and social justice dimensions underpinning these practices, accord fully with many of the widely valued characteristics of EBL.

Implementing EBL in formal education is generally associated with negotiated curricula, and leads to growth in student self-concept, and a greater awareness of the implicit ethical considerations in teaching and learning. EBL has been embraced at many levels in higher education, from whole programs to sections of courses, and through the use of the practicum and internships in university courses and by professional bodies for admission purposes (engineering, teaching, chartered accountancy, nursing, law, medicine). Many professional bodies are collaborating with educational providers to design relevant courses which take account of the experience of their constituency and thus are more cost-efficient. EBL subjects may be studied at Masters level, and there is a Graduate Certificate in Experiential Learning offered by one major adult and professional education provider.

At the national level, professional bodies, networks and publications are now well-established and have been instrumental in providing a professional base for developing innovative activities in the EBL field. On the world scene, several major international conferences on experiential learning have now been held. These provide a forum for presenting research and theory developments and demonstrating techniques and methods, but also for highlighting the directions EBL is taking across the world. At recent conferences it has become evident that EBL is being increasingly understood in terms of a future-oriented project to tackle global educational issues, such as those involved in forwarding multi-racialism and multiculturalism, respect for the environment, non-aggression and coexistence, and world literacy (see Freire). Pettman (1996) captures this personal/international connection well:

> Learning about the international, about difference, is learning about the experiences of others who, on the whole, are not where we are, and often have not written their own accounts. Connecting these with our own experiences is hard work. The international is personal; and the personal is international.

DISPUTES AND DILEMMAS

An innovative field of practice like EBL inevitably generates controversy, and the examples below illustrate two faces of this phenomenon. It is probably not coincidental that the contested issue in each case turns on the question of the uncertainty, unpredictability and indeterminacy inherent in learning through experience.

A site of disputation

The essential indeterminacy of what learning *outcomes* an individual's own private experiences and their personal reflection on them will lead to underlies the contested territories of both independent studies and work-based studies. Independent studies was first established at the North East London Polytechnic under the leadership of Tyrrell Burgess in 1974. Unique degree programs were constructed for each student through negotiation with the institution. The issue that immediately arose, and which remains the object of the major criticisms of such approaches, was how confident one could ever be that any student's own negotiated curriculum would connect coherently with the established disciplines or fields of study, and hence be able to be assessed as equal to a program studied along conventional lines (e.g. Robbins 1988). In a more recent manifestation of this debate, work-based learning renders the problem even more sharply, as here not only is the curriculum negotiated, but study takes place more or less completely outside the accrediting and responsible institution (and, hence, at some distance from its monitoring and control). The characteristics of work-based learning are, broadly, that (Boud 1998):

> Students study for a degree or diploma through activities conducted primarily in their workplace and within topic areas for which there may be no immediate equivalence with university subjects. Learning opportunities arise from the circumstances of normal work; work is the curriculum foundation. One effect of such study is to directly advance the work-enterprise itself; the university, however, is ultimately responsible for any qualification. The system offers unqualified people already in employment and unable to take time off the opportunity to do part-time studies, a chance to become more expert at their job, develop lifelong learning skills, and an educational qualification, all through a negotiated curriculum unique to each student. Since employers support such study financially, universities welcome it as an added strand to the diversification of their own funding sources.

Whether such programs can satisfy the general requirements of a university education is clearly a moot point. The other side to the controversy is, however, that they may well represent the cutting edge of rapid changes taking place in how the nature of a university education is itself defined.

A field of dilemmas

These relate to the ethics of facilitating EBL, and here the unknown and unpredictable element lies not so much in the curriculum as in the kinds of experiences learners may be required to undertake, and the (possibly uncomfortable, unwanted, dangerous and/or distressing) effects these may have on them. Some current practice is premised on the notion that it is acceptable to introduce participants to activities without fully explaining the details or the possible consequences of the activities. Justifications include the idea that to reveal particular outcomes prematurely would fundamentally change the character of the experience, or that it would not be meaningful to provide an account of possible outcomes because it could not be understood independently of the experience. A key challenge for EBL relates to developing ethical standards applying to such situations.

As yet there is no widely accepted code of ethics for EBL, and it is not clear what would constitute acceptable and workable standards for practice. A rigid adherence to the concept of informed consent would inhibit so many modes of learning (experiential or otherwise) that it does not seem likely to provide an appropriate model. However, there are situations where informed consent *should* be mandatory to minimise danger that might result from no forewarning. These include laboratory experiences, field trips and adventure training, as well as activities designed to mislead or trigger anger, fear and other strong emotional responses. There are also legal responsibilities for health, safety and physical welfare involved in some of these activities. Strategies available for dealing with such situations include the use of written learning agreements and the negotiation of explicit ground rules which enable participants easily to opt out of activities when they wish. More effective training of facilitators highlighting ethical issues is also needed.

Ethical concerns are exacerbated in situations where participation is, in effect, mandatory. In some situations, employers' or teachers' strong expectations of participation by individuals in training events or formally assessed courses can lead to outcomes counter to those desired and can antagonise those who participate. Participants may be inappropriately confronted and feel required to reveal aspects of themselves which they regard as occupying the private domain. Even with formal disclaimers that such activities are not compulsory, participants may believe that they will be disadvantaged in some way (e.g. through lack of access to promotions or assessments) if they refuse to become involved. The implicit power of organisations operates in ways that can undermine the whole basis of EBL. Learners can, consequently, become confused about boundaries between the personal and professional, act in ways that play to an external audience rather than responding to their own needs and interests, or inadvertently disclose aspects of themselves which can cause them continuing embarrassment within the organisation. As EBL becomes more popular and is taken up with enthusiasm in the corporate context, the need for a code of practice in this area becomes more urgent.

CONCLUSION

This chapter has argued that EBL is a distinctive field of educational theory and practice. It is a normative stance towards the entire educational process, whose implications range from the private appropriation of personally significant learning to social transformation and global educational renewal. At the personal level it draws on learners' previous life experience, engages the whole person, and stimulates reflection on experience and openness towards new experience and, thence, continuous learning. At the social level it emphasises critical social action and a stance embodying moral accountability and sociopolitical responsibility.

The roots of EBL lie in both classical philosophy and the work of an eclectic sample of modern thinkers. Various models of EBL exist, and are being applied in a variety of educational and workplace settings, using diverse methodologies. Like any field of radical educational practice, EBL generates disputes and dilemmas. Among these are questions about the adequacy of learner-negotiated curricula, the ethics of working with deeply felt experience, and the difficulty of operating within organisational contexts in which there are expectations of learner participation that potentially undermine the intended learning.

NOTES

1 The terms experience-based learning, experiential learning and learning from experience are used interchangeably in this chapter. While some authors use these terms with slightly different emphases, the similarities between them are far greater than the differences.
2 In writing this overview, the authors are indebted to Richard Kraft (n.d.) for his valuable account of the historical foundations of experiential learning.

FURTHER READING

Boud, D., Cohen, R. & Walker, D. (eds) 1993 *Using Experience for Learning*. Buckingham: SRHE & Open University Press.
Boud, D. & Miller, N. (eds) 1996 *Working with Experience: Animating Learning*. London: Kogan Page.
Dewey, J. 1938 *Experience and Education*. New York: Collier Books.
Freire, P. 1973 *Pedagogy of the Oppressed*. New York: Seabury Press.
——1994 *Pedagogy of Hope: Reliving Pedagogy of the Oppressed*. Transl. R.R. Barr. New York: Continuum.
Heron, J. 1993 *Group Facilitation*. London: Kogan Page.
Higgs, J. (ed.) 1988 *Experience-Based Learning*. Sydney: Australian Consortium on Experiential Education.

Kolb, D. 1984 *Experiential Learning: Experience as the Source of Learning and Development.* Englewood Cliffs, NJ: Prentice Hall.

Robbins, D. 1988 *The Rise of Independent Study: The Politics and the Philosophy of an Educational Innovation, 1970–87.* SRHE & Open University Press.

Weil, S. & McGill, I. 1989 *Making Sense of Experiential Learning.* Milton Keynes: Open University Press.

15

Women and learning
Susan Knights

Women make up the vast majority of students in community-based adult education and a growing proportion of participants in workplace training. Adult education has been relatively slow to follow school-based education in considering the influence of gender on access to learning opportunities and on approaches to learning once access has been gained. However, the literature in relation to women's learning is growing fast. Any attempt to provide an overview of the current understanding of issues relating to women and learning must first acknowledge the differences among women and the problems involved in making generalisations which disguise the enormous range of life experiences and situations that affect women as learners and in every other way. The idea that any specific characteristics are inherently female (or male) is problematic but, in any society, as Patti Lather points out, 'gender is a central factor in the shaping of our consciousness, skills and institutions as well as in the distribution of power and privilege' (Lather 1991a: 17). It is appropriate therefore that this book should contain a chapter looking at the current position of women as learners.

The chapter provides an overview of some of the issues identified as significant in relation to women's learning, starting with questions of access and curriculum, and moving on to discussion of women's needs as learners and their implications for educational practice.

WOMEN'S PARTICIPATION IN ADULT EDUCATION

Although women make up the majority of participants in community-

240

based adult education, significant barriers to their participation still exist, mainly because of the responsibility women generally take for child care and housework. Whereas men can expect to move from school to higher education or employment and to pursue a work life uninterrupted by family responsibilities, women's work life and education are far more likely to be seen as secondary. In the current economic climate, unemployment is a disruptive influence on the employment prospects of both men and women, but the rates of unemployment are disproportionately high for women. The most obvious barriers to women's access to adult education (assuming it is available to them) are lack of child care and lack of transport, both of which have significant economic components. For certain groups of women there are significant additional problems: for example, rural women face geographical barriers on a scale far greater than city women, and women whose first language is not English often have severely limited opportunities for involvement in adult learning. In addition to these concrete barriers, it is likely that negative experience of schooling acts as an inhibitor to many women's participation in adult education.

Recognition of the existence and effects of gender discrimination in schooling grew throughout the 1970s and 80s. School systems have been coming to grips with the implications of gender bias and taking a variety of steps to improve the situation for girls. In some countries the performance of girls in high school examinations has improved so markedly that calls for assistance for boys are now being heard. However, these recent improvements have come too late to assist women who have already left school and who, however well they did there, are likely to carry with them some feelings of inadequacy acquired in their early education.

Susan Kelly's study of women returning to study at Melbourne College of Advanced Education (Kelly 1987) indicated that, for some of them, entering tertiary study was the fulfilment of an ambition they had held for over 20 years and that they were overwhelmingly motivated by a desire for self-fulfilment and achievement. Often this ambition was related to the feeling that they had not been given a chance to fulfil their intellectual potential at school. Similar feelings were expressed by the mainly working-class women from the Second Chance for Women courses offered at the University of Southampton during the early 1980s in a book called *Learning the Hard Way*, which a group of these students wrote as a collective (Taking Liberties Collective 1989). Although there are similarities between the largely middle-class women in Kelly's book and the women of the Taking Liberties Collective, the combination of class and racial disadvantage with what the subtitle of their book calls 'women's oppression in men's education' had made the struggle of the latter group for access to education particularly hard. Both these studies report on difficulties women faced owing to family opposition to their studying—opposition from partners, parents and children in varying degrees. This opposition was compounded by the pressure of the socialisation that leads women to feel guilty if they spend time and energy on themselves rather than their families (Davies 1989). The situation of some women students undertaking week-long residential courses was graphically described by an indigenous Australian university student (Gwen Millar 1998, quoted with permission):

> I have seen men come to residentials and beat their wives and drag them home; I have seen women crying on the phone from the abuse of husbands who are demanding that they get home immediately; and I have seen women with huge potential leave their courses because of this kind of pressure.

NEIGHBOURHOOD HOUSES

The 1970s in Australia saw the emergence of a new site for women's learning—the neighbourhood house, community house or community learning centre. These were often located in suburban houses and usually managed by committees of members. The neighbourhood houses were open to all but overwhelmingly used by women, thus providing a learning environment managed by women for women. As well as offering learning opportunities, the houses offer support for families and individuals and work from a perspective often closer to community development than to traditional adult education provision. The neighbourhood houses have been far more successful than other adult education providers in securing the participation of migrant women, who are generally very poorly represented in the statistics of community-based adult education. By providing a place for both women and children, they made access to education a possibility for women who would otherwise have been severely limited by child care responsibilities.

The learning opportunities in settings like neighbourhood houses go beyond those available in formal education. The incidental learning gained through participation in neighbourhood house activities such as play groups and management committee meetings, and in the conflict often encountered in such activities, has been described by Foley as follows (1993: 34, see Sanguinetti 1994):

> This is learning that enables people to make sense of and act on their environment, and to come to understand themselves as knowledge-creating, acting beings. Through their participation in neighbourhood houses, women have learned to overcome the fear and lack of confidence instilled in them by their gender socialisation, to fight for something for themselves and to participate in difficult collective decision-making.

VOCATIONAL EDUCATION AND TRAINING FOR WOMEN

Neighbourhood houses have provided a first step for many women in acquiring the skills and confidence needed to move back into the workforce after years of working only in the home. Technical and further education (TAFE) has also made important contributions here. Although provision has differed from state to state, there has been a significant commitment to courses tailored to the real-life needs of women in their curriculum, in their teaching processes and in timetabling. Sometimes there has been provision of child care to take account of women's child care responsibilities. TAFE has also taken on the long-term project of increasing the numbers of girls and women who take up vocational education and training (VET) in 'non-traditional' areas.

Nevertheless, there are still major barriers to women's participation and success in VET. These are recognised by the Australian National Training Authority and categorised in ANTA's National Women's Vocational Education and Training Strategy (1996) as follows:

- attitudinal barriers
  - societal, industry, school, parents;
  - media images;
  - inadequate marketing;
- learning environment barriers
  - gender harassment;
  - inappropriate learning materials;
  - lack of support, counselling, child care;
- structural barriers
  - transport;
  - inadequate use of recognition of prior learning;
  - timetabling;
  - course selection procedures;
  - resource allocation;
  - fees;
  - accommodation.

The Strategy seeks to achieve four specific outcomes in relation to women's participation in VET:

- an increase in the number of women completing VET programs;
- an increase in the number of women with VET qualifications at all levels;
- women distributed more broadly across fields of study;
- an increase in participation and improved outcomes for specific groups of women.

WOMEN'S ACCESS TO TRAINING AT WORK

Although there have been some improvements in women's access to training schemes which may help them to gain work (no doubt influenced by the political pressure generated by alarmingly high rates of unemployment), once they are in the workforce women face a range of barriers in accessing training that might help them to improve their skills and gain promotion.

The progressive dismantling of the training schemes which previously gave unemployed men and women some opportunity to enter or re-enter the workforce means that the impact of globalisation in workplaces continually undermines the likelihood of any further progress towards gender equity in access to work or training. As Elaine Butler (1997: 64) has pointed out: 'Education, and so therefore gender equity in education is now . . . firmly located within the markets and market places of global restructuring, and the privileging of the economic over the social'. Moreover, many employers are still reluctant to invest in training for their female workers. The idea that women will inevitably marry and have children and be lost to the workforce persists, and many women are working part-time or on a casual basis and thus often ineligible for training.

Australian statistics indicate that women and men receive on-the-job training and attend training courses in about the same proportions, but these statistics do not tell us whether they receive equivalent amounts of training in terms of type of course undertaken. Both in-house and external courses attended by women tend to be shorter than those taken by men (ABS 1993: 131).

Often there are age barriers related to support for training, such as study leave or financial allowances, and women who have left the workforce to have and care for children may find they are too old to benefit from these provisions once they return to work. They may also find that they do not have the necessary technical qualifications to make them eligible for training in new technology. Training opportunities which offer an entry test rather than a demand for previous educational requirements and offer job-related remedial education, especially in maths, can be very helpful for women.

Although equal opportunity provisions have made training opportunities apparently equally available to male and female workers, workplaces are still affected by gender divisions. Women may well decide that there is no point in undertaking training which would lead to their working in a position traditionally occupied by men when neither their employer nor their fellow workers would support such a move.

Decisions about selection for training, or for the informal learning available from undertaking special projects or job rotation, are often made by men in relation to female employees, and may well be influenced by gender-biased assumptions (e.g. assumptions about how long an employee will be with the organisation). Women with family responsibilities may be unable to undertake off-the-job training which requires residential attendance or simply attendance at times that do not fit with child care responsibilities. In many countries these kinds of barriers are gradually being overcome, especially in the public sector, but once again there are wide differences between the opportunities available for different groups of women depending on the size of the organisation they work for, their own family circumstances and educational background, their age and their language. International covenants offer women some hope. For example, ILO Convention 156 on Workers with Family Responsibilities aims to ensure that workers do not suffer discrimination or conflict as a result of their responsibilities to their families. As women bear a disproportionate weight of responsibility for family care, this convention may eventually be of particular assistance to them.

This brief discussion of women and training has concentrated on the issue of access to existing training opportunities in the workplace. Mechtild Hart argues that adult educators need to rethink the whole question of work and education and recognise what she calls 'the miseducative reality of work under patriarchal-industrial conditions' (Hart 1992: 199). Like other feminist commentators, she questions the claim that skills are value-free, technical and individual attributes, and calls on adult educators (1992: 200):

> to see the current troubled experience of work, accompanied by doubts, problems, dissatisfactions and sufferings as an opportunity for asking critical questions, and for opening up at least the

conception of new possibilities for living and working . . . Instead of simply adjusting people to the hierarchical and divided reality of work, adult educators need to ask the question of how we could and how we should work in a manner that contributes to the maintenance and improvement of life rather than profit.

The experience of women in relation to vocational training has been the subject of increasing interest among researchers and some policy makers, but the basic inequalities remain. The past decade has seen a plethora of reports, projects and strategies, which have resulted in a wealth of new and vital information and understandings. Little of this information has touched the everyday lives and opportunities of women (Butler 1997).

WOMEN AS LEARNERS

But gaining access to education is only part of the story. In a range of settings, women suffer disadvantage as learners because of the curriculum they are offered and the domination of a traditional, one-way-transmission-of-information approach to teaching.

In her 1983 book *Learning Liberation*, Jane Thompson provided a strong critique of the curriculum of traditional adult education in England, locating the problem firmly in the wider conditions of a patriarchal society (Thompson 1983: 86):

> As with the sexual division of labour generally, the adult education relationship is essentially a relationship of female tutor and students' subordination to male organisation and control. In the process, women's real needs (i.e. the definition women would make about themselves and their lives if men were not around or if men were not structurally in charge) are not being recognised or met. It is not distractions that women seek, but space; not confidence, but autonomy.

Helen Gribble made a similar point about the curriculum of adult education almost 10 years later, pointing out that most adult education ignores the struggle involved in women's lives where they do a double shift of work inside and outside the home, have low-status jobs, unequal pay and unequal access to education (Gribble 1992: 231):

> Read through the list of offerings of many adult education programs and you'd never guess that women's lives involve such struggle. On the whole adult education seems to be designed to quieten them down and give them an outlet so they stay contented with their

unjust lot—the educational equivalent of Valium rather than a walk in a brisk wind.

The problem for women entering tertiary education, as they have been doing in growing numbers since the early 1970s, is not that they are faced with a curriculum oriented towards domesticity but that they are working within academic disciplines that have traditionally ignored or distorted the experience of women. The growth of women's studies as a discipline in its own right is one response to this situation, but alongside this feminist academics in all disciplines have contributed to the process of uncovering and including the perspectives and contributions of women. This is a revolutionary process for the academy, as the American feminist educator Frances Maher points out (1985: 33):

> In every scholarly discipline wherein the female experience has been explored, the new scholarship on women has challenged not only the scope, the content, and the conclusions of the field but also the research methods by which the knowledge in the field has been derived in the first place.

The feminist critique of traditional disciplines that began in the 1960s now overlaps with the poststructuralist and postmodernist debates which have preoccupied academics in the 1980s and 90s (see Lather 1991a, b for an overview of these debates). The methodology Maher describes as being characteristic of a feminist approach to the construction of knowledge could equally well apply to a postmodernist approach (1985: 33):

> This methodology involves a conceptualisation of knowledge as a comparison of multiple perspectives leading towards a complex and evolving view of reality . . . This methodology replaces the search for a single, objective, rationally derived 'right answer' that stands outside the historical source or producer of that answer.

The recognition of the validity of multiple perspectives and respect for difference underlines the dangers of implying a unitary feminist viewpoint on anything, let alone anything as complex as teaching and learning. A useful paper by Sue Blundell, 'Gender and the curriculum of adult education' (1992), outlines four different varieties of feminist discourse and their implications for adult education. Differences, for example, between those who believe that women suffer from discrimination and those who believe that women suffer oppression in the existing conditions of society lead to different ideas about appropriate strategies for adult education. The former, liberal feminist approach tends to emphasise issues of equity and access to an education system dominated by men,

247

whereas the latter, radical feminist approach tends to assert the need for women-centred knowledge and curriculum.

The range of ideas that fall under the heading of 'feminist pedagogy' points out that women have not been well-served by traditional models of education, such as the valuing of the ability to assert and defend individual points of view in competitive debate, nor by the emphasis on 'objective' truth at the expense of knowledge which comes through connection and personal experience. The kinds of processes advocated by feminist pedagogy are not unfamiliar to adult educators. In fact Paulo Freire, with his emphasis on dialogue and respect for the experience of the learner, is cited by some feminist educators as providing a good model of the educational process (e.g. Allman 1994). Explorations of women's experience in traditional learning situations have illuminated the ways in which collaboration and mutuality are often undermined by the traditional process of one-way transmission of information and the silencing of women's voices in discussion.

A vivid example of the dynamics of a mixed-gender classroom is given in a paper in which Magda Lewis and Roger Simon (female student and male teacher) describe and analyse the process of silencing of female students as it happened in a graduate seminar designed to explore the relationship between language and power. Lewis describes the class process as follows (Lewis & Simon 1986: 462):

> men were allowed to speak at length—and did. Their speaking was seldom if ever interrupted. When a woman and a man began speaking at the same time, the woman always deferred to the man. Women's speaking was often reinterpreted by the men through phrases such as 'what she really means' . . . More than just a few times the actual talk of women was attributed in a later discussion by a man to a man. Women's ideas—sometimes reworded, sometimes not—were appropriated by men and then passed off as their own. Whenever a woman was able to cut through the oppressive discourse, the final attempt at silencing took the form of aggressive yelling. It became clear to us that the reversal of this dynamic would have been totally unacceptable to those who held the power of legitimation.

The dynamics of a learning group like this are clearly opposed to the interests of the women learners. Research in both psychology and linguistics has indicated that gender socialisation has significant impact on the ways in which women and men are likely to approach classroom interaction. Gilligan and others have identified women's valuing of and capacity for connection and interdependence, in contrast to the male movement towards separation and independence (Gilligan 1982; Jordan 1991). Gilligan's work on moral development has led to the recognition that girls and women focus on relationships, whereas boys and men tend to focus on rules and rights. These differences have significant implications for classroom dynamics in mixed-gender groups, as do the differences in conversational modes identified by the growing literature on gender and language. Tannen notes that women see conversation and discussion as an opportunity for connection and relationship, whereas men's socialisation leads them to see discussion as a competitive arena (Tannen 1990), a situation graphically illustrated in Lewis' description of her graduate class.

An influential study, which aimed to illuminate the experiences of women as learners, was carried out in the USA by Belenky and her colleagues in the late 1970s and early 80s. The research consists of detailed interviews with 135 women from a range of socioeconomic and educational backgrounds, and focuses on their approaches to knowledge and conceptions of themselves as learners. The authors use the metaphor of 'voice' to indicate how the women in their study saw themselves in relation to knowledge and learning. They discuss the different ways the women in their study approached learning under the following headings:

- *silence*: where women feel passive, reactive and dependent and see authorities as being all-powerful, if not overpowering;
- *received knowledge*: women think of words as central to the knowing process and are open to taking in what others have to offer. They equate receiving, retaining and returning the words of authorities with learning;
- *subjective knowledge*: a conception of truth as personal, private and subjectively known or intuited;
- *procedural knowledge*: the recognition that knowing requires careful observation and analysis;
- *constructed knowledge*: the understanding that all knowledge is constructed and the knower is an intimate part of the known.

Although the authors are careful not to compose these different conceptions of knowing as another set of 'developmental stages', the women who were subjects in the study could often identify movement in their experience of learning from one phase to another. The kinds of processes that were identified as helping women to find a voice as learners were ones that the women saw as helping them to recognise and expand their latent knowledge, valuing connection over separation, providing acceptance rather than assessment, and emphasising collaboration and participation rather than competition.

In my own experience this kind of interdependent learning is harder for the students who have been longest (and most successful) in traditional learning environments. Collaboration seems reasonably easy to achieve in community-based, non-accredited learning and in the beginning stages of higher education with 'non-traditional students' (i.e. those who have not come direct from a successful school career). Women students given the opportunity to work in all-women learning groups typically express great enthusiasm for the process. Talking about their experience in mixed-gender groups, they often express frustration about the difficulty of achieving genuine collaborative learning with their male peers.

WOMEN-ONLY COURSES

Given the differences in male and female socialisation, and the power differences between the sexes, one obvious way of providing an appropriate environment for women's learning is to set up courses and even centres for women only. In the early days of adult education provision it was inconceivable that any provision for women could be other than in single-sex groups, and in some cultures this is still taken for granted. Currently, however, the provision of either community or workplace education for women alone is often the subject of intense opposition and is, in some cases, forbidden by legislation.

In many countries the commonest area in which women-only classes are provided is in courses for women returning to study after periods away from paid work of being fully engaged in child-rearing. Educational systems seem to be able to cope with an argument that women who have been at home caring for children for some years need the support of an all-women environment as they move back into formal studies. However, on the basis of research such as Gilligan's and that of Belenky et al., it would also be possible to argue that women's learning in any area is likely to be enhanced by the absence of men.

Arguments for women-only education do not rest solely on women's lack of confidence or preference for a particular type of pedagogical process. There is also the question of providing adequate space for women to share and explore their own experience in relation to the topic of study and to create their own knowledge in doing so. This type of exploration is far more difficult in mixed-gender groups, where the experience in question is so different and there is often little respect for the value of personal experience of any kind. In the light of these arguments, the success of women-only provision, where it has been possible, is understandable (Coats 1994). However, as well as clear advantages there are dangers. As Blundell points out, 'Our education does not exist in isolation, but is an element within social and cultural structures which persistently undervalue women' (Blundell 1992). She fears that if significant numbers of women opt for separation in learning, 'then we could end up with a kind of educational apartheid, involving a traditional, high-status curriculum for men, and an innovative but low-status curriculum for women'. Such an arrangement, she points out, would do nothing to transform the situation of women in a patriarchal society.

CONCLUSION

This chapter has considered some of the implications of the different life experiences of women for their experience as adult learners. Some of the ideas about providing appropriate learning environments for women's learning are familiar to adult educators; the value of the work of Paulo Freire in particular is acknowledged by several writers on feminist pedagogy. The apparent parallels between general theories about facilitating adult learning and some of the ideas of feminist pedagogy should not blind us to the difficulties of providing effective learning opportunities for women, especially in mixed-gender groups. The effects of socialisation are subtle. Many women successfully make use of less than ideal learning opportunities, and changes to existing practices often provoke intense opposition. These facts all militate against the careful review of program offerings and processes that is necessary to ensure that women's learning needs are being served. The literature of adult education has long ignored the fact that the majority of participants in all areas except workplace training are women, and that this has significant implications for the organisation, curriculum and learning processes of adult education. Once gender is recognised as a central factor in shaping our consciousness, skills and institutions (Lather 1991a: 17), it is clear that consideration of the needs of women learners can no longer be ignored in any area of adult education.

FURTHER READING

Belenky, M., Clinchy, B., Goldberger, N. & Tarule, J. 1986 *Women's Ways of Knowing: The Development of Self, Voice and Mind*. New York: Basic Books.

Gribble, H. 1992 'A big proportion of them were women', in R. Harris & P. Willis (eds), *Striking a Balance: Adult and Community Education in Australia Towards 2000*. Adelaide: Centre for Human Resource Studies, University of South Australia.

Hart, M. 1992 *Working and Educating for Life: Feminist and International Perspectives on Adult Education*. London: Routledge.

Lather, P. 1991a *Feminist Research in Education: Within/Against*. Geelong: Deakin University.

—— 1991b *Getting Smart: Feminist Research and Pedagogy with/in the Postmodern*. New York: Routledge.

Robinson, V. & Richardson, D (eds) 1997 *Introducing Women's Studies: Feminist Theory and Practice* 2nd edn London: Macmillan.

Thompson, J. 1983 *Learning Liberation: Women's Response to Men's Education*. London: Croom Helm.

16

Adult education and Indigenous Australians

Michael McDaniel & Rick Flowers

In this chapter we treat Australia as an exemplar of the difficulties faced by indigenous people in institutionalised education around the world. Indigenous people constitute about 2 per cent of Australia's 19 million people. Australia has rich traditions of precolonial indigenous education, and a long and often sorry history of Aboriginal education post-White settlement. This chapter examines four aspects of these pre- and postcolonial histories. The first section discusses relationships of Indigenous culture and adult education policy and programs. The second provides a historical outline of Australian indigenous adult education, and discusses ways in which indigenous people contested attempts by governments and churches to use adult education for assimilation and social control purposes. The third section draws on theoretical perspectives that have been used by writers to critique recent federal government policies and programs. The fourth discusses the difficulties indigenous people continue to face in trying to obtain a quality adult education.

CULTURE AND ADULT EDUCATION

There is a commonly held but misleading impression in Australia that indigenous adult education, and more generally indigenous culture, is a homogeneous entity. It further misleads to suggest that indigenous adult education and indigenous culture should be defined as distinct in relation to 'mainstream' adult education and culture. It is more useful to focus on the notion that there is a wide variety of indigenous cultures which, through increasingly vigorous processes of contestation, are resisting traditions of White cultural hegemony and contributing to new notions of national culture. For governments and institutional adult education providers it is, therefore, less a matter of identifying what policies and programs should be developed and implemented for some monolithic notion of 'Aboriginal adult education' and more of recognising that adult education will be more meaningfully built by a diversity of indigenous efforts.

Indigenous peoples, by choice and through necessity, have developed a wide range of vibrant and dynamic cultural forms. Indigenous people—in common with other people who have been forced to survive in, and resist, colonialist systems—are capable of 'speaking in many voices'. Moreover, an individual Aboriginal or Torres Strait Islander learner may have many voices, with no single voice being identified as more or less authentic. The insistence on finding one voice, one definitive style of learning, one style of talking, fits all too neatly with an exotic but misleadingly static and voyeuristic notion of identity and culture.

It is not being suggested that there is not a common indigenous cultural reality: there are common histories of invasion, resistance and dispossession; there are shared histories of poverty, exploitation, racism and exclusion from many institutions. But the commonality exists alongside difference, and both must be recognised. The reason for making this point is to direct the adult educator's attention to an examination of:

- why the notion—a colonialist mindset—of an exotic, static, monolithic culture is still so dominant;
- how this dominant notion reinforces a liberal or institutional curriculum approach;
- how dominant educational policies and programs retain their dominance, therefore continuing to marginalise the diversity of indigenous, independently managed adult education initiatives;
- relationships between culture, politics, history and adult education practice.

HISTORICAL OUTLINE: CONTESTATION AND SOCIAL CONTROL1

The history of adult education and training for Indigenous people is characterised by struggle or 'contestation' (on contestation, see Foley 1993a: 22–4, 33–5). The state has struggled to exercise social control over indigenous peoples. Adult education has been a key element in the state's efforts at exercising control. Indigenous people have resisted these attempts, and have tried to develop forms of adult education that are compatible with their perspectives and interests.

Until the early 1970s, shortly after indigenous people had finally (in 1967) won citizenship rights and Aboriginal affairs became for the first time a federal government responsibility, adult education had an explicit—to the point of being brutal and crude—aim of assimilation and social control. State and federal governments, mostly in the name of benevolence, sought to educate and train indigenous adults:

- to learn English and abandon their own languages;
- to take on the mores and values of British society and to ignore Australian history before European invasion and the conflicts between Black and White Australians;
- to be productive workers in an economy controlled by non-indigenous interests;
- to accept that they were not entitled to land and power;
- to believe that they are not competent or ready to manage their own affairs and therefore should rely on White expertise.

From the time of invasion in 1788, indigenous people have resisted this sort of adult education and training, in many ways. Armed resistance had to be abandoned by the early part of the 19th century in the face of overwhelming odds. Subversion and lack of cooperation became less effective as it became clear that the colonisers were not going to leave. Indigenous people were forced to live and survive in a colonialist and capitalist state. Indigenous people learned to contest dominant adult education and training interests. Together with non-Aboriginal allies, they developed strategies:

- to maintain and develop indigenous languages;
- to retain indigenous perspectives on Australian history;
- to help their people gain skills and knowledge for community development and economic enterprise;
- to help their people organise politically and assert their right to land and power;
- to combat dependency and develop competence for self-management.

Since the mid-1980s there has been a significant expansion of adult education provision for indigenous people across Australia. The field of higher education has established new, or expanded existing, academic support programs specifically for Indigenous students. Technical and further education provision for Indigenous students has expanded considerably. Significant, too, has been the heightened commitment of federal government departments to training and employment programs for indigenous people. Particularly notable was the establishment of the Aboriginal Employment Development Policy (AEDP), with its commitment of significant funds to support community organisations and land councils to develop economic enterprises.

This rapid expansion of adult education provision from the mid-1980s is the subject of considerable controversy in both government and indigenous political circles. The significant investment of resources has yet to yield clear results. Unemployment rates for indigenous people remained disproportionately high in the mid-1990s. Poor health, family violence, and substance abuse remained as deep-seated as before. Critics of the delivery of programs at a local level point to shortcomings in planning and management. Some claim that government agencies are intent only on rhetorical shows of community consultation and that their adult education programs are ill-conceived and irrelevant. From the mid-1980s one can speak of a new phase in indigenous adult education, in which debate focuses not just on the quantity of provision but also on the quality and control of the provision.

The lines of struggle in this most recent phase are perhaps more difficult to delineate than previously. There has been a considerable increase in the number of people who work in indigenous adult education in government agencies and universities. Those who work in the independently managed providers and community organisations, however, remain comparatively marginalised—poorly funded, mostly on short-term grants. It is now less clear who is contesting whom. While the issue of control of indigenous adult education continues to be crucial, we would argue that it is not always useful to pitch community control against mainstream control. After all, provision in community organisations is dependent on government funding and therefore government directions. It is more useful to contrast adult education which is generally managed by independent indigenous interests with adult education which is managed by state interests that are, to use Garbutcheon-Singh's (1990) terms, 'conservative, capitalistic and favourable to long-continued paternalism'. The central current issue in indigenous adult education is the intensifying struggle between the state and indigenous people over control of education and training. This mirrors the wider political struggle between state and indigenous people which in recent years has taken a disturbingly revanchist turn, with the accession to power of a conservative federal government.

THE POLICY RHETORIC OF THE 1990S: NEW OPPORTUNITIES FOR INDIGENOUS ADULT EDUCATION?2

Following the establishment of the Aboriginal Employment Development Policy, the federal government introduced a second major policy initiative in 1989, the National Aboriginal and Torres Strait Islander Education Policy (NATSIEP). Like other policy statements of its kind, NATSIEP presented progressive rhetoric that sought to break from earlier crude policy intentions of assimilation and social control. It asserted the importance of recognising and harnessing indigenous educational practices and set clear goals for the expansion of provision of various forms of adult education.

The policy document indicated a potential for change. But in his analysis of the discourse of NATSIEP, Nakata (1991, see Snow 1993) argues that the document constructs a romantic and misleading image of Indigenous Australians. It refers to the 'nation's living heritage' as opposed to the 'Aboriginal and Torres Strait Islander peoples'; 'historically developed education processes' as opposed to 'Western education arrangements and procedures'; and 'Australian society' as opposed to 'specific historical conditions and practices of colonial law' (Snow 1991: 5). Nakata argues that NATSIEP avoids addressing racism and the other historical factors that have contributed to the marginalisation of indigenous peoples in education.

Nakata refers to NATSIEP's 'cultural agenda': 'To read the Islander's educational situation as culturally inappropriate, mismanaged, deprived of their rights, under represented, disadvantaged, and suffering inequitable situations also enables the cultural agenda to be supported'. The danger of the cultural agenda is that it diverts attention away from the real problem, which, according to Nakata, is the colonial education system: 'Culturally relevant programs then, at best, become 'add-ons' to unchanged mainstream practices in the education system' (Snow 1991: 11).

Nakata's analysis illustrates how deep-seated and pervasive the notion is that indigenous people have some sort of exotic, static and monolithic culture. It is a liberal and paternalistic discourse that views indigenous people as victims rather than as creative, active people (see Moore 1993). The language of NATSIEP may be understood as an expression of wider and changing political and historical conditions. The colonial state, some would argue, has retreated. After all, governments now officially proclaim policies of self-determination for indigenous peoples. We would argue, however, that the colonial state has not so much retreated but changed the conditions and terms of contestation. No longer is the state brutal and stern as it was until the 1970s; no longer is it nonchalant and dismissive as it was from the 1970s to the mid-80s; in the 1990s it has been concerned and caring. But whose interests is it most concerned and caring about? Specifically, whose interests are served by reinforcing an image of indigenous culture as exotic and unchanging—by not acknowledging the dynamism, diversity and political dimension of modern, indigenous cultural reality?

The reproduction of this subtly paternalistic approach in indigenous adult education is a complex process. On one level are the interests of those who hold on dearly to the model of interventionist, 'expert'-oriented strategies of program or curriculum development. Bureaucrats with responsibility for managing the comparatively new and large amounts of funding for Indigenous education, employment and training see their task from a technical perspective. Indigenous people and communities are perceived as objects with cultural characteristics that should be worked with in a sensitive way. Any suggestion that Aboriginal people and communities are political forces who would prefer to define their culture and adult education needs on their own terms is met with impatience and hostility. This is one way of understanding the entrenched lack of understanding between independent, Indigenous adult education providers and major funding bodies.

On another level, the interests of institutional providers are also served by the continued dominance of a liberal discourse. It is in their interests not to dwell on the question of whether the dominant education system can accommodate the political and cultural agendas of indigenous peoples, but to insist that they have the means and the responsibility to adapt their curricula in ways that are responsive to the 'identified' needs of Indigenous adults.

THE STRUGGLE FOR INDIGENOUS CONTROL OF EDUCATION

How, in practice, does Indigenous control of education come about in what is still, for all its caring rhetoric, a White-settler capitalist political economy and culture? The following critique of current practices in university education demonstrates both the complexity of the struggle for indigenous control of education and, paradoxically, how straightforward some of the solutions are.

In recent years, in the push to ensure access and equity for Aboriginal people there has been a significant increase in the number of Aboriginal people participating in both 'mainstream' and 'Aboriginal' courses. However, in the pursuit of numbers, an educational experience of equal quality to that being provided to non-Aboriginal people is sometimes denied to Aboriginal people. What is more, this quality-compromised educational experience is more often than not delivered by those who purport to be committed to the empowerment of Aboriginal people and consider themselves to be acting out of the best intentions.

What is meant by a 'quality-compromised' educational experience? As Aboriginal people, we invariably enter tertiary institutions not for an Aboriginal education. This we appropriately receive elsewhere and certainly not from non-Aboriginal institutions. We come to universities and colleges, non-Aboriginal educational institutions, to acquire the means to successfully participate and compete in a non-Aboriginal-dominated world. While valuing our own forms of knowledge, we come knowingly for a non-Aboriginal education. It is non-Aboriginal skills and forms of knowledge we seek, in the full realisation that without them we remain a dependent and disempowered people. It may not be the best form of education—this we are fully aware of—but it is a powerful one, one we have chosen, one we pay for in more than monetary terms, and one we expect to be delivered in its fullest.

A quality-compromised educational experience is one that does not require Aboriginal students to perform at the same level as non-Aboriginal students studying towards the same award or same level of award. Graduates of such courses have extreme difficulty competing in an open job market with non-Aboriginal graduates. While it is to their credit that most Aboriginal graduates at enrolment express a wish to work in Aboriginal-identified positions for the betterment of their own people, the reality is that, having experienced such an education, they have little choice but to move into such positions. Once employed in identified positions, such graduates often come to the realisation that they cannot independently perform tasks based on non-Aboriginal skills and forms of knowledge to the level required.

This inability to perform to expectation, apart from creating a sense of insecurity, does not escape the notice and contempt of peers, a situation that in turn undermines the credibility of affirmative-action employment policies. To realise that one is unable to perform at the same level as one's peers is to recognise that one's employment is based not on merit but on sufferance and charity or legality. To come to the realisation that despite the possession of a tertiary qualification you are simply 'a guest at the white man's table' is a disempowering experience.

Aboriginal people in this situation often and understandably adopt a defensive position—one which, combined with co-worker resentment and alienation, often leads to stress, avoidance behaviour in the form of irregular attendance and/or job resignation. Alternatively, graduates of such courses establish a number of dependent relationships, usually with non-Aboriginal graduates of academically rigorous courses.

The overall consequence of a quality-compromised, though well-intended, education is the antithesis of an empowering and positive experience: it is cruel and alienating. The product of dishonesty, it is a form of theft both financially and experientially. It is colonialism in its truest sense—the farming of a people and their resources (*colonia*, the Latin for settlement or colony). It is not about access and equity; it is about the denial of access and equity in the broader and long-term sense.

While this is the experience of the individual graduate, the experience has implications far beyond that of the individual. As already suggested, the employment of less than fully competent Aboriginal people undermines the credibility of affirmative-action policies, and reinforces racist and stereotypical attitudes, all of which translates into resentment and innuendo towards the many competent Aboriginal employees occupying positions on the basis of institutionally acquired merit as well as that of Aboriginality.

Another consequence of such educational provision is that the whole of what is termed 'Aboriginal education' and its graduates come under the suspicion of being second-rate. As many Aboriginal people will tell you, there is a cultural and historical predisposition among many in non-Aboriginal society to 'tar all Aborigines with the same brush'. Regardless of the cultural origins of the deliverers of such educational experiences, it is solely Aboriginal participants, providers and recipients who will bear the stigma.

So who loses from the lowering of assessment criteria and presumably course content? The answer is all Aboriginal people. Graduates lose financially, experientially, emotionally and career-wise. Clients of graduates, who are almost invariably Aboriginal, also lose when providers, administrators and coordinators are unable to perform to task. Within education, people with a quality-compromised experience, ignorant of what is normally involved in the delivery of a particular level of study, in turn perpetuate through ignorance and lack of skills their own compromised experience for other Aboriginal students. The farmed become farmers. In short, a very real and long-term cycle of oppression, disempowerment and dependency is set up, in which old stereotypes are reinforced and the colonised are enlisted in the colonising process. Providers of such an experience may consider themselves to be acting out of the best of intentions, but history demonstrates that much of the short- and long-term suffering imposed on Aboriginal individuals and communities has been imposed by those with the best of intentions.

How does such a situation arise (i.e. the compromising of performance expectations and therefore the quality of education for Aboriginal people)? The reasons are numerous, overlapping and easily identified. They are also corrigible.

At the level of the deliverer, the compromising of standards and expectations normally required of non-Aboriginal students may be due to the deliverer's fear of the possibility of being confronted or questioned by a group of powerful Aboriginal adults over such things as the demand for a certain level of performance or the enforcement of course assessment policy. This fear may be due to a self-serving wish to avoid possible unpleasantness. Alternatively, compromise may be due to a sometimes cited and well-intentioned concern that to enforce educational standards is to impose non-Aboriginal cultural expectations on Aboriginal people and thereby engage them in an assimilative process. It is true that expectations or performance indicators in formal education are non-Aboriginal. However, provided students are fully informed as to the course expectations and their rationale prior to enrolment, the acceptance of non-Aboriginal cultural expectations is purely on a voluntary basis.

While well-informed and voluntary application of non-Aboriginal standards and performance expectations is far from an 'imposition', neither is the same process culturally subversive. To believe otherwise is to condescendingly underestimate the intelligence and perceptiveness of Aboriginal participants as well as the depth and strength of Aboriginal culture and identity. In our experience, Aboriginal adults are far more aware of, and resistant to, the hidden cultural agenda of the Western educational process than their non-Aboriginal peers or, for that matter, the deliverers themselves. Furthermore, if light is shone on the dominant cultural agenda, its presumptions and value orientation, while at the same time the immediate value of the education to one wanting to enter and change the existing order is discussed, the participant is in an even better situation to avoid its possibly pacifying agenda. Remember that, as Aboriginal people, we have maintained our culture and identity through far more violent and less voluntary experiences than a tertiary education.

Another possible cause of compromise is the personal and

usually subconscious emotional agenda of deliverers. The fact is that sometimes non-Aboriginal people choose to work with Aboriginal people in order to meet their own emotional needs. They desire to nurture in order to be needed, to be seen to be generous and in return appreciated. Sometimes these people identify with the marginalised because they themselves feel marginalised. An inability to identify with the perceived harshness or competitiveness of their own society or a sense of disillusionment can result in a quest to be accepted by what they perceive to be a far more accepting and tolerant society. Hence any possibility of confrontation or rejection is avoided. While any leniency may be well-received, it is often accepted knowingly and with a degree of contempt.

Alternatively, deliverers may compromise standards because they want to avoid the very real emotional difficulty of, in the worst scenario, having to 'fail' a student who has experienced, or is experiencing, a great deal of personal hardship. That is, they do not want to provide another negative experience to the student. The unavoidable reality of such an act of self-serving cowardice is that a far greater negative experience will result when in the workplace graduates become aware of the quality of their education, not to mention the long-term 'negative' consequences of such graduates for all Aboriginal people.

Another common reason for compromise is peer or institutional pressure. Having inherited the compromises of another deliverer, Aboriginal or otherwise, it is easier to compromise oneself—particularly when the upholding of standards may result in sanction from misguided or complacent peers. Furthermore, to be the first and only one of numerous staff to refuse to compromise student performance expectations is to increase the potential for student confrontation. In addition, the professional career and economic agendas of course coordinators may result in a push to produce greater graduate numbers. Therefore the fear of a pressured coordinator aligning her/himself with a disgruntled student to the detriment of a staff member is a genuine concern. Compromise (for the deliverer) is an easier path.

In all, a mesh of economic, professional and emotional agendas as well as a number of misguided assumptions operate at the level of the deliverer in such a way as to justify the compromising of academic standards.

Providers need to question their personal motives and assumptions and take full responsibility for their own actions and the consequences of such actions. But there is also a single factor operating at the institutional level which places the deliverers in a situation in which the temptation to compromise is far greater for Aboriginal students than for non-Aboriginal students. This is the Department of Employment, Education and Training's policy of funding Aboriginal courses by the number of participants through the granting to universities of API (Aboriginal Participation Initiative) funding. The stated aim of API is to provide access and equity to Aboriginal people by funding the university per Aboriginal student in order to cover the costs of creating additional positions for Aboriginal people. The funding is to cover all the material, administrative and academic resources required by a student.

Once a course is conceived, established, staffed and funded through API, the personal economic/employment interests of staff at various levels are directly tied to student numbers. Hence the potential for compromise towards Aboriginal students is dramatically increased, particularly in regard to those students enrolled in all-Aboriginal and predominantly API-funded programs. In addition, providers' reputations are invested in the 'success' of their courses (whose pragmatic institutional measure is usually number rather than quality).

These two factors can influence staff decisions all the way, from student selection at enrolment to the point of graduation. For example, if a course seems unlikely to attract a sufficient number of applicants who are able to meet the essential academic or skills criteria for entrance to the program, the often-realised temptation is to compromise entrance criteria to achieve the numbers. From this single compromise a host of others will ensue over the length of the students' enrolment.

When students are enrolled in courses without the academic or skills prerequisites, not only are entrance and inevitably assessment criteria compromised but the quality of classroom education is lowered. This in turn results in a loss of enthusiasm by the more competent (and originally targeted) students, who become disheartened and/or resentful towards both weaker students and staff. They also invariably lower their own level of performance. If lesson delivery is pitched towards the centre or top of the skills range, the less capable feel alienated, incompetent and consequently come under considerable personal stress. As a result, students usually engage in avoidance behaviour in regard to both attendance and the submission of work, in turn creating further temptation on the part of staff to compromise course requirements.

Our experience is that two major consequences arise at this point. First, staff begin to engage in an emotionally exhausting and time-consuming welfare role. Apart from placing the staff under considerable emotional pressure, the need to spend time 'chasing up' and encouraging students to hand in work or attend class removes the staff member from more productive and personally rewarding activities. Is it, then, any wonder that the staff turnover in Aboriginal programs is so high (a factor that is particularly destabilising for students whose cultural prerequisite is the establishment of a personal relationship with the deliverer)? Further, the counselling itself is often self-serving and negative in effect. Often students who have assessed their lack of sufficient skills, personal emotional resources and/or family or employment commitments, and who would wisely seek to withdraw from the course, are encouraged by staff to stay on. In effect they are kept in crisis mode. This often results in the establishment of an overdependence on tutorial assistance programs and tutorial staff.

The second consequence of enrolling less academically prepared students and having to compromise quality of delivery as well as assessment criteria is that disappointed and disgruntled competent graduates will, even to their own professional detriment, speak badly of the course. At the same time, the quality of less competent graduates out in the workplace and in the community will speak for itself. The end result is a poor course reputation among a community of people who are largely attracted to courses by word of mouth. Such a course is unlikely ever to attract a sufficient number of desirable applicants, and will forever be pursuing numbers.

In summary, the temptation to meet enrolment quotas and compromise entrance criteria creates further potential for compromise. This compromise, extended to quality of delivery and student performance expectation, is rationalised at the personal level partly out of misguided and condescending attitudes and/or partly out of a variety of conscious and subconsciously held personal agendas. These compromises in turn not only create further potential for compromise, they reduce the quality of student-to-student and student-to-staff relations, and engage staff in a welfare model of education which is draining on staff and damaging to students.

We have discussed the long-term and broader implications of such a model not only for graduates in regard to their workplace and their peers and for their clients, but for all Aboriginal people. What is more, such a model is cyclical. A course with a poor reputation or incapable of considering its irrelevance to Aboriginal people will forever be short of applicants and will therefore continually compromise quality at all levels.

However, while the system of funding Aboriginal student positions per head does create potential for compromise, it does not predetermine it. Blame should not be attributed solely to the API funding process. Rather, individual providers need to consider the role of their own actions, their assumptions and their underlying agendas.

While the process discussed above is complex, damaging and far-reaching, the solution is relatively simple. Deliverers need only engage in a degree of self-examination and exercise uncompromising honesty and a degree of personal fortitude. This is a path which is straightforward, yet personally challenging.

Many of the frustrations and difficulties experienced by both providers and students in the field of Aboriginal adult education are perceived to be primarily cultural in origin and largely unavoidable—an inevitable part of the scene in Aboriginal adult education. Here we have proposed that the difficulties experienced by deliverers and students stem more from institutional agendas than from cultural difference. They are not cultural issues, they are institutional and administrative issues. If the same compromising decisions were made in regard to the enrolment of non-Aboriginal students, the same difficulties, tensions and levels of stress would exist.

Neither are the 'difficulties' unavoidable. By claiming to be well-meaning yet impotent victims of greater cultural systems, institutions and government agendas, providers (Aboriginal and non-Aboriginal alike) unknowingly (presuming their ignorance of their role), though conveniently, abrogate responsibility for their contribution to the 'difficulties', and with this fail to recognise their personal and significant ability to create change.

CONCLUSION

This chapter has argued that there is a long-running struggle in Australia between the colonial capitalist state, which has attempted to use indigenous adult education and training as a means of social control, and Indigenous people, who have attempted to use adult education and training to maintain their political and cultural autonomy. There are a number of dimensions to this struggle. There is the attempt by the state, and many individual adult educators, to define Indigenous education as a monolithic entity in opposition to 'mainstream' culture. The educational task then becomes either to 'help' Indigenous people move away from their own culture or to integrate their own and 'mainstream' culture, or both. During the past two centuries, this perspective on Indigenous education has spawned a plethora of programs, ranging from the total institutionalisation of the 19th-century reserve system to contemporary 'concerned and caring' practices, which purport to offer support to Aboriginal self-determination.

It has been argued here that, while these later policies and practices do offer Indigenous people opportunities to gain more control over their lives, they also generate new complexities, including more subtle forms of control, new resistances and negative educational outcomes. These complexities have been demonstrated through a critique of current practices in Indigenous tertiary education programs. While these difficulties have largely institutional origins, many of them can be overcome by courageous action by individual educators.

NOTES

1 The following analysis is based in part on Lane (1994), and Foley & Flowers (1990).
2 This analysis draws on Bin Sallik et al. (1994).

FURTHER READING

Bin-Sallik, M., Blomeley, N., Flowers, R. & Hughes, P. 1994 *Review and Analysis of Literature Relating to Aboriginal and Torres Strait Islander Education.* Canberra: Department of Employment, Education & Training.
Folds, R. 1987 *Whitefella School.* Sydney: Allen & Unwin.
Foley, G. & Flowers, R. 1990 *Strategies for Self-Determination: Aboriginal Adult Education, Training and Community Development in NSW.* Sydney: University of Technology.
——1992 'Knowledge and power in Aboriginal communities', *Convergence*, 12(2), pp. 31–9.
Garbutcheon-Singh, M. 1990 'Curriculum knowledge and Aboriginality: conservative, capitalistic and favourable to long-continued paternalism', *Curriculum Perspectives*, 10(2), pp. 10–19.
Lane, J. 1984 'Tuition before rights: Aboriginal adult education in Australia 1800–1983', *The Aboriginal Child at School*, 12(3), pp. 3–11.
Luke, A., Nakata, M., Garbutcheon-Singh, M. & Smith, R. 1993 'Policy and politics of representation: Torres Strait Islanders and Aborigines at the margins', in R. Lingard, J. Knight & P. Porter (eds), *Schooling Reform in Hard Times*. London: Falmer Press.
Nakata, M. (1998) 'Culture in education: for us or for them?', in N. Loos & T. Osani (eds), *The Struggle for Human Rights: Reading in the History, Culture, Education and Future of the Ainu of Japan and the Aborigines and Torres Strait Islanders of Australia.* Tokyo: San You-Sha.
Welch, A.R. 1988 'Aboriginal education as internal colonialism: the schooling of an indigenous minority in Australia', *Comparative Education*, 24(2), pp. 203–15.

17

Learning, education and social action

Michael Newman

In this chapter our focus is on the learning and education that occur when people with a shared history or political interest act on their environment to gain more control over their own lives. Such learning can take a number of forms: incidental learning; informal learning; informal education; and formal education (see also the Introduction to this volume).

FORMS OF LEARNING

Incidental learning occurs during action, and it may be only in hindsight that we recognise that the learning has taken place. People in community organisations and community development projects learn to write submissions, run an office, canvass community opinion, and lobby bureaucrats and politicians. Activists in a campaign to stop the mining of uranium learn about the mining industry, the workings of different levels of government, legal aspects of the leasehold and ownership of land, indigenous land rights, international trade, the nuclear power industry and the arms industry, as well as how to organise and take direct action. This kind of learning is very real and can be empowering, but it is incidental to the action taken by the members of a community group or the activists, and may not be articulated as learning (Foley 1991b, 1993a, 1999).

Non-formal learning occurs when people become aware of the potential for learning in their activities and make a decision to learn from those experiences. A group campaigning for the ordination of women priests may regroup after a day of demonstration and action to consider what they have learnt from the day and what new strategies they may try in the next phase of their campaign. There is no planned and structured educational program, but learning is very consciously done.

Informal education is organised, but not in a recognisably educational context, and perhaps not in a particularly structured format. Women in a neighbourhood centre may form a consciousness-raising group, or Green activists might undertake non-violent direct-action training in the midst of a campaign. This kind of education is normally participant-directed and often one-off or sporadic (Foley 1991b, 1993a).

Formal education is systematic and structured. What started as a consciousness-raising group at a neighbourhood centre may become a women's studies class at a local college (Foley 1991a). Members of a management committee of a community organisation may decide they need training in group work and financial management. They may seek the help of a trainer for a series of sessions on group dynamics, meeting procedures and problem-solving techniques, and buy and then work their way through a number of self-paced learning modules on bookkeeping and budgeting for community organisations.

VARIOUS HISTORIES

The examples given above are contemporary ones, but adult education in its various forms has a long history of being put to the service of social action. In Britain in the 19th century, working-class people engaged in adult education in order to improve their lot and gain a greater say in their own affairs and the political and economic affairs of the country. Labourers from farms attended adult schools to learn to read. The new urbanised working class went to schools of the arts and mechanics institutes to learn the new sciences that were influencing and altering their lives on the factory floor. Members of the 'artisan and working classes' went to working people's colleges (Kelly 1970).

Adult schools, mechanics institutes and working people's colleges were, by and large, initiated by middle-class philanthropists, and were shunned by some of the more radical working-class activists. The radicals—Owenites, trade unionists and Chartists—saw these kinds of institution as offering 'useful knowledge'—that is, knowledge helpful to those who wanted to improve their lot within the class-based, propertied state of the time. The radicals in their turn established classes, meetings and adult education

institutions that offered 'really useful knowledge'. This they understood as knowledge concerned with defining and protecting
natural rights, extending democracy, critically examining the propertied nature of the state, promoting concepts of community and
cooperation, and explaining the continued existence of poverty
amid the production of great wealth (Johnson 1988).

In the 20th century, the Workers Educational Association
sought to provide a liberal education for working people, while
the Plebs League and its associated National Council of Labour
Colleges provided a radical alternative, offering adult education
for working people based on an analysis of class conflict (Brown
1980; Armstrong 1988).

North America had its own adult education movements associated with middle-class values and with radical working-class
movements. But in North America we also find examples of adult
education flourishing in rural areas and contributing to the development of impoverished rural communities. The departments of
agriculture in various US states and Canadian provinces provided
education for rural and agrarian development. In Nova Scotia,
Canada, in the 1920s and 30s, educators in the Antigonish
movement used adult education processes to help people of the
region establish fishing and farming cooperatives, credit unions,
and other community facilities and projects. These programs of
meetings, kitchen circles, radio discussion groups and leadership
schools were aimed at giving people control over the processing
and distribution of their produce, therefore more control over their
own lives and the affairs of their communities. Moses Coady, a
central figure in the Antigonish movement, saw adult education
as 'an aggressive agent of change, a mass movement of reform,
the peaceful way to social change' (Lovett 1988: xix; Newman
1993: 204–5; Lotz & Welton 1987, 1997).

In 1932 in the American South, in the Appalachian mountains,
a White American called Myles Horton founded the Highlander
Folk School. Highlander since then has offered workshops and
educational advice to Black and White activists and community
organisations. In the 1930s Highlander worked with people in the
mining and cotton industries to establish unions. In the 1940s and
50s it helped establish adult schools in the South to help people
learn to read in order to register to vote, and in the late 1950s
and early 60s it provided workshops for activists who prepared
for and then engaged in the civil rights movement (Horton et al.
1990). Highlander's focus since the late 1960s has been on
environmental issues, issues relating to indigenous people, and

the struggle of local Appalachian people against the intrusion of transnationals and the ownership of land by absentee landlords. In Latin America over the past 40 years there have been many examples of adult education in social action. Against a background of repressive governments, military dictatorships and client states of the superpowers, educators have worked in varying ways to give people a say in their own lives, to help people combat poverty and struggle for some kind of human dignity. These educators and activists—sometimes referred to as 'popular educators'—have drawn eclectically from socialism, liberal education and liberation theology. Adult education in social action in Latin America includes the work of Paulo Freire with shanty-town dwellers and peasant communities in Brazil and Chile (Taylor 1993), the work of many others using and developing his methods throughout the region, the national literacy and basic education campaign in Nicaragua under the Sandinistas (Miller 1985), the Christian base communities (*communidades de base*) throughout Latin America (Wickham-Crowley 1992; Dickson 1994), and the work of theatre activist Augusto Boal (1979).

There have been many examples of adult education in social action in other parts of the world. One can interpret the work of Gandhi in the struggle to liberate the Indian subcontinent from British colonial rule as a vast exercise in education for social action. Foley (1993b) writes of the intense and transformative kinds of learning that took place in China during a 'democratic moment' in the Chinese liberation struggle in the 1930s and 40s. And it can be argued that education played a significant part in liberation struggles and the social change that followed in countries like Zimbabwe (Foley 1993c).

From the 1970s, through the writings of Paulo Freire, the Latin American experience of 'popular education' became widely known among adult educators working for social change in other parts of the world. This form of education in social action has spread, fused with indigenous forms of educational action, and developed in differing ways in both industrialised and non-industrialised parts of the world. In the years preceding the abandonment of apartheid in South Africa, White and Black educators, operating out of universities, trade unions, community organisations and health centres, used adult education to inform and develop a critical awareness in learners. In an inner city area of Edinburgh in Scotland, adult educators employed a Freirean framework to provide an educational program tackling local problems of poverty and inequity (Kirkwood & Kirkwood 1989). And in countries like

India, for example, cultural and development programs have been inventively linked with adult education (Rogers 1992).

In Australia it has been forcefully argued that adult education has a part to play in the struggle by Aboriginal people for recognition and equity (Foley & Flowers 1992). Community development projects constructed around the provision and support of indigenous adult educators within Aboriginal communities have been implemented. And several Aboriginal adult education institutions have been established. Tranby Aboriginal Cooperative College in Sydney was established in 1952 with the help of church and trade union groups, and became fully Aboriginal-controlled in 1962. Tranby provides courses aimed at helping individual Aboriginal people enter the mainstream educational system, courses and activities aimed at encouraging Aboriginal people to learn in order to contribute to their communities, and educational support and consultancy to Aboriginal communities and organisations. Non-Aboriginal people help at Tranby, but to a visitor walking into the college it is immediately clear that this is an Aboriginal organisation committed to an activist form of adult education on behalf of Aboriginal people (Newman 1993).

SOCIAL CONTROL

Tranby provides an example of Aboriginal people resisting White control. As social action is concerned with helping people gain more influence over events that affect their lives, adult education in social action will often involve people learning to understand and then resist social control.

Social control can take different forms. People can be controlled through brute force. People also submit themselves to institutional forms of control. We give over a range of our freedoms to institutions in exchange for membership of those institutions, or for the services those institutions can provide us, or the protection those institutions will afford us. We submit to the order and regulations imposed by governments. We abide by the requirements of our employment. We follow the educational paths set by schools, colleges and universities. We accept intrusions on our privacy by the forces of regulation, law and order in exchange for the protection these various forces provide us (Foucault 1980).

Control by brute force and institutional control are normally relatively easy to identify. There is another form of social control—hegemonic control—that can be all-pervading and more difficult to identify. This is a form of control by consent, in which

271

one group of people accept as normal, and therefore not to be questioned, conditions that are in the interests of another group altogether.

Hegemonic control can be detected in 'commonsense truths' that both the oppressors and the oppressed mouth. If we live in a part of the city poorly serviced by schools but say 'Talent will always win out', we remove pressure from the authorities to provide universally available schooling. If people say 'Change is inevitable. It's foolish to stand in the way of progress', then they may more easily be moved out of their homes to make way for the construction of a freeway. And if enough people say 'The private sector is more efficient than the public sector', then the sale of essential public utilities, even in the face of conflicting evidence from other countries, is more easily achieved.

Hegemonic control is also reinforced by ridiculing opposing ideas as extreme, or ruling opposing ideas out altogether. Thus: 'Those who criticise the competency movement are either on the far right or the far left'; 'It's obvious that competition will improve the quality of a service'; 'Everyone knows you can get a job if you really want to'; and 'Growth is the only way to go'.

DIFFERENT KINDS OF LEARNING IN SOCIAL ACTION

As people struggle against intrusive, unwarranted or oppressive forms of social control, different kinds of learning and education are generated. Mezirow (1991), drawing on Jurgen Habermas' analysis of the generation of knowledge, describes three domains of learning: instrumental learning, interpretive or communicative learning, and critical or emancipatory learning (see also chapters 1 and 8).

Instrumental learning enables us to manage and control our environment, to do a job and earn a living, to build things and to manage people when we consider those people as functions and part of the physical environment. In this domain we examine and learn about cause and effect. We learn to solve problems by the application of 'commonsense logic', by weighing up the options and choosing the most appropriate one. This learning can be complex but is essentially about getting the skills and information necessary to construct systems and devise methods for making those systems work. For social activists, learning in this domain will provide them with the skills and information to help them deal with practical matters; use existing structures and systems such as governmental and legal processes to bring about change; and oppose the physical, practical and more obvious forms of social control.

Interpretive learning helps us understand the human condition. It is the learning that focuses on people, on what they are and how they relate, on symbolic interaction and the social construction of meaning—how people's interaction is mediated by language and other symbols. In this domain we learn to solve problems through exchanging ideas and opinions, through reflection and insight, and by seeking consensus. Learning in this domain enables activists to understand thinking and values, the character, background and motives of the people they are working with and those they may be seeking to change.

Critical learning helps us understand the psychological and cultural assumptions that constrain the way we see the world and that influence the way we think, feel and act. In this domain, we learn not only to see the world more clearly but *to see ourselves seeing* the world. This learning involves a kind of meta-awareness, in which we come to know what 'makes us tick', what the influences are that make us adopt particular positions, think in particular ways, react and feel the way we do, and take the actions we take. In this domain we learn to solve problems by a form of self-reflection that may transform our whole way of thinking— our perspectives. In this kind of learning we can learn to see through ourselves, and so may be enabled to understand others as well.

Most manifestations of social control will be a complex mix of coercion, different kinds of institutional authority, and various attempts to influence people's thinking. Learning in social action is, in turn, likely to range across Habermas' three domains. Robert Regnier (1991) describes the public relations campaign by the nuclear power industry in the Canadian province of Saskatchewan and the counter-campaign by community groups opposed to the nuclear industry. It is an excellent example of social activists engaging in adult education in all three domains. Griff Foley (1991b), in his research into the struggle to save a rainforest in New South Wales, Australia, interviewed a number of the environmental activists involved. From his analysis it is clear that they and others involved in the campaign engaged in significant action and learning in all three domains.

THE DYNAMICS OF LEARNING IN SOCIAL ACTION[1]

Foley (1999) offers a framework for analysing the detailed dynamics of learning in social action—who learns what, how, and with what outcomes. This framework emerged from case study research on informal and incidental learning in social action in diverse sites in Australia, Zimbabwe, China, the USA and Brazil—workplaces, community centres, local campaigns to protect the environment and social services, and national liberation struggles. Foley concludes that in all these situations emancipatory learning occurred—learning which freed people from various sorts of domination and enabled them to exercise more control over their lives. But he argues that such emancipatory learning and the political struggles in which it occurs are complex, ambiguous and contradictory. His starting point is the assumption that conflict and contradiction are integral to social life. History, he argues, is characterised by attempts by ruling groups to dominate and people's struggles against these attempts. So domination and emancipation are *learned*. To understand them their detailed dynamics need to be documented and put in context.

Foley further argues that domination and emancipation are constructed in economic and political relationships but they are also constructed in ideologies and discourses, in the ways in which people make sense of situations and explain them in speech, writing or in other ways. People learn dominative and emancipatory ideologies and discourses, and they do this within politically laden local situations which are in turn shaped by broader economic and political influences. So satisfactory accounts of informal and incidental learning in social action will make connections between learning and education on the one hand, and micropolitical factors, 'macro' political and economic factors, ideologies and discourses (or 'discursive practices') on the other. These connections are represented in Figure 17.1.

The framework in Figure 17.1 suggests some key questions. In a particular situation:

- What forms and expressions do social action take?
- What are the crucial features of the political and economic context? How do these shape the social action?
- What are the micropolitics of the situation?
- What are the discursive practices and struggles of the people involved? To what extent do these practices and struggles facilitate or hinder emancipatory learning and action?
- What does all this mean for education?
- What interventions are possible and helpful?

In the New South Wales rainforest campaign, activists learned a new discourse which was composed of instrumental, interpretive

Figure 17.1   A framework for analysing learning in social action

Political economy	Micro politics
	Learning in social action
Educational interventions	
Learning	Discursive practices Ideologies

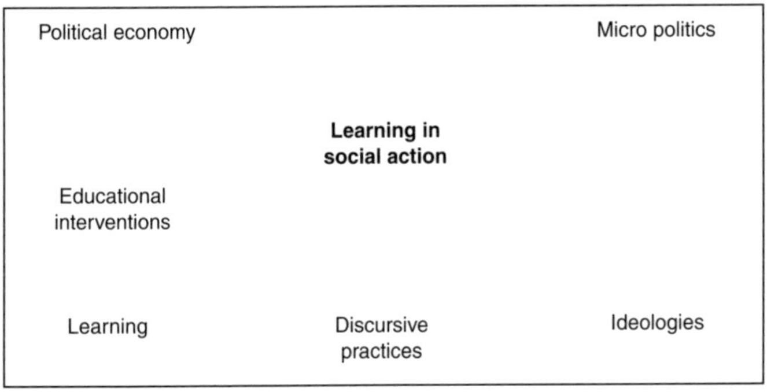

and critical elements. They gained knowledge and skills in rain-forest ecology, lobbying and advocacy. They learned a great deal about their own value assumptions and those of others such as foresters, bureaucrats and politicians. They developed a more critical view of authority and expertise, and a recognition of their own ability to influence decision making. All this was *incidental* learning—it was embedded in the social action and not articulated until the activists were interviewed some years after the campaign. And this learning took place in a broader political context in which for various reasons growing importance was being placed on the natural environment, and within a micropolitical context characterised by struggle between the conservationists and other interest groups, and among and within the conservationists themselves. Finally, the activists learned their new environmentalist discourse in relationship with and in opposition to a dominant discourse of 'scientific' expertise, profit making and political fixing (Foley 1991b, 1999).

Another study, of women's learning in two women's 'neighbourhood houses' or community centres, showed that struggles there—within individuals, among members, between workers and committee members and between the centres and the state—generated instrumental skills and knowledge, self-awareness and social and political understanding (Foley 1993a, 1999). This research also showed that such learning is not inevitably emancipatory. People's everyday experience and learning can as easily reproduce ways of thinking and acting which support the often oppressive status quo as it can produce recognitions that enable people to critique and challenge the existing order. And even when learning is emancipatory it is not so in some linear, developmental

275

sense: it is complex and contradictory, shaped as it is by intra-personal, interpersonal and broader social factors.

ANALYSIS OF POWER

Social action of the above kind is a struggle over power. It is a struggle over who should wield it and how much power different parties should have. Social activists are commonly trying to gain more power for themselves or the people they represent or are working with. Often, as in the case of the struggle against the nuclear power industry in Saskatchewan, they see their struggle as an attempt to redress a gross imbalance of power. Part of the role of learning and education in social action, therefore, is to help people understand the way power can be exercised.

Power can be perceived in different ways. As a result of the debate on postmodernity, two sharply opposing views have emerged about the location of power. Foucault (1980), for example, suggested that power is dispersed and expressed in a myriad locations, events, relations and groupings of people, rather than being centrally located in large structures such as the state or the judiciary or a union or a large corporation. He maintained that power is exercised and circulates among actors rather than being possessed by one person or group, and that power can be enabling as well as repressive (Gore 1993: 52).

Some of the more recent social movements seem to have recognised this interpretation of power in their own structures and processes. The feminist movement has no organisational centre but is rather a vast array of semiformal and informal groupings at all levels of the social and political structures. The environmental movement has no one dominant body, nor any one headquarters. Thousands of organisations and groupings around the world form the movement, most with their own particular and often singular focus, be it the preservation of a wetland, the curbing of the discharge of chemical effluent, the recycling of manufactured products, or the protection of whales. Yet all these movements clearly *are* movements, and the members know they are part of them. Both these movements, through action in a myriad locations, have contributed to major social change in many parts of the world.

Adult education, then, can play a role in social action by providing people with the opportunities to analyse power in this way, examine modes of communication and cooperation in these kinds of movement, and plan this kind of localised action.

However, we cannot conclude that centralised power is an illusion. Localised sites of power may proliferate, but considerable power continues to reside in state apparatuses that have extensive bureaucracies and sophisticated surveillance technologies, in huge enterprises that have the wealth and expertise to buy and do what they want, and in legal systems that have prisons and police to enforce their decisions.

Nor can we conclude that mass cohesive political or social action is an illusion. Some of the more recent social movements— the women's movement, the environmental movement and the peace and human rights movements—may take the form of untidy patchworks of activist groups, but there are times when faiths, ideas, fashions, anxieties and ideologies will grip whole populations and, as the events in 1989 in Eastern Europe demonstrated, people will take to the streets and bring about sweeping social change.

Adult education can also contribute to social action by helping activists increase their understanding of this kind of centralised power and develop the political skills of lobbying, organisation, advocacy, representation and the like that go with centralised action.

SOCIAL ANALYSIS

Social action involves people working together to bring about change in the groupings, communities and organisations that make up their social context. In effect, social activists want to influence the social histories of themselves and the people they may be working with. Some adult education processes are aimed at helping learners shift from a passive or reactive role in the affairs of their societies to a proactive role. Consciousness-raising, for example, is a process through which people move from a fatalistic or naive consciousness to a critical consciousness, to a state of mind in which they are aware of themselves within their social context and capable of acting on that context in order to change it. In a sense, consciousness-raising is the process by which the learners become active in the flow of social history. They cease being objects and become writers of their own and their communities' stories (see Hart 1990; Freire 1972a, b).

Adult education in social action, therefore, has a role in providing learners with the tools and information they need to understand their own histories, to analyse and understand their social contexts, and to begin acting on those contexts.

ECONOMIC ANALYSIS

And social action often involves intervening in or affecting economies. Trade unionists strike, and their action has a direct bearing on the finances of themselves, their employers and the communities of which they and the employers are a part. At a micro level, environmental activists will sometimes try to interrupt the business activities of organisations they see as damaging the environment. At a macro level, environmentalists engage in action and argument that go to the heart of the management of whole national and international economies. Can a particular form of industrial development be environmentally sustainable? Can the planet sustain continual economic growth? And some of the major struggles by the feminist movement have been to do with access and equity in work, and therefore with gaining an equal say and influence in the economic affairs of society.

ISSUES FOR THE ADULT EDUCATOR

Helping people learn in a context of social action presents the adult educator with a number of challenges. On what condition does the adult educator engage with a community, community group or group of activists? Does the educator engage only by invitation? Does she/he intervene? Does she/he 'invade'?

Articulate, organised activists might invite an adult educator to help them with the learning and training that might be needed in a campaign. Trade unions, in preparation for campaigns, have invited in educational and training consultants. But less organised groups may not know how to make use of adult educators and others who could help them. In this case, there are community adult educators who make contact with groups, call meetings in communities, talk to local community leaders and the providers of local services, and offer their services. By suggesting what they might be able to help people do, these adult educators actively seek an invitation. For example, a community education worker entered a caravan park on the fringes of Sydney, made contact with some of the residents and the caravan park owners, and then organised a meeting. People perceived that they, in the park, were less well-served by the welfare and social services in the area. The worker undertook to help them examine these perceptions and, if they proved true, to help them petition for improvements.

Some adult educators intervene in the lives of others. They enter a community or group on their own initiative and use processes to gain people's attention and get them thinking and learning. Sometimes their entry into the lives of others will be negotiated, but sometimes it is not. Some educators, ostensibly using techniques based on Freire's thinking, simply engage with groups they perceive as oppressed and try to motivate them to change.

Interventionist adult educators often have a mission—a belief that the learning they can offer will benefit a community or group of people. There are times, for example, when also adult health educators intervene uninvited. Through research, from statistics, as a result of their own or their own organisation's judgment, they identify a health risk among a particular group of people or in a particular social class or community, and they intervene in order to mobilise people through learning and action to combat the risk. In Rajasthan, India, a non-government organisation used puppetry followed by discussion to alert villagers to the dangers of alcohol abuse and to mobilise people to take action (McGivney & Murray 1991: 32–3). The results of the intervention by the puppeteer-educators varied from village to village. In one village the women decided to smash any bottles of drink they came across. In another a group decision was made by the villagers to stop drinking alcohol. In a third, villagers imposed fines on drinkers, the revenue going to the village fund for seed and fertiliser.

Campaigns related to skin cancer, for example, can take the form of interventionist adult or public education. Campaigns involve advertising on television, exhortation by radio and television commentators, and intervention in the form of teams of health workers and educators who set up camp on beaches or at sporting events and provide information and instruction on skin protection.

But, as Head (1977) argues, education can be invasion. Certainly, if a team of educators, driven by their own sense of mission and perhaps from another social class, enter the lives of a group of disadvantaged people uninvited, their action does begin to look like invasion. This kind of adult education initiative can all too easily become an exercise in propaganda and another form of social control.

In adult education in social action, the relationship of the adult educator to the learners can also become a problem. Is he/she simply the neutral provider of information and skills, the dispassionate facilitator of learning? Is he/she a stirrer, a person who provokes? Or does he/she abandon any efforts at detachment and objectivity, espouse the learners' cause, and join with them in the action? Thompson (1983, 1988), a feminist adult educator, makes it quite clear in her call for a separatist form of education for women that she acts in solidarity with her learners. (For further discussion of this issue, see chapter 15.) A union trainer will in all likelihood be a member of the same union as the participants in the union course, and so will formally be acting in solidarity with her/his learners. And an educator working with Christian base communities in Latin America will no doubt share the Christian viewpoint with his/her learners.

Some adult educators may, however, be coopted by the learners but not be members of their group or expected to be party to the group's action: Aboriginal groups make use of non-Aboriginal educators. And some educators stand completely apart: environmental activists will from time to time make use of scientific experts in educational roles without expecting them necessarily to commit themselves to the environmentalist cause.

Some adult educators themselves see virtue in maintaining a form of detachment to better help the learners. Mezirow, in a discussion of adult education and social action, proposes that the adult educator be 'an empathic provocateur' (1990: 360) and that he 'should strive to stay outside the dominant culture to be better able to see taken-for-granted assumptions for what they are: common and uncritically assimilated assumptions that need to be critically examined through discourse' (1992: 231).

However, whether the adult educator remains detached or not, he/she is working with learners who are involved in or may decide to take action. And as this action may be part of a struggle against oppression or some other form of social control, the adult educator may well find him/herself helping people decide on action that could lead to violence. Horton tells the story of 'facilitating' a group of striking miners in 1933 who had to decide whether to kill two professional killers or let them go ahead and kill the mine workers' leader. Whichever way the decision went, someone would be killed. In recounting the story, Horton comments: 'Of course any person in their right mind would be for non-violence over violence if it were a simple choice, but that's not the problem the world has to face' (Horton et al. 1990: 41).

Horton seems to have resolved the educator's dilemma by having no qualms about helping people arrive at a decision to take action, so long as that action, *would lead to further learning.* Horton's emphasis was on the *adult learning* in social action.

CONCLUSION

In this chapter we have discussed various forms and histories of learning in social action. We have paid particular attention to the role of power in such learning and have offered a framework for understanding and facilitating it. We have also pointed to the potentially invasive effects of educators' would-be emancipatory interventions in social action.

NOTE

1   Griff Foley wrote this section.

FURTHER READING

Foley, G. 1999 *Learning in Social Action: A Contribution to Understanding Informal Learning.* London: Zed.

Hart, M. 1990 'Liberation through consciousness-raising', in J. Mezirow (ed.), *Fostering Critical Reflection in Adulthood.* San Francisco: Jossey-Bass.

Lovett, T. (ed.) 1988 *Radical Approaches to Adult Education.* London: Routledge.

Newman, M. 1994 *Defining the Enemy: Adult Education in Social Action.* Sydney: Stewart Victor.

18

Conclusion: critical theory and adult education

Griff Foley

As noted in chapter 1 and discussed elsewhere in this book, in recent years there has been a flourishing of critical scholarship in adult education. There is also an ongoing debate in adult education and the social sciences more generally about different critical perspectives, some of it productive and some of it quite confused and confusing. The purpose of this brief chapter is to give readers an overview of critical perspectives.

CRITICAL THEORY/IES

'Critical theory' is a label often attached to a group of German social theorists collectively known as the 'Frankfurt School'. This group, whose most influential members were Max Horkheimer, Theodor Adorno, Herbert Marcuse and Jurgen Habermas, emerged in the 1920s. Escaping Nazi persecution, many of these scholars moved to the USA. After World War II and particularly in the 1960s and 70s Frankfurt School critical theory became very influential in Western social science, including in education studies. (For a useful discussion of Frankfurt School critical theory, see Held 1980.)

Critical theory focuses on the critique of ideology, taken to mean systems of ideas which (a) help people to make sense of the world and to explain it to themselves, and/or (b) distort reality. Theorists attached to or inspired by the Frankfurt School were interested in the ways in which the institutions of modern mass society—governments, the mass media, the family, education— systematically manipulated and directed people through their control of ideas. One highly influential theorist, Habermas, also became interested in how such ideological domination could be overcome, in how processes and institutions could be developed which would enable people to develop 'communicative competence' (i.e. the capacity to communicate with each other in non-distorting and clarifying ways). This goal, of course, is the same as that aspired to by adult educators who seek to promote ethical principles and practices in discussion (see chapter 3). (For a compact summary of Habermas' position, see Morrow & Torres 1995: 233–41; for extended applications to education of Habermas' ideas and other Frankfurt School theory, see Carr & Kemmis 1986; Mezirow 1991; Welton 1995; Collins 1991.)

It is useful to begin a discussion of critical theory with the Frankfurt School, because much discussion in contemporary critical educational scholarship revolves around debates set off by this group. But I think it is unhelpful to equate critical theory with the Frankfurt School; it is much more useful to recognise that there are critial *theories* which, while they have fundamental differences in epistemological and value assumptions, have a common interest in critique, in the sense of scrutinising and making judgments about social processes and philosophical assumptions (ethical, epistemological, ontological), or, to put it in plain language, 'getting to the bottom of things'. In general, critical theories also have an emancipatory intent: that is, they seek to generate knowledge and practices which will release people from various oppressions—gender, class, race and so forth. What has characterised critical theory as it has emerged over the past 150 years is a growing recognition of the complexities and contradictions of emancipatory efforts. Postmodernist and postructuralist theorists have paid particular attention to the oppressive effects of would-be emancipatory efforts (see below, and chapters 3 and 8) and now approach the question of emancipation with great caution—they are 'haunted' by the hope and the prospects for it rather than confidentally expecting it (Usher & Edwards 1994: 4).

But if one expands the scope of critical theory in this way it is difficult to know where to start and stop, because there are so many critical theories and theorists. So, practically, one has to put limits on any discussion of critical theory. In this chapter I restrict discussion to the Frankfurt School, historical materialism and poststructuralism/postmodernism, as so many major contemporary debates in critical adult education scholarship revolve around these three groups of theories. (And note that in using the term 'groups of theories' I recognise that there are important debates and differences within each of these problematics.) These debates are of great practical importance, because they shape what is written and read in the field and thereby influence how other adult educators think and act. I recognise that limiting discussion to these three groups of theories leaves a lot out, for other critical social theorists (e.g. Weber and Durkheim) and theoretical frameworks (e.g. hermeneutics, phenemenology) have contributed greatly to our understanding of learning and education. (For these thinkers and theories, see Giddens 1993; for an example of an application of sociological theory to education, see Archer 1979, who makes good use of Weber.)

HISTORICAL MATERIALISM

Historical materialism, or Marxism,[1] holds an ambiguous place in adult education theory. It hardly features in recent adult education scholarship, except as a strawman to be knocked down by rival theories. Yet historically it has had a considerable influence on the thinking of many adult educators and adult students (as a reading of Fieldhouse and associates' 1996 collection on British adult education history, or McIlroy & Westwood's 1993 book on the Welsh adult educator Raymond Williams make clear, for example), and has been an important influence in adult education theory and practice in many parts of world—until recently in Eastern Europe and China, and still today in Latin America (Youngman 1986; Gadotti 1996; Morrow & Torres 1995).

Historical materialism does what its name implies: it focuses on the ways in which material factors, and especially economic and political factors, are played out in and shape history. Its founding and still most influential theorist is Marx, so it is useful to begin with a (radically simplified) sketch of his basic theoretical concepts and account of history.[2]

The fundamental concept in historical materialism is production. To exist, people must produce—their labour, assisted by technology, transforming raw materials into products. Production is both a material and a social activity: people act on nature, but they do so in relationship with other people. To understand production and society you must analyse both the material or economic level (the 'forces of production') and the political relationships and ideologies that develop around it (the 'social relations of production'). All this together—the material and the social, the economic, political and ideological—constitutes a 'mode of production'.

The bulk of Marx's scholarship and journalism was an analysis and critique of the predominant mode of production of his era, capitalism. This remains the analytical starting point for contemporary historical materialists, who argue that if we are going to understand adult education or any other aspect of social life we must analyse it within the context of capitalism. In what follows I outline an historical materialist analysis of the general direction of contemporary adult education.

THE ESSENCE OF CAPITALISM

In a capitalist economy a proportionately small group of people (capitalists) own and control the means of production, and another, much larger group (workers) survives by selling its labour. Under this arrangement, workers produce goods and services which are sold in the market. Capitalists extract the surplus of workers' labour: the capitalist takes whatever profit remains after the costs of production (including labour costs) have been met. If capitalists cannot make a profit, or if they see an opportunity to increase profits, they seek to reorganise (or restructure) production, usually by lowering the cost of labour and/or applying new technology. Workers both accommodate to and resist this process. Conflict— class struggle between labour and capital—is consequently endemic in capitalism.

Capitalism therefore is a system of economic, political and cultural domination, based on two processes: the alienation of labour (the separation of workers from the process and product of their labour); and reification (the commodification of all relationships). The effects of these processes include constant and accelerating exploitation of labour and the environment, and continual conflict as workers and citizens resist this exploitation and money values progressively displace use values in all spheres of life, including adult education.

LEARNING, EDUCATION, CAPITALISM

The analysis of adult education and learning in capitalism that I sketch here begins with the following assumptions:

- Learning is a dimension of human life and occurs in many forms (formal and non-formal education, informal and incidental learning) and sites (workplaces, communities, social action, families, educational institutions).
- Education and learning are shaped by economic and political forces beyond participants' immediate influence.
- Emancipatory learning and education are possible, but are also complex, ambiguous and continually contested.

285

• It is both possible and necessary to develop an analysis of this complexity and to act strategically.

I have fleshed out this analytical framework elsewhere in a series of case studies of learning in social action and in discussion of the political economy of adult education (see Foley 1998, 1999). In what follows, given restrictions of space, I am able only to provide the briefest outline of a political economy of contemporary adult education.

THE REORGANISATION OF THE ECONOMY

In capitalism, reorganisation of education accompanies reorganisation of the economy. In the early 1970s the accord between capital, labour and the state which had held in advanced industrial countries since World War II broke down in the face of currency crises, stagflation and competition from newly industrialised countries. Demand management of the economy was replaced by supply-side economics, which argued that the source of the economic crisis was a long-term decline in productivity caused by a growing taxation burden, accelerating costs of government and increased government regulation, all of which discouraged investment and entrepreneurial activity. The solution was said to be to stimulate the economy by reorganising its supply side—that is, the way production is organised. In this approach to economic management, investment and production are stimulated by letting 'market forces' rule. This means, in particular, cutting government expenditure and lowering taxes, especially higher tax rates on corporations and entrepreneurs, so as to stimulate investment and production. It also involves paying close attention to the organisation of production at enterprise level and the promotion of innovations (such as continuous quality improvement and organisational learning) intended to enhance labour productivity.

The purpose of this reorganisation is to enable national economies to compete more effectively in the global economy. The primary role of the state is to manage this reorganisation, rather than to regulate the economy and provide social services as in the welfare state (see chapter 6).

THE REORGANISATION OF EDUCATION

The impact of all this on education is dramatic. Education ceases to be seen as a citizen's right and is redefined as a support to the economy. A century of extending public provision of education, beginning with free and compulsory education in the late 19th century, ends. Politicians and policy makers articulate the theory that if a nation is to maintain or enhance its standard of living, its efforts in education must focus on helping its economy to become internationally competitive. The primary role of education—including universities and community-based adult education—is redefined as the production of human capital. The state decrees that education must become more vocational, and more efficient and effective. A training market is created in which public and private providers compete. In an attempt to compete in this market on an equal basis, public education undergoes constant organisational restructuring and adopts private sector managment techniques like quality assurance and performance enhancement. Formal education attempts to become more immediately job-related, flexible and portable through the construction of national competency standards, the introduction of modular curricula, the use of information technology, and the creation of a bureaucracy to foster and regulate the process.

In this attempt to demonstrate the applicability of historical materialist concepts to the study of adult education and learning. I will finish with two points.

First, historical materialist analysis is radically underdeveloped in the adult education literature. If until recently the literature has been largely silent on issues of gender and race, it is still equally or more silent on questions of political economy and class. To date there have been few sustained applications of historical materialism in the adult education literature, the notable exceptions being the work of Ettore Gelpi (1979, 1985) (and Frank Youngman 1986, 1999; Wangoola & Youngman 1996).

Second, historical materialism is often misinterpreted by scholars who subscribe to other problematics. The most frequently employed error is to equate 'Marxism' with economic determinism, thus ignoring the century of debate around this issue within historical materialism, and the seminal theoretical advances in the understanding of the relationship of economy, politics and culture achieved by scholars like Lukacs (1968), the Frankfurt theorists and cultural studies scholars like Raymond Williams (1961, 1983, 1989), and historians such as E.P. Thompson (1968) and Ellen Meiksins Wood (1986, 1991, 1995).

POSTSTRUCTURALISM/POSTMODERNISM

It is difficult to present this third theoretical problematic succinctly, as it encompasses a range of perspectives and has its own quite difficult language. Here I try to give some sense of how postmodern/

poststructuralist perspectives can enhance our understanding of adult learning and education. (Those who want to read further will find the following references useful: Smart 1993 for an overview of postmodernism; Usher & Edwards 1994 for an extended discussion of the applicability of postmodernist and poststructuralist approaches to the analysis of education; Weedon 1987 and Stacey 1997 for feminist poststructuralism; Weiner 1994 for feminist poststructuralism in education; Gore 1993 for an extended poststructuralist analysis of a particular educational practice, critical pedagogy.)

Obviously, *post*structuralism and *post*modernism must each come after phenomena called 'structuralism' and 'modernism'. Structuralists, the best-known of whom was probably Claude Levi-Strauss, analysed the structure of language. Their fundamental theoretical assumption was that pre-existing linguistic structures shape thought. This assumption has been inherited by poststructuralism, which is concerned more broadly with forms of representation (speech, writing, visual, electronic) and how these 'construct' (shape, determine) what people do and think. Poststructuralism asserts that particular instances of representation (such as a film, a newspaper article, a classroom discussion) need to be studied as 'texts', which have their own logic and rules. Such texts are not 'logocentric', they do represent the world 'as it is'. And it is not just the form of the text that needs to be studied but also the ways in which texts are 'read' or interpreted by particular people in particular situations, thus producing new texts (Usher & Edwards 1994: 18–19).

Modernism was the intellectual movement and paradigm which emerged from the 18th-century European Enlightenment, and which involved an attempt to develop 'objective', 'scientific' forms of thinking and social organisation, 'in order to liberate human beings from their chains'. Modernism can be seen as a concomitant of capitalism and its drive to control and exploit natural and human resources. For all its emancipatory aspirations, modernism came to be seen as inherently totalitarian. As the Frankfurt School critical theorists put it, 'the lust to dominate nature entailed the domination of human beings, and that could only lead, in the end, to "a nightmare condition of self-domination"' (Harvey 1989: 12–13, 35–7).

The origins of postmodernism lie in resistance to the standardising and 'totalising' (to use one of the postmodernists' favourite terms) tendencies of modernism. This resistance manifested itself first in a protracted struggle within modernism itself (see Harvey 1989: 10–38), and ultimately flowered in the cultural and political movements of the 1960s. The essence of postmodernism is its problematising of the rational, the stable and the uniform, and its celebration of difference, 'fragmentation, ephemerality, discontinuity, and chaotic change' (1989: 44). Foucault, one of the most interesting (for adult educators) postmodernist thinkers, urges us to 'develop action, thought and desires by proliferation, juxtaposition, and disjunction', and 'to prefer what is positive and multiple, difference over uniformity, flows over unities, mobile arrangements over systems. Believe what is productive is not sedentary but nomadic' (in Harvey 1989: 44).

Foucault also argues that it is futile to try (as did the 'grand narratives' of modernist 'social science') to identify ultimate sources of power and domination in capital, state, ruling class, patriarchy, or wherever. It is more productive, he argues, to identify the way power is constructed, often in subtle and unrecognised ('soft and secret') ways, at the local or 'micro' level, in social institutions (hospitals, classrooms, families), social relationships (e.g. of gender, class and race), as well as in the social sciences.

For Foucault, power and knowledge are intimately related. In the modern world, people's lives are increasingly regulated by the practices and discourses of the professions. Discourses are about 'what can be said and thought, but also about who can speak, when, and with what authority' (Foucault 1974: 49, in Ball 1990: 2). Discourses are of central importance in how people understand their own identities and place in society (Fairclough 1992: 64). Domination is constructed in particular social sites, through discourses. So domination must be struggled with locally—dominant discourses must be countered by insurgent discourses: 'The only way to "eliminate the fascism in our own heads" is to explore and build upon the open qualities of human discourse, and thereby intervene in the way knowledge is produced' in particular situations (Harvey 1989: 45–6).

Poststructuralists and postmodernists are thus particularly interested in relations of language and power, encapsulated in the key concept: 'discourse'. As Stephen Ball, a British scholar who has developed interesting poststructuralist analyses of the policy-making process in education, points out, in dominant discourses (Ball, in Patton 1987: 228–33):

> . . . the possibilities for meaning and for definition are pre-empted through the social and institutional position of those who use them. Meanings thus arise not from language but from institutional practices, from power relations. Words and concepts change their meaning and their effects as they are deployed within different discourses. Discourses constrain the possibilities of thought. They

order and combine words in particular ways and exclude or displace other combinations.

The notions of subject and discourse are linked to another of Foucault's core concepts: 'governance'. Foucault sees subjects as being governed, or controlled, by discourses. In his historical studies, Foucault (1973, 1977) traced the replacement of violent control of populations with gentler means, including the key modern social institutions of the prison and the mental asylum. The discourses and practices of such institutions—which by extension include education—subtly control people (Philp 1985: 68–78). So, for example, the discourse of competency-based education is said to construct the curriculum in a particular fragmented, controlling and commodified way, with concomitant effects on teaching and learning (Usher & Edwards 1994: 101–18).

The discourse of competency-based education is thus an example of what Foucault calls 'totalising discourses', ways of thinking and acting which speak for and take over whole areas of human life. It can be argued that over the past two centuries the learning dimension of human life has been colonised by the discourse of institutionalised education, and that in the 20th century thinking about the organisation of work has come to be dominated by the discourse of management. As already noted, poststructuralists pay particular attention to the ways in which discourses operate 'behind the backs' of their speakers. This secret, unconscious aspect of discourses means that people can participate in their own subjugation by absorbing the rules of a discourse or by taking something that is socially constructed as 'truth'—the construction of managerialism in education over the past decade being a good example of this. Often, even when people resist totalising discourses, they do so in ways that do not challenge the power of the discourse to set the boundaries of thought, as for example when students resist teachers by 'mucking up' in class, thus sentencing themselves to menial, poorly paid jobs (Willis 1978). And the bearers of a discourse generally do not recognise the totalising power of what they are transmitting, and so are the unaware bearers of oppression, as for example when educators in supervisory positions learn and then are in a real sense 'constructed by' (another key poststructuralist term) managerialist discourses.

Its focus on the ways in which people actively construct their own oppression can give poststructuralism a bleak and deterministic cast. But certain strands of poststructuralist theory also pay close attention to the ways in which people construct their own meanings in and against dominant discourses. Here power is seen both as relational and in constant flux. The emphasis is on analysing the possibilities and relations of power in particular sites and how these shift over time. Particular attention is paid to the role of discourse in constructing, challenging and changing power relations (Gore, 1993, pp. 50–66; Usher & Edwards, 1994, pp. 97–100. So, for example, a number of feminist educators and researchers (Lather, Gore, Ellsworth, Durie: see chapter 3) have noted the ways in which students resist the would-be emancipatory educational efforts of their teachers. And case studies of informal learning in social action (in workplaces, women's community centres, an environment campaign and national liberation struggles) show how people 'unlearn' (i.e. learn to see through and then discard) dominant discourses which mystify and oppress them and learn new discourses of rights and assertion (Foley 1999; and chapter 17).

CONCLUSION

While this discussion merely scratches the surface of critical theory, it gives some indication of the contribution critical analyses can make to our understanding of education and learning. These theories help us understand the wider economic and political contexts of adult education and training, as well as the subtle ways in which we produce particular sorts of relationships and outcomes in our day-to-day lives and work. What we need now are many more applications of concepts drawn from critical theory to the analysis of specific educational histories, systems, policies, institutions, courses, classrooms, and informal learning processes.

NOTES

1   I prefer the former term, for while Marx remains the most influential historical materialist thinker he is by no means the only one. Moreover, subsequent theorists have critiqued and moved beyond significant aspects of Marx's original theorising.
2   For fuller expositions of core historical materialist concepts and their application to adult education, see Youngman (1986) and Foley (1999).

Bibliography

ACAL 1989 *Policy Statement August 1989* Melbourne: Australian Council for Adult Literacy

ACTRAC 1993 *National Framework of Adult English Language, Literacy and Numeracy Competence* Melbourne: Australian Committee for Training Curriculum

Adams, F. 1975 *Unearthing Seeds of Fire: The Idea of Highlander* Winston-Salem: John Blair

Adult Literacy Information Office NSW (ALIO) 1983 *Broadsheet no. 10*, November

Allman, P. 1994 'Paulo Freire's contribution to radical adult education' *Studies in the Education of Adults* 26(2), pp. 144–61

Archer, M. 1979 *The Social Origins of Educational Systems* London: Sage

Argyris, C. & Schon, D. 1974 *Theory in Practice: Increasing Professional Effectiveness* San Francisco: Jossey-Bass

——1978 *Organisational Learning: A Theory of Action Perspective* Reading, MA: Addison-Wesley

Armstrong, P. 1988 'The long search for the working class: socialism and the education of adults, 1850–1930' in T. Lovett (ed.) *Radical Adult Education: A Reader* London: Routledge

Arnold, R. & Burke, B. 1984 *A Popular Education Handbook: An Educational Experience Taken from Central America and Adapted to the Canadian Context* Toronto: CUSO

Ashenden, D. 1991 *Progress and Prospects in Improved Skills Recognition* Canberra: AGPS

Athanasou, J.A. 1997 *Introduction to Educational Testing* Wentworth Falls: Social Science Press

——1998 'A framework for evaluating the effectiveness of technology-assisted learning', *Industrial and Commercial Training* 30, pp. 96–103

Atkinson, E. 1996 'Some observations on how the open learning initiative is facilitating change in Australian tertiary education' *Hot Topics, Australian Council for Educational Administration* 2, 15 November

Atkinson, J. & Meager, N. 1990 'Changing working patterns: how companies achieve flexibility to meet new needs' in G. Esland (ed.) *Education, Training and Employment, vol. 1,* Wokingham: Addison-Wesley

Australian Committee on Technical and Further Education 1974 *TAFE in Australia: Report on Needs in Technical and Further Education* Canberra; Australian Government Printing Service

Australian National Training Authority (1996) *The National Women's Vocational Education and Training Strategy—An Implementation Guide* Brisbane: ANTA

Ausubel, D.P. 1963 *The Psychology of Meaningful Verbal Learning: An Introduction to School Learning* New York: Grune & Stratten

Ausubel, D.P. et al. 1968 *Educational Psychology: A Cognitive View* New York: Holt, Rinehart & Winston

Avis, J. 1996 'The myth of the post-Fordist society' in J. Avis, M. Bloomer, G. Esland, D. Gleeson & P. Hodkinson *Knowledge and Nationhood,* London: Cassell

Bagnall, R. 1994 'Performance indicators and outcomes as measures of educational quality: a cautionary critique' *International Journal of Lifelong Education* 13(1), pp. 19–32

Ball, S.J. 1987 *The Micro-politics of the School: Towards a Theory of School Organisation* London: Methuen

Ball, S. 1990 *Foucault and Education* London: Routledge

Baltes, P.B. 1968 'Longitudinal and cross-sectional sequences in the study of age and generation effects' *Human Development* 11, pp. 145–71

——1987 'Theoretical propositions of lifespan developmental psychology: on the dynamics between growth and decline' *Developmental Psychology* 23(5), pp. 611–26

Baltes, P.B. & Smith, J. 1990 'Towards a psychology of wisdom and its ontogenesis' in R.J. Sternberg (ed.) *Wisdom: Its Nature, Origins and Development* Cambridge: Cambridge University Press

Baltes, P., Cornelius, S. & Nesselroade, J. 1980 'Cohort effects in developmental psychology' in J. Nesselroade & P. Baltes (eds) *Longitudinal Research in the Study of Behaviour and Development* New York: Academic Press

Baltes, P.B. & Willis, S.L. 1982 'Plasticity and enhancement of intellectual functioning in old age: Penn State's adult development and enrichment project' in F.I.M. Craik & S.E. Trehub (eds) *Aging and Cognitive Processes* New York: Plenum

Barer-Stein, T. & Draper, J. (eds) 1994 *The Craft of Teaching Adults* Malabar, Fla: Krieger

Barr, R. & Dreeben, R. 1978 'Instruction in classrooms' in L.S. Shulman (ed.) *Review of Research in Education, vol. 5* Itasca, IL: F.E. Peacock

Bateson, G. 1973 *Steps to an Ecology of Mind* London: Paladin

Beach, K. 1984 'The role of external cues in learning to become a bartender' *Quarterly Newsletter of the Laboratory of Comparative Human Cognition* 16(1&2), pp. 42–3

Beazley, H. 1997 'Inventing individual identity in the Australian language and literacy policy' *Literacy and Numeracy Studies* 7(1) pp. 46–62

Bee, B. 1982 *Migrant Women and Work: An ESL Program* Sydney: Randwick Technical College

——1984 *Women's Work, Women's Lives: An ESL Program* Sydney: Randwick Technical College

——1989 *Women and Work* Sydney: NSW TAFE

Belenky, M., Clinchy, B., Goldberger, N. & Tarule, J. 1986 *Women's Ways of Knowing: The Development of Self, Voice and Mind* New York: Basic Books

Bengtsson, J. 1993 'Labour markets of the future: the challenge to education policy makers' *European Journal of Education* 28(2), pp. 135–58

Bennett, K. 1991 *Cross-Cultural Diversity: Trainer's Manual* Seattle, WA: Department of Social and Health Services

Berman, P. & McLaughlin, W.M. 1977 *Federal Programs Supporting Educational Change Vol. III: Implementing and Sustaining Innovations* Santa Monica: The Rand Corporation

Bernstein, B. 1971 'On the classification and framing of educational knowledge' in M.F.D. Young (ed.) *Knowledge and Control: New Directions for the Sociology of Education* London: Collier Macmillan

Beven, F. 1994 'Pressing TAFE learners for far transfer within a CBT framework' in J.C. Stevenson (ed.) *Cognition at Work* Leabrook, SA: National Centre for Vocational Education Research

Bhavani, K. 1997 'Women's studies and its interconnection with "race", ethinicity and sexuality' in V. Robinson & D. Richardson (eds) *Introducing Women's Studies: Feminist Theory and Practice, 2nd edn* London: Macmillan

Biddle, B.J. & Dunkin, M.J. 1987 'Effects of teaching' in M.J. Dunkin (ed.) *The International Handbook of Teaching and Teacher Education* Oxford: Pergamon Press

Billett, S. 1993 'What's in a setting? Learning in the workplace' *Australian Journal of Adult and Community Education* 33(1), pp. 4–13

——1994 'Authenticity in workplace settings' in J. Stevenson (ed.) *Cognition at Work* Adelaide: National Centre for Vocational Education Research, pp. 36–75

——1996 'Situated learning: bridging sociocultural and cognitive theorising' *Learning and Instruction,* 6, pp. 263–80

Binney, G & Williams, C. (1995) *Leaning into the Future: Changing the Way People Change Organisations* London: Brearley

Bin-Sallik, M., Blomeley, N., Flowers, R. & Hughes, P. 1994 *Review and Analysis of Literature Relating to Aboriginal and Torres Strait Islander Education* Canberra: Department of Employment, Education and Training

Bird, G. n.d. *Cross-Cultural Communication and the Law* Unpublished training program

Blachford, K. 1986 *Orientations to Curriculum in TAFE* Melbourne: Hawthorn Institute of Education

Blundell, S. 1992 'Gender and the curriculum of adult education' *International Journal of Lifelong Education* 11(3), pp. 199–216

Boal, A. 1979 *Theatre of the Oppressed* London: Pluto

Boone, E.J. 1985 *Developing Programs in Adult Education* New Jersey: Prentice-Hall

Boud, D. 1985 'Problem-based learning in perspective' in D. Boud (ed.) *Problem-Based Learning in Education for Professions* Sydney: HERDSA

———(ed) 1998 *Current Issues and New Agendas in Workplace Learning* Leabrook SA: National Centre for Vocational Education Research

Boud, D. & Felletti, G. 1991 (eds) *The Challenge of Problem-based Learning* London: Kogan Page

Boud, D. & Griffin, V. (eds) 1987 *Appreciating Adults Learning: From the Learner's Perspective* London: Kogan Page

Boud, D. & Miller, N. (eds) 1996 *Working with Experience: Animating Learning* London & New York: Kogan Page

Boud, D. & Pascoe, J. 1978 'Conceptualising experiential learning' in D. Boud & J. Pascoe (eds) *Experiential Learning: Developments in Australian Post-Secondary Education* Sydney: Australian Consortium on Experiential Education

Boud, D. & Walker, D. 1990 'Making the most of experience' *Studies in Continuing Education* 12(2), pp. 61–80

———1991 *Experience and Learning: Reflection at Work* Geelong: Deakin University Press

———1993 'Barriers to reflection on experience' in D. Boud, R. Cohen, & D. Walker (eds) *Using Experience for Learning* Buckingham: SHRE and Open University Press

Boud, D., Keogh, R. & Walker, D. (eds) 1985 *Reflection: Turning Experience into Learning* London: Kogan Page

Boud D., Cohen, R. & Walker, D. (eds) 1993 *Using Experience for Learning* Buckingham: SRHE and Open University

Bourdieu, P. 1977 *Outline of the Theory of Practice* Cambridge: Cambridge University Press

Bowles, S. & Gintis, H. 1976 *Schooling in Capitalist America: Educational Reform and the Contradictions of Economic Life* London: Routledge & Kegan Paul

Brandt, G.L. 1986 *The Realisation of Anti-Racist Teaching* London: Falmer Press

Bredo, E. & Feinberg, W. (eds) 1982 *Knowledge and Values in Social and Educational Research* Philadelphia: Temple

Brenner, R. 1998 'The economics of global turbulence: a special report on the global economy, 1950–1998' *New Left Review* 229, May/June

Bright, B. 1989 'Epistemological vandalism: psychology in the study of adult education' in B. Bright (ed.) *Theory and Practice in the Study of Adult Education: The Epistemological Debate* London: Routledge

Brookfield, S. 1984 'Self-directed adult learning: a critical paradigm' *Adult Education Quarterly* 35(2), pp. 59–71

———1985 *Self-Directed Learning: From Theory to Practice* San Francisco: Jossey-Bass

———1986 *Understanding and Facilitating Adult Learning* San Francisco: Jossey-Bass

——1987 'Eduard Lindeman' in P. Jarvis (ed.) *Twentieth Century Thinkers in Adult Education* Beckenham, UK: Croom Helm
——1989 *Developing Critical Thinkers* San Francisco: Jossey-Bass
——1990 *The Skilful Teacher* San Fransisco: Jossey-Bass
——1995 *Becoming a Critical Reflective Teacher* San Francisco: Jossey-Bass
Brown, G. 1980 'Independence and incorporation: the Labour College Movement and the Workers' Educational Association before the Second World War' in J. Thompson (ed.) *Adult Education for a Change* London: Hutchinson
Brown, G.A. 1987 'Lectures and lecturing' in Dunkin, op. cit., pp. 284–5
Brundage, D. & Mackeracher, D. 1980 *Adult Learning Principles and their Application to Program Planning* Toronto: Ontario Ministry of Education
Buckley, R. & Caple, J. 1990 *The Theory and Practice of Training* London: Kogan Page
Bureau of Industry Economics 1994 *Job Growth and Decline: Recent Changes in Large and Small Business* (occasional paper 21, April) Canberra: AGPS
Burrell, G. & Morgan, G. 1986 *Sociological Paradigms and Organisational Analysis* 2nd edn London: Heinemann
Burke, J.W. (ed.) 1989 *Competency-Based Education and Training* London: Falmer Press
Butler, E. (1997) *Beyond Political Housework: Gender Equity in the Post-School Environment* Sydney: NSW Premier's Council for Women
Buzan, T. 1978 *Use Your Head* London: BBC Productions
Cabral, A. 1974 *Revolution in Guinea: An African People's Struggle* London: Stage 1
Campbell, D.T. & Fiske, D.W. 1959 'Convergent and discriminant validation by the multitrait-multimethod matrix' *Psychological Bulletin* 56, pp. 81–105
Campbell, D.T. & Stanley, J.C. 1966 *Experimental and Quasi-Experimental Designs for Research* Chicago: Rand McNally
Candy, P.C. 1991 *Self-Direction for Lifelong Learning* San Fransisco: Jossey-Bass
Candy, P.C., Crebert, R.G. & O'Leary, J. 1994 *Developing Lifelong Learners through Undergraduate Education* Report to the Higher Education Council, NBEET, Canberra: AGPS
Canterbury–Bankstown Migrant Resource Centre 1989 *Multicultural Access Training Kit: A Trainer's Manual* Sydney: Canterbury-Bankstown Migrant Resource Centre
Carnoy, M. 1974 *Education as Cultural Imperialism* New York: David McKay
Carr, W. & Kemmis, S. 1986 *Becoming Critical: Education, Knowledge and Action Research* Geelong: Deakin University Press
Carraher, T.N., Carraher, D.W. & Schliemann, A.D. 1985 'Mathematics in the streets and schools' *British Journal of Developmental Psychology* 3, pp. 21–9
Carroll, J. & Mack, R. 1985 'Learning to use a word processor: by doing, by thinking and by knowing' in J. Thomas & M. Schneider (eds) *Human Factors in Computer Systems* Norwood, NJ: Ablex Publishing

Cattell, R.B. 1971 *Abilities: Their Structure, Growth and Action* Campaign, IL: IPAT

Ceci, S. & Liker, J. 1985 'Academic and non-academic intelligence: an experimental separation' in R.J. Sternberg & R.K. Wagner (eds) *Practical Intelligence: Nature and Origins of Competence,* Cambridge: Cambridge University Press

Centre for Continuing Education 1992 *Higher Education and the Competency Movement* Canberra: Australian National University

Centre for Skill Formation Research and Development 1993 *After Competence: The Future of Post-Compulsory Education and Training* Brisbane: Griffith University

Cerny, P. (1990) *The Changing Architecture of Politics: Structure, Agency and the Future of the State* London: Sage

Chaiklin, S. & Lave, J. (eds) 1993 *Understanding Practice: Perspectives on Activity and Context* Cambridge: Cambridge University Press

Chambers, J. & Pettman, J. 1986 *The Anti-Racism Handbook: A Guide for Adult Educators* Canberra: Australian Government Publishing Service

Chandler, M.J. & Holliday, S. 1990 'Wisdom in a post apocalyptic age' in R.J. Sternberg (ed.) *Wisdom: Its Nature, Origins and Development* Cambridge: Cambridge University Press

Chase, W.G. 1983 'Spatial representation of taxi drivers' in D. Rogers & J.A. Sloboda (eds) *The Acquisition of Symbolic Skills* New York: Plenum

Chase, W.G. & Simon, H.A. 1973 'Perception in chess' *Cognitive Psychology* 4, pp. 55–81

Chi, M.T.H., Glaser, R. & Farr. M.J. (eds) 1988 *The nature of expertise* Hillsdale, NJ: Erlbaum

Clare, R. & Tulpule, A. 1994 *Australia's Ageing Society* Canberra: Economic Planning Advisory Council

Clyne, M. 1991 'Australia's language policies: are we going backwards?' *Australian Review of Applied Linguistics* Series S, 8, pp. 3–22

Coats, M. 1994 *Women's Education* Buckingham: SRHE/OU Press

Cohen, R., Flowers, R., McDonald, R. & Schaafsma, H. 1994 'Learning from experience counts' in Higher Education Division, DEET *Recognition of Prior Learning in Australian Universities* Canberra: Australian Government Publishing Service

Coleman, J.S. et al. 1966 *Equality of Educational Opportunity* Washington DC: US Government Printing Office

Collard, S. & Law, M. 1989 'The limits of perspective transformation: a critique of Mezirow's theory' *Adult Education Quarterly* 39(2), pp. 99–107

Collins, C. (ed.) 1993 *Competencies: The Competencies Debate in Australian Education and Training* Melbourne: Australian College of Education

Collins, J. 1991 *Migrant Hands in a Distant Land* Sydney: Pluto Press

Collins, M. 1991 *Adult Education as Vocation: A Critical Role for the Adult Educator* London: Routledge

Commonwealth of Australia, Committee on Employment Opportunities 1993 *Restoring Full Employment: A Discussion Paper* Canberra: Australian Government Publishing Service

Commonwealth of Australia 1989b *National Aboriginal and Torres Strait*

Islander Education Policy Canberra: Australian Government Publishing Service

——1991 *Australia's Language: The Australian Language and Literacy Policy* Canberra: Australian Government Publishing Service

Connell, R.W., Ashenden, D.J., Kessler, S. & Dowsett, G.W. 1982 *Making the Difference* Sydney: George Allen & Unwin

Cooksey, R.W. 1996 *Judgment Analysis. Theory, Methods and Applications* San Diego: Academic Press

Cope, B. 1991 *Mistaken Identity* Sydney: Pluto Press

Cope, B. & Kalantzis, M. 1997 *Productive Diversity: A New Australian Model for Work and Management* Sydney: Pluto Press

Cope, B., Kalantzis, M. & Castles, S. 1991 *Immigration, Ethnic Conflicts and Social Cohesion* Canberra: Bureau of Immigration Research

Cope, B., Pauwels, A., Slade, D., Brosnan, D. & Neil, D. 1994 *Local Diversity, Global Connections* Canberra: Office of Multicultural Affairs

Courtney, S. 1992 *Why Adults Learn: Towards a Theory of Participation in Adult Education* London & New York: Routledge

Cousins, J.B. & Earl, L.M. 1992 'The case for participatory evaluation' *Educational Evaluation and Policy Analysis* 14, pp. 397–420

Cronbach, L.J. 1963 'Course improvement through evaluation' *Teachers College Record* 64, pp. 672–83

Cross, R. & Woozley, A. 1964 *Plato's Republic: A Philosophical Commentary* London: Macmillan

Cross-Durrant, A. 1987 'John Dewey and lifelong education' in P. Jarvis (ed.) *Twentieth Century Thinkers in Adult Education* Beckenham, UK: Croom Helm

Cunneen, C. 1990 *Aboriginal–Police Relations in Redfern: With Special Reference to the 'Police Raid' of 8 February 1990* Sydney: Human Rights & Equal Opportunity Commission

Curtain, R. et al. 1991 *Award Restructuring and Workplace Reform: An Appraisal of Progress Based upon 33 Case Studies* Melbourne: National Key Centre for Industrial Relations

Darkenwald, G. & Merriam, S. 1982 *Adult Education: Foundations of Practice* New York: Harper & Row

Darkenwald, G.G. & Merriam, S.B. 1982 Ch. 4, 'Participation', in *Adult Education: Foundations of Practice*. New York: Harper & Row.

Davies, I. 1973 *Competency-Based Learning: Technology, Management, and Design* New York: McGraw-Hill

Davies, K. 1989 *Women and Time: Weaving the Strands of Everyday Life* Sweden: University of Lund

Davis, L. & Kambouris, N. 1989 *Multicultural Access Training Kit: A Trainer's Manual* Sydney: Canterbury Bankstown Migrant Resource Centre

Dawkins, J. 1989 *Towards a Skilled Australia* Canberra: AGPS

de Groot, A. 1966 'Perception and memory versus thought: some old ideas and new findings' in B. Kleinmuntz (ed.) *Problem Solving* New York: Wiley

Delmont, S. 1983 *Interaction in the Classroom*, 2nd edn London: Methuen

Dempster, P. & Rooney, J. 1991 *Networks: A Third Form of Organisation*

Bureau of Industry Economics: Discussion Paper no. 14. Canberra: Australian Government Publishing Service

Denzin, N.K. & Lincoln, Y.S. (eds.). 1994 *Handbook of qualitative research*. Thousand Oaks: Sage Publications.

Deshler, D. & Hagan, D. 1990 'Adult education research: issues and directions' in S. Merriam & P. Cunningham (eds) *Handbook of Adult and Continuing Education* San Francisco: Jossey-Bass

Dewey, J. 1938 *Experience and Education* New York: Collier Books

Dickson, J. 1994 'Adult education for liberation: the Christian base communities in Latin America' *Student Showcase Conference* Sydney: School of Adult and Language Education, University of Technology

Drucker, P. 1993 *Post-Capitalist Society* Oxford: Butterworth-Heinemann

Dube, E.F. 1982 'Literacy, cultural familiarity and "intelligence" as determinants of story recall' in U. Neisser (ed.) *Memory Observed: Remembering in Natural Contexts* San Francisco: W.H. Freeman, pp. 274–91

du Gay, P. 1996 *Consumption and Identity at Work* London: Sage.

Duke, C. 1984 'Australian adult education: origins, influences and tendencies' in *Canberra Papers in Continuing Education* Canberra: Centre for Continuing Education, Australian National University

Dunkin, M.J. & Biddle, B.J. 1974 *The Study of Teaching* New York: Holt, Rinehart & Winston

Durie, J. 1996 'Emancipatory education and classroom practice: a feminist post-structuralist perspective' *Studies in Continuing Education* 18(2), pp. 135–46

Dwyer, P. 1991 *Training a Multicultural Workforce* Hobart: Hobart Technical College

Edwards, R. 1993 'Multi-skilling the flexible workforce in post-compulsory education and training', *Journal of Further and Higher Education*, 17(1), pp. 44–51

——1997 *Changing Places? Flexibility, Lifelong Learning and a Learning Society* London: Routledge

Eisner, E. 1976 'Educational connoisseurship and criticism: their form and functions in educational evaluation' *Journal of Aesthetic Education* 10 (3&4), pp. 135–50

Eitington, J. 1989 *The Winning Trainer, 2nd edn* Houston: Gulf Publishing

Ellsworth, E. 1989 'Why doesn't this feel empowering? Working through the repressive myths of critical pedagogy' *Harvard Educational Review* 59(3), pp. 297–324

Emery, F. 1991a 'From Bear Mountain to workplace Australia' in *Designing the Future: Workplace Reform in Australia* Melbourne: Workplace Australia Conference Papers

——1991b 'The light on the hill' in *Designing the Future: Workplace Reform in Australia* Melbourne: Workplace Australia Conference Papers

Emery, M. (ed.) 1993 *Participative Design for Participative Democracy* Canberra: Centre for Continuing Education, Australian National University

Emery, F. & Trist, E. 1978 'The causal texture of organisational environments' in W. Pasmore & J. Sherwood (eds) *Sociotechnical Systems: A Sourcebook* San Diego: University Associates

Employment and Skills Formation Council (ESFC) 1992 *The Australian Certificate Training System* Canberra: Australian Government Publishing Service

Entwistle, N. 1984 *Styles of Learning and Teaching* Chichester: Wiley

Evans, G. (ed.) 1991 *Learning and Teaching Cognitive Skills* Hawthorn, Victoria: Australian Council for Educational Research

Evans, M.D. 1988 *A Nation of Learners: National Social Science Survey Report* Canberra: Australian National University

Ewer, P. (ed.) (1991) *Politics and the Accord,* Sydney: Pluto Press

Fairclough, N. 1992 *Discourse and Social Change* Cambridge: Polity Press

Faure, E. (chair) 1972 *Learning to Be: The World Education Today and Tomorrow* Paris: UNESCO/Harrup

Field, J. 1991 'Competency and the pedagogy of labour' *Studies in the Education of Adults* 23, pp. 41–52

Field, L. 1989 'An investigation into the structure, validity and reliability of Guglielmino's self-directed learning readiness scale' *Adult Education Quarterly* 39(3), pp. 125–39

——1990 *Skilling Australia: A Handbook for Trainers and TAFE Teachers* Melbourne: Longman Cheshire

——1997 'Impediments to empowerment and learning within organizations', *The Learning Organization,* 4(4), pp. 149–58

——1998 'The challenge of empowered learning' *Asia Pacific Journal of Human Resources* 36(1), pp. 72–85

Field, L. & Ford, B. 1995 *Managing Organisational Learning: From Rhetoric to Reality* Melbourne: Longman

Fieldhouse, R. & Associates 1996 *A History of Modern British Adult Education* Leicester: NIACE

Finkel, D. & Monk, 1981 'Teachers and learning groups: dissolution of the Atlas complex' in C. Bouton & R.Y. Garth (eds) *Learning in Groups* San Francisco: Jossey Bass

Foley, G. 1989 *Adult Education for the Long Haul* Sydney: ITATE Monographs

——1991a 'Radical Adult Education' in M. Tennant (ed.) *Adult and Continuing Education in Australia: Issues and Practices* London: Routledge

——1991b 'Terania Creek: learning in a green campaign' *Australian Journal of Adult and Community Education* 31(3), pp. 160–76

——1992a 'Adult education and the labour market' in R. Harris & P. Willis (eds) *Striking a Balance: Adult and Community Education in Australia Towards 2000* Adelaide: University of South Australia

——1992b 'Self-directed learning in vocational adult education' in A. Gonczi (ed.) *Teaching and Learning for the Productive Society* Adelaide: TAFE National Centre for Research and Development

——1992c 'Going deeper: some insights into teaching and group work in adult education' *Studies in the Education of Adults* 24(2), pp. 143–61

——1993a 'The neighbourhood house: site of struggle, site of learning' *British Journal of Sociology of Education* 14(1), pp. 21–37

——1993b 'Political education in the Chinese liberation struggle' *International Journal of Lifelong Education* 13(1), pp. 323–42

——1993c 'Progressive but not socialist: political education in the Zimbabwe liberation struggle' *Convergence* 23(4), pp. 79–88

——1994 'Adult education and capitalist reorganisation' *Studies in the Education of Adults* 26(2), pp. 121–43

——1998 'Clearing the theoretical ground: elements in a theory of popular education' *International Review of Education* 44(2–3), pp. 139–53

——1999, *Learning in Social Action: A Contribution to Understanding Informal Learning* London: Zed

Fonow, M. & Cook, J. 1991 *Beyond methodology: Feminist scholarship and lived research.* Bloomington: Indiana University Press.

Foley, G. & Flowers, R. 1990 *Strategies for Self-Determination: Aboriginal Adult Education, Training and Community Development in NSW* Sydney: School of Adult Education, University of Technology

——1992 'Knowledge and power in Aboriginal adult education' *Convergence* 25(1), pp. 61–74

Foley, G., Ingram, N., Flowers, R. & Camilleri, S. 1991 'Towards an Aboriginal community controlled adult education' in M. Tennant (ed.) *Adult and Continuing Education in Australia: Issues and Practices* London: Routledge & Kegan Paul

Ford, B. 1991 Civil & Civic Workplace Reform Strategies: A Submission to the NSW Royal Commission into Productivity in the Building Industry p. 15

Ford G.W. 1986a *Diversity, Change and Tradition: The Environment for Industrial Democracy* Canberra: Australian Government Publishing Service

——1986b 'Cross-cultural differences in enterprise skill formation: can Australia learn from Japan?' *Economic and Industrial Democracy* 7, pp. 205–13

——1989 'Conceptual changes and innovations in skill formation at the enterprise level' in *Technological Change and Human Resource Development: The Services Sector* Netherlands: OECD

——1991a 'Integrating technology, work organisation and skill formation: lessons from manufacturing for ports' in M. Costa & M. Easson (eds) *Australian Industry: What Policy?* Sydney: Pluto Press

——1991b 'Technology transfer, technocultures and skill formation: learning from the Australian experience' *Asia Pacific Journal of Human Resource Management* 29(4), pp. 67–73

Ford, M.E. 1982 'Social cognition and social competence in adolescence' *Developmental Psychology* 18(3), pp. 323–40

Foster, L. & Stockley, D. 1988 *Australian Multiculturalism: A Documentary History and Critique* Clevedon: Multilingual Matters

Foucault, M. 1972 *The Archaeology of Knowledge* London: Tavistock

——1973 *The Birth of the Clinic* London: Tavistock

——1977 *Discipline and Punish: The Birth of the Prison* London: Allen Lane

——1980 *The History of Sexuality* New York: Vintage Books

—— 1983 'Afterword: the subject and power' in H. Dreyfuss & P. Rabinow (eds) *Michel Foucault: Beyond Structuralism and Hermeneutics, 2nd edn* Chicago: University of Chicago Press

Freire, P. 1973 *Pedagogy of the Oppressed* New York: The Seabury Press

———1972b *Cultural Action for Freedom* Harmondsworth: Penguin

———1976 *Education: The Practice of Freedom* London: Writers & Readers

Fullan, M. 1991 *The New Meaning of Educational Change* New York: Teachers College Press

———1993 *Change Forces: Probing the Depths of Educational Reform* Bristol, PA: The Falmer Press

Fullan, M & Hargreaves, A. 1991 *What's Worth Fighting For: Working Together for Your School* Toronto: Ontario Public School Teachers' Federation

Fullan, M. & Stiegelbauer, S. 1991 *The New Meaning of Educational Change*, 2nd edn London: Cassell

Gadotti, M. 1996 *Pedagogy of Praxis: A Dialectical Philosophy of Education* Albany, NY: State University of New York Press

Garbutcheon-Singh, M. 1990 'Curriculum knowledge and Aboriginality: conservative, capitalistic and favourable to long-continued paternalism' *Curriculum Perspectives* 10(2), pp. 10–19

Garratt, B. 1990 *Creating a Learning Organisation* Cambridge: Director Books

Garrick, J. & Solomon, N. 1997 'Technologies of compliance in training' *Studies in Continuing Education* 19(1)

Garvin, D. 1993 'Building a learning enterprise' *Harvard Business Review* July–August, pp. 78–91

Gee, J.P. 1990 *Social Linguistics and Literacies: Ideology in Discourses* London: Falmer Press

Gee, J., Hull, G. & Lankshear, C. 1996 *The New Work Order: Behind the Language of the New Capitalism* Sydney: Allen & Unwin

Gelpi, E. 1979 *A Future for Lifelong Education* Manchester: University of Manchester Department of Adult and Higher Education

———1985 *Lifelong Education and International Relations, Vols 1 & 2* London: Croom Helm

Gergen, M. 1997 'Life stories: pieces of a dream' In M. Gergen, & S. Davis (eds) *Toward a new psychology of gender* New York: Routledge, 203–21

Gibbs, G. 1996 *Improving Student Learning: Using Research to Improve Student Learning* Oxford: Oxford Centre for Staff Development

Giddens, A. 1990 *The Consequences of Modernity* Cambridge: Polity Press

———1993 *Sociology*, 2nd edn Cambridge: Polity Press

Gilligan, C. 1982 *In a Different Voice* Cambridge, MA: Harvard University Press

Giroux, Henry 1988 *Teachers as Intellectuals: Toward a Critical Pedagogy of Learning* New York: Bergin & Garvey

Glaser, R. & Chi, M.T.H. 1988 'Overview' in M.T.H. Chi, R. Glaser & M.J. Farr (eds) *The Nature of Expertise* Hillsdale, NJ: Erlbaum

Gonczi, A. 1993 *Developing a Competent Workforce* Adelaide: TAFE National Centre for Research and Development

Gonczi, A., Hager, P. & Oliver, E. 1990 *Establishing Competency-Based Standards in the Professions* National Office of Overseas Skills Recognition Research Paper no. 1, Canberra: Australian Government Printing Service

Gonczi, A., Hager, P. & Heywood, I. 1992 *A Guide to Development of Competency Standards for Professions* Research Paper no. 7, Canberra: Australian Government Printing Service

Gonczi, A., Hager, P. & Palmer, C. 1994 'Performance Based Assessment and the NSW Law Society Specialist Accreditation Program', *Journal of Professional Legal Education*, 12(2), pp. 135–48

Goodnow, J.J. 1985 'Some lifelong everyday forms of intelligent behaviour: organising and reorganising' in R.J. Sternberg & R.K. Wagner (eds) *Practical Intelligence: Nature and Origins of Competence* Cambridge: Cambridge University Press

——1990 'The socialisation of cognition: what's involved?' in J.W. Stigler, R.A. Schweder & G. Herdt (eds) *Cultural Psychology* Cambridge: Cambridge University Press

Gore, J. 1992 'What we can do for you! What *can* "we" do for "you"? Struggling over empowerment in critical and feminist pedagogy' in C. Luke & J. Gore (eds) *Feminisms and Critical Pedagogy* New York: Routledge

——1993 *The Struggle for Pedagogies: Critical and Feminist Discourses as Regimes of Truth* New York: Routledge

Grant, A. 1986 *Opportunity to Do Brilliantly: TAFE and the Challenge of Literacy Provision in Australia*, 2nd edn, Canberra: Australian Government Publishing Service

Gribble, H. 1992 'A big proportion of them were women' in R. Harris & P. Willis (eds) *Striking a Balance: Adult and Community Education in Australia Towards 2000* Adelaide: Centre for Human Resource Studies, University of South Australia

Griffin, C. (1987) *Adult Education as Social Policy.* London: Croom Helm.

Grundy, S. 1987 *Curriculum: Product or Praxis?* London: Falmer Press

Gumperz, J., Jupp, T. & Roberts, C. 1991 *Crosstalk at Work: Cross-Cultural Communications in the Workplace* London: BBC Training Video

Habermas, J. 1971 *Knowledge and Human Interest* Boston: Beacon Press

Hager, P. 1994 'Is there a cogent philosophical argument against competency standards?' *Australian Journal of Education* 38(1), pp. 3–18

——1995 'Competency standards—a help or a hindrance?: an Australian perspective' *Journal of Vocational Education and Training* 47(2), pp. 141–51

Hager, P. & Beckett, D. 1995 'Philosophical underpinnings of the integrated conception of competence' *Educational Philosophy and Theory* 27(1), pp. 1–24

Hager, P. & Gonczi, A. 1991 'Competency-based standards: a boon for continuing professional education?' *Studies in Continuing Education* 13, pp. 24–40

——1996 'What is competence?' *Medical Teacher* 18(1), pp. 15–18

Hall, B. & Kassam, Y. 1988 'Participatory research' in T. Husen & T.N. Postlethwaite (eds) *International Encyclopaedia of Education* Oxford: Pergamon

Halpin, D. & Troyna, B. (eds.) 1995 *Researching Educational Policy.* London: The Falmer Press.

Hammersley, M. & Atkinson, P. 1995 2nd ed. *Ethnography: Principles into Practice* London and New York: Routledge.

Hammond, J., Wickert, R., Burns, A., Joyce, H. & Miller, A. 1992 *The Pedagogical Relationship between Adult Literacy and Adult ESL* Sydney: University of Technology Language and Literacy Centre

Hampson, I. 1991 'Post-Fordism, the "French Regulation School", and the work of John Mathews' *Journal of Australian Political Economy* 28, pp. 92–130

Harris, R. 1989 'Reflections on self-directed learning: some implications for educators of adults' *Studies in Continuing Education* 11(2), pp. 102–16

Harris, R. & Willis, P. (eds) 1992 *Striking a Balance: Adult and Community Education in Australia Towards 2000* Adelaide: Centre for Human Resource Development, University of South Australia

Hart, M. (1990) 'Liberation through consciousness-raising' in J. Mezirow (ed.) *Fostering Critical Reflection in Adulthood* San Francisco: Jossey-Bass

——1992 *Working and Educating for Life: Feminist and International Perspectives on Adult Education* London: Routledge

Harvey, D. 1989 *The Condition of Post-Modernity* Oxford: Basil Blackwell

Hayes, E. 1979 'Insights from women's experiences for teaching and learning' in E. Hayes (ed.) *Effective Teaching Styles* New Directions for Continuing Education no. 43, San Francisco: Jossey-Bass

Head, D. 1977 'Education at the Bottom' *Studies in Adult Education* 9(2), pp. 127–52

——1978 *There's No Politics Here* London: The City Lit

Held, D. 1980 *Introduction to Critical Theory* Berkeley, CA: University of California Press

Heron, J. 1989 *The Facilitator's Handbook* London: Kogan Page

——1993 *Group Facilitation* London: Kogan Page

Higgs, J. (ed.) 1998 *Writing Qualitative Research.* No 2 in the Centre for Professional Education Advancement R &D Series. Sydney: Hampden Press.

Hilmer, F. 1989 *New Games, New Rules* Sydney: Angus & Robertson

Horn, J.L. 1970 'Organisation of data on lifespan development of human abilities' in L.R. Goulet & P.B. Baltes (eds) *Lifespan Development Psychology: Research and Theory* New York: Academic Press

——1982 'The aging of human abilities' in P.B. Wolman (ed.) *Handbook of Developmental Psychology* Englewood Cliffs, NJ: Prentice-Hall

Horne, D. (ed.) 1992 *The Trouble With Economic Rationalism* Melbourne: Scribe

Horton, M. & Freire, P. 1990 *We Make the Road by Walking* Philadelphia: Temple University Press

Horton, M., Kohl, J. & Kohl, H. 1990 *The Long Haul* New York: Doubleday

Houle, C. 1972 *The Design of Education* San Francisco: Jossey-Bass

——1976 'Deep traditions of experiential learning' in M. Keeton (ed.) *Experiential Learning: Rationale, Characteristics and Assessment* San Francisco: Jossey-Bass

Howard, D.V. 1988 'Implicit and explicit assessment of cognitive aging' in

M.L. Howe & C.J. Brainerd (eds) *Cognitive Development in Adulthood* New York: Springer-Verlag

Human Rights & Equal Opportunity Commission 1993a *Diversity Makes Good Business: A Training Package for Managing Cultural Diversity in the Workplace* Sydney: Australian Government Publishing Service

——1993b *Diversity Makes Good Business: A Report on Piloting the Human Rights and Equal Opportunity Commission's Diversity Makes Good Business Training Program* Sydney: Australian Government Publishing Service

Hunt, D.E. 1987 *Beginning with Ourselves: In Practice, Theory and Human Affairs* Toronto: OISE Press

Hyman, R. 1991 '*Plus ca change?* The theory of production and the production of theory' in A. Pollert (ed.), *Farewell to Flexibility?* Oxford: Basil Blackwell

International Labour Organisation 1966 *Conventions and Recommendations Adopted by the International Labour Conference, 1919–1996* Geneva: International Labour Office

Issaris, M. 1991 *Managing a Culturally Diverse Workforce Workshop* Sydney: Qantas Airways

Jackson, N. 1989 'The case against competence: the impoverishment of working knowledge' in M. Brown (ed.) *A Collection of Readings Related to Competency-based Training* Geelong: Faculty of Education, Deakin University, pp. 243–9

Jarvis, P. 1993 *Adult Education and the State. Towards a Politics of Adult Education.* London: Routledge.

Jarvis, P. 1983 *Adult and Continuing Education—Theory and Practice* London: Croom Helm

Jessop, B. 1991 'The welfare state in the transition from fordism to post-fordism', in B. Jessop, H. Kastendiek, K. Nielsen & O. Pedersen (eds) *The Politics of Flexibility* Aldershot: Edward Elgar

——1995 'The regulation approach, governance and post-fordism: perspectives on economic and political change' *Economy and Society* 24(3) pp. 307–33

Johnson, R. 1983 *The Provision of External Studies in Australian Higher Education* Canberra: CTEC Evaluations and Investigations Program

Johnson, R. 1979 '"Really useful knowledge": radical education and working class culture' in J. Clarke, C. Critcher & R. Johnson (eds) *Working Class Culture: Studies in History and Theory* London: Hutchinson

——1988 'Really useful knowledge 1790–1850: memories for education in the 1980s' in T. Lovett (ed.) *Radical Approaches to Adult Education* London: Routledge

Johnson, T.R. & Geller, D.M. 1992 Experimental evidence on the impacts of computer-aided instruction in the Job Corps program *Evaluation Review* 16, pp. 3–22

Johnson, R. & Hinton, F. 1986 *It's Human Nature: Non-Award Adult and Continuing Education in Australia* Discussion paper prepared for the Commonwealth Tertiary Education Commission, Canberra, July

Johnston, B. & Lunvall, B. 1991 'Flexibility and institutional learning' in

B. Jessop, H. Kastendiek, K. Nielsen & O. Pedersen (eds) *The Politics of Flexibility* Aldershot: Edward Elgar

Joint Committee on Standards for Educational Evaluation 1981 *Standards for Evaluation of Educational Programs, Projects and Materials* New York: McGraw-Hill

——1994 *The Program Evaluation Standards* Newbury Park, CA: Sage

Jordan, J. 1991 'The meaning of mutuality' in *Women's Growth in Connection: Writings from the Stone Centre* New York: The Guilford Press

Kalantzis, M., Brosnan, D. & Cope, B. 1992a *Managing Cultural Diversity: Culture* Sydney: NLLIA Centre for Workplace Communication and Culture, University of Technology

——1992b *Cultural Diversity: Training Manual: Migration* Sydney: NLLIA Centre for Workplace Communication and Culture, University of Technology

Kanu Kogod, S. 1991 *A Workshop for Managing Diversity in the Workplace* San Diego: Pfeiffer

Karpin, D. (1995) *Enterprising Nation* Canberra: Australian Government Publishing Service

Keating, P.J. 1994 *Working Nation: Policies and Programs* (Presented by the Prime Minister, The Honourable P.J. Keating, MP, to the House of Representatives) Canberra: Australian Government Publishing Service

Keddie, N. 1971 'Classroom knowledge' in M. Young (ed.) *Knowledge and Control* London: Collier Macmillan

Keeves, J.P. 1988 'The unity of educational research' *Interchange*, 19(1), pp. 14–30

Kelly, S. 1987 *The Prize and the Price: The Changing World of Women Who Return to Study* Sydney: Methuen Haynes

Kelly, T. 1970 *A History of Adult Education in Great Britain* Liverpool: Liverpool University Press

Kemmis, S. 1980 'Program evaluation in distance education: against the technologisation of reason' *Open Campus* 2

Kemmis, S. & McTaggart, R. (eds) 1988 *The Action Research Planner, 3rd edn* Geelong: Deakin University

Kennedy, H. 1997 *Learning Works: Widening Participation in Further Education* Coventry: FEFC

Kerlinger, F. 1994 *The Foundations of Behavioural Research, 4th edn* New York: Rinehart & Winston

Kimberley, H. 1987b *The Outcomes Report* Melbourne: TAFE Board of Victoria

King, S. 1992 'Module 2: culture and language' in *Multicultural Skills for Adult Educators* Sydney: School of Adult and Language Education

Kinsman, M. 1992 'Competency-based education in TAFE' in Centre for Continuing Education *Higher Education and the Competency Movement* Canberra: ANU

Kirkpatrick, D. 1997 'Becoming flexible: contested territory' *Studies in Continuing Education* 19(2), pp. 160–73

Kirkpatrick, D.L. 1996 *Evaluating Training Programs: The Four Levels* San Francisco, CA: Berret-Koehler

Kirkwood, G. & Kirkwood, C. 1989 *Living Adult Education: Freire in Scotland* Buckingham: Open University Press

Knight, J., Lingard, B. & Porter, P. 1991 'Restructuring schooling towards the 1990s' in B. Lingard, J. Knight & P. Porter (eds) *Schooling Reform in Hard Times* London: Falmer

Knowles, M. 1978 *The Adult Learner: A Neglected Species* Houston: Gulf Publishing

——1980 *The Modern Practice of Adult Education, 2nd edn* Chicago: Follett

Knowles M. and Associates 1984 *Andragogy in Action* San Francisco: Jossey-Bass

Kogod, S. 1991 *A Workshop for Managing Diversity in the Workplace* San Diego: Pfeiffer

Kohlberg, L. & Ryncarz, R.A. 1990 'Beyond justice reasoning: moral development and consideration of a seventh stage' in C.N. Alexander & E.J. Langer (eds) *Higher Stages of Human Development* Oxford: Oxford University Press

Kolb, D. 1984 *Experiential Learning: Experience as the Source of Learning and Development* Englewood Cliffs, NJ: Prentice-Hall

Kovel, J. 1987 *A Complete Guide to Therapy* Harmondsworth: Penguin

Kraft, R. (n.d.) 'Towards a theory of experiential learning' in R. Kraft & M. Sakofs (eds) *The Theory of Experiential Education, 2nd edn* Boulder, CO: Association for Experiential Education

Kroenhert, G. 1990 *Basic Training for Trainers: An Australian Handbook for New Trainers* Sydney: McGraw-Hill

Kuhn, T.S. 1970 *The Structure of Scientific Revolutions, 2nd edn* Chicago: University of Chicago Press

Labouvie-Vief, G. 1990 'Wisdom as integrated thought: historical and developmental perspectives' in R.J. Sternberg (ed.) *Wisdom: Its Nature, Origins and Development* Cambridge: Cambridge University Press

Lancy, D.F. 1993 *Qualitative Research in Education. An Introduction to the Major Traditions.* New York: Longmans.

Lane, J. 1984 'Tuition before rights: Aboriginal adult education in Australia 1800–1983' *The Aboriginal Child at School* 12(3), pp. 3–11

Langenbach, M. 1993 *Curriculum Models in Adult Education* Malabar, FL: Krieger

Lather, P. 1991a *Getting Smart: Feminist Research and Pedagogy with/in the Postmodern* New York: Routledge

——1991b *Feminist Research in Education: Within/Against* Geelong: Deakin University

Lave, J. & Wenger, E. 1991 *Situated Learning: Legitimate Peripheral Participation* Cambridge: Cambridge University Press

Lave, J., Murtaugh, M. & de la Rocha, O. 1984 'The dialectic of grocery shopping' in B. Rogoff & J. Lave (eds) *Everyday Cognition: Its Development in Social Context* Cambridge, MA: Harvard University Press, pp. 67–94

Lawler, E. 1994 'From job-based to competency-based organisations' *Journal of Organisational Behaviour* 15(1)

Lawless, K.A. & Brown, S.A. 1997 'Multimedia learning environments: issues of learner control and navigation' *Instructional Science* 25, pp. 117–31.

Lawrence, J. 1988 'Expertise on the bench: modelling magistrates' judicial decision-making' in M.T.H. Chi, R. Glaser & M.J. Farr (eds) *The Nature of Expertise* Hillsdale, NJ: Lawrence Erlbaum

Lee, A. 1994 'Countering "oppressive simplification": feminism and the left in radical pedagogy *Education Links* 48, pp. 9–19

Lee, A. & Poynton, C. (1998) *Discourse and Text* Sydney: Allen & Unwin

Lessem, R. 1993 *Business as a Learning Community* London: McGraw-Hill

Levin, H.M. 1983 *Cost-Effectiveness: A Primer* Beverley Hills, CA: Sage

Levinson, D. 1997 *The Seasons of a Woman's Life* New York: Ballantine

Leviton, L. & Hughes, E. 1981 'Research on the utilisation of evaluations: a review and synthesis' *Evaluation Review* 5, pp. 525–48

Lewin, K. 1951 *Field Theory in Social Science: Selected Theoretical Papers* New York: Harper & Row

Lewis, M. & Simon, R. 1986 'A discourse not intended for her' *Harvard Educational Review* 56(4), pp. 457–72

Limerick, D. & Cunnington, D. 1993 *Managing the New Organisation: A Blueprint for Networks and Strategic Alliances* Sydney: Business and Professional Publishing

Lincoln, Y. & Guba, E.G. 1985 *Naturalistic Inquiry* Beverley Hills, CA: Sage

Lingard, B. 1991 'Corporate federalism: the emerging approach to policy-making for Australian schools' in B. Lingard, J. Knight & P. Porter (eds) *Schooling Reform in Hard Times,* Falmer

Locke, J. 1690 *An Essay Concerning Human Understanding* A.D. Woozeley (ed.) 1964 New York: The New American Library

Long, H.B. 1983 Ch 4. Reasons, motives and barriers in participation, and Ch 5, Models of adult participation, in *Adult Learning: Research and Practice.* New York: Cambridge.

Lotz, J. & Welton, M. 1987 'Knowledge for the people: the origins and development of the Antagonish movement' in M. Welton (ed.) *Knowledge for the People* Toronto: OISE Press

——1997 *Father Jimmy: The Life and Times of Jimmy Tompkins* Cape Breton Island: Breton Books

Lovett, T. 1975 *Adult Education: Community Development and the Working Class* London: Ward Lock Educational

——(ed.) 1988 *Radical Approaches to Adult Education* London: Routledge

Lukacs, G. 1968 *History and Class Consciousness: Studies in Marxist Dialectics* London: Merlin Press

Luke, A. & Gilbert, P. (eds) 1993 *Literacy in Contexts* Sydney: Allen & Unwin

Lyotard, J. 1993 *Political Writings* London: UCL Press.

Mackie, R. (ed.) 1980 *Literacy and Revolution: The Pedagogy of Paulo Freire* London: Pluto Press

Maher, F. 1985 'Classroom pedagogy and the new scholarship on women' in M. Culley & C. Portugues (eds) *Gendered Subjects: The Dynamics of Feminist Teaching* Boston: Routledge & Kegan Paul

Maher, F. & Tetreault, M. 1994 *The Feminist Classroom* New York: Basic Books

Mansfield, B. & Mitchell L. 1996 *Towards a Competent Workforce* Aldershot: Gower

Mao Tse-tung 1968 'On practice' in *Four Essays on Philosophy* Peking: Foreign Language Press

Marginson, S. 1993 *Education and Public Policy in Australia* Cambridge: Cambridge University Press

Marshment, M. 1997 'The picture is political: representation of women in contemporary popular culture' in V. Robinson & D. Richardson (eds) *Introducing Women's Studies: Feminist Theory and Practice*, 2nd edn London: Macmillan

Marsick, V. (ed.) 1987 *Learning in the Workplace* London: Croom Helm

——1988 'Learning in the workplace: the case for reflectivity and critical reflectivity' *Adult Education Quarterly* 38(4), pp. 187–98

Marsick, V. & Watkins, K. 1991 *Informal and Incidental Learning in the Workplace* London: Routledge

Marton, F., Hounsell, D. & Entwistle, N. (eds) 1984 *The Experience of Learning* Edinburgh: Scottish University Press

Mathews, J. 1989a *Tools of Change* Melbourne: Pluto Press

Mathews, J. 1989b *Age of Democracy: The Politics of Post-Fordism* Melbourne: Oxford University Press

Mathison, S. 1988 'Why triangulate?' *Educational Researcher* 17, pp. 13–17

Mayer, R.E. 1981 *The Promise of Cognitive Psychology* San Fransisco: Freeman

McAdams, D. 1996 'Personality, modernity, and the storied self: a contemporary framework for studying persons' *Psychological Inquiry* 7(4), pp. 295–321

McDonald, R. & Bishop, R. 1990 *Guidelines for ETF Project Evaluation, Training and Development Services* Sydney: UTS

McConnell, S. & Trealor, A. (eds) (1993) *Voices of Experience: A Professional Development Package for Adult and Workplace Literacy Teachers* Melbourne: Deakin University

MCEETYA (n.d.) *National Collaborative Adult English Language and Literacy Strategy* Sydney: NSW Adult Literacy Information Office

McGivney, V. 1990 *Education's for Other People: Access to Education for Non-Participant Adults.* Leicester: NIACE and Hillcroft College.

McGivney, V. & Murray, F. 1991 *Adult Education Development: Methods and Approaches from Changing Societies* Leicester: National Institute of Adult and Continuing Education

McGregor, A.L. & Williams, R.T. 1984 'Cross-cultural communication in the employment interview' *Australian Review of Applied Linguistics* 7(1), pp. 203–19

McHoul, A. 1994 *A Foucault Primer* Melbourne: Melbourne University Press

McIlroy, J. & Westwood, S. (eds) 1993 *Border Country: Raymond Williams in Adult Education* Leicester: National Institute of Adult Continuing Education

McIntyre, J. 1993 'Research paradigms and adult education' *Studies in Continuing Education* 15(2), pp. 80–97

——1994 'Researcher understanding and qualitative methodology' in B. Neville et al. (eds) *Qualitative Research in Adult Education* Adelaide: Centre for Research in Education and Work, University of South Australia

McIntyre, J. & Crombie, C. 1996 *Who are Australia's Adult Learners: Report of National Household Survey Data Collected by the ABS Population Survey for the AAACE*, Canberra: Australian Association of Adult and Community Education

McIntyre, J., Foley, G., Morris, R. and Tennant, M. 1995 *ACE Works: The Vocational Outcomes of ACE Courses in NSW.* Sydney: Board of Adult and Community Education.

McIntyre, J., Morris, R. & Tennant, M. 1993 *The Vocational Scope of ACE* Research report commissioned by the NSW Board of Adult and Community Education, Sydney: University of Technology

McKeon, R. (ed.) 1948 *Aristotle: The Basic Works of Aristotle* New York: Random House

McLaren, P. 1988 'Foreword: critical theory and the meaning of hope' in H. Giroux *Teachers as Intellectuals: Toward a Critical Pedagogy of Learning* New York: Bergin & Garvey

McLaren, P. & Hammer, R. 1995 'Media knowledges, warrior citizenry and postmodern literacies' in P. McLaren, R. Hammer, D. Scholle & S. Reilly (eds) *Rethinking Media Literacy: A Critical Pedagogy of Representation* New York: Peter Lang

McLaughlin, M.W. (1976) Implementation as mutual adaptation: change in classroom organisation *Teachers' College Record* 78, pp. 339–51

McTaggart, R. 1991 'Principles for participatory action research' *Adult Education Quarterly* 41(3), pp. 168–82

Merriam S. 1991 'How research produces knowledge'. In J. Peters & P. Jarvis (eds) *Adult Education: Evolution, Achievements in a Developing Field of Study* San Francisco and Oxford: Jossey Bass.

Merriam, S. & Simpson, E. 1989 *A Guide to Research for Educators of Adults and Trainers* revd edn Malabar, FL: Krieger

Metcalfe, A. 1988 *For Freedom and Dignity: Historical Agency and Class Structures in the Coalfields of NSW* Sydney: Allen & Unwin

Mezirow, J. 1991 *Transformative Dimensions of Adult Learning* San Francisco: Jossey-Bass

——1992 'Understanding transformation theory' *Adult Education Quarterly* 44(4), pp. 222–32

Mezirow, J. et al. 1990 *Fostering Critical Reflection in Adulthood: A Guide to Transformative and Emancipatory Learning* San Francisco: Jossey-Bass

Miles, M.B. & Huberman, A.M. 1984 *Qualitative Data Analysis: A Source Book of New Methods* California: Sage

Miller, N. 1993 *Personal Experience, Adult Learning and Social Research: Developing a Sociological Imagination in and beyond the T-Group* Adelaide: Centre for Research in Adult Education for Human Development, University of South Australia

Miller, V. 1985 'The Nicaraguan literacy crusade: education for transformation' in C. Duke (ed.) *Combating Poverty through Adult Education* London: Croom Helm

Ministerial Council on Education, Employment, Training and Youth Affairs 1993 *National Policy Adult and Community Education* Canberra: MCEETYA

Miura, S., Matsushita, T., Nakamura, M. & Suezaki, F. 1991 *Lifelong Learning in Japan: An Introduction* Tokyo: National Federation of Social Education

Moore, B. 1993 *The Politics of Victim Construction in Australian Social Justice Policies* Paper delivered at the Australian Curriculum Studies Association Conference, June

Morgan, C. 1994 *The Train the Trainers Program in Cross-Cultural Awareness Training—Five Day Program* Adelaide: Cross Cultural Communications

——1995 *The Three Day Cross-Cultural Awareness Training Program* Adelaide: Cross Cultural Communications

Morley, D. & Robins, K. 1995 *Spaces of Identity: Global Media, Electronic Landscapes and Cultural Boundaries* London: Routledge

Morris, R. 1991 'Trade union education in Australia' in M. Tennant (ed.) *Adult and Continuing Education in Australia: Issues and Practices* London: Routledge

——1992 'The great tradition revisited: a revisionist view of the history of adult education in Australia' in R. Harris & P. Willis (eds) *Striking the Balance: Adult and Community Education in Australia Towards 2000* Adelaide: University of South Australia, Centre for Human Resource Studies

Morrison, M. 1992 'Part-time: whose time? Women's lives and adult learning' *CEDAR Papers 3* Coventry: University of Warwick

Morrow, R. & Torres, C. 1995 *Social Theory and Education: A Critique of Theories of Social and Cultural Reproduction* Albany, NY: State University of New York Press

Moses, I. 1995 'Tensions and tendencies in the management of quality and autonomy in Australian higher education' *Australian Universities' Review* 38(1), pp. 11–15

Moyers, B. 1981 *Adventures of a Radical Hillbilly* video New York: WNET

Multicultural Centre, Sydney College of Advanced Education, 1984 *Communication, Cultural Diversity and the Health Professional*, 2nd edn Sydney: Multicultural Centre, Sydney College of Advanced Education

Nadler, L. & Wiggs, G.D. 1986 *Managing Human Resource Development* San Fransisco: Jossey-Bass

Nakata, M. 1991 *Constituting the Torres Strait Islander: A Foucauldian Discourse Analysis of the National Aboriginal and Torres Strait Islander Education Policy* BEd Honours thesis, Townsville: James Cook University of North Queensland

NCSHITAB 1993 *Developing National Competency Standards in the Community Services Industry* Sydney: National Community Services and Health Industry Training Advisory Board

National Training Board 1990 *National Competency Standards Policy and Guidelines, 1st edn* Canberra: National Capital Printing

——1993 *National Competency Standards Policy and Guidelines, 2nd edn* Canberra: National Capital Printing

Nelson A.J. & Dymock D. (eds) 1986 *Adult Literacy and Community Development* Armidale: University of New England Press

Neville, B., Willis, P. & Edwards, M. (eds) 1994 *Qualitative Research in*

Adult Education Adelaide: Centre for Research in Education and Work, University of South Australia

New London Group 1995 *A Pedagogy of Multiliteracies: Designing Social Futures* Sydney: NLLIA Centre for Workplace Communication and Culture, Occasional Paper no. 1

Newman, M. 1979 *The Poor Cousin* London: Allen & Unwin

——1986 *Tutoring Adults* Melbourne: Council of Adult Education

——1993 *The Third Contract: Theory and Practice in Trade Union Training* Sydney: Stewart Victor

——1994 *Defining the Enemy: Adult Education in Social Action* Sydney: Stewart Victor

Nicoll, K. 1998 'Fixing the facts: "Flexible learning" as policy invention', *Higher Education Research and Development* 17(3)

Nicoll, K. and Edwards, R. (1997) 'Open learning and the demise of discipline?' *Open Learning* 12(3) pp. 14–24

Nielson, K. 1991 'Towards a flexible future—theories and politics' in B. Jessop, H. Kastendiek, K. Nielsen & O. Pedersen (eds) *The Politics of Flexibility* Aldershot: Edward Elgar

Nonaka, I. 1993 'The knowledge-creating company' in R. Howard (ed.) *The Learning Imperative: Managing People for Continuous Innovation* Boston: Harvard Business School Press

Norris, N. 1990 *Understanding Educational Evaluation* London: Kogan Page

Norwegian Association of Adult Education Organisations (NAAEO) 1982 *Adult Education in Norway: A Brief Introduction* Trondheim Norwegian Institute of Adult Education

NSWALC 1988 *The Policy of the NSW Adult Literacy Council* February, Sydney

NSW Government 1990 *A Literacy Strategy for the People of NSW* Sydney: Office of Education and Youth Affairs

NSW TAFE 1992 *An Emerging National Curriculum: English Literacy for Adults Project Report* Sydney: NSW TAFE Commission

NSW VETAB 1994 *Accreditation of Competency Based Education and Training for a Qualification: Review of Literature* vol. 1 Sydney: New South Wales Vocational Eduation and Training Accreditation Board

O'Brien, G.E. & Plooij, D. 1973a *Cultural Training Manuals for Medical Workers in Aboriginal Communities* Adelaide: Flinders University School of Social Sciences

——1973b *Cultural Training Manuals for Technical Workers in Aboriginal Communities* Adelaide: Flinders University School of Social Sciences

O'Brien, G.E., Plooij, D. & Whitelaw, A. 1973 *Cultural Training Manuals for Teachers in Aboriginal Communities* Adelaide: Flinders University School of Social Sciences

OECD 1992 *Adult Illiteracy and Economic Performance* Paris: OECD Centre for Educational Research and Innovation

Office of Multicultural Affairs 1989 *National Agenda for a Multicultural Australia* Canberra: Australian Government Printing Service

——1992 *Value in Diversity: A Management Training Resource Kit for Multicultural Situations* Canberra: AGPS

——1994 *National Directory of Cross Cultural Training* Canberra: AGPS

Owen, J.M. 1993 *Program Evaluation* Sydney: Allen & Unwin

Ozolins, U. 1993 *The Politics of Language in Australia* Cambridge: Cambridge University Press

Parlett, M. 1990 'Illuminative evaluation' in H.J. Walberg & G.D. Haertel (eds) *The International Encyclopaedia of Educational Evaluation* Oxford: Pergamon Press

Parlett, M. & Dearden, G. 1977 'Introduction to illuminative evaluation' *Studies in Higher Education* Cardiff-by-the-Sea, CA: Pacific Soundings Press

Parlett, M. & Hamilton, D. 1977 'Evaluation in illumination: a new approach to the study of innovative programs' in D. Hamilton et al. (eds) *Beyond the Numbers Game* London: Macmillan

Patton, P. 1987 'Michel Foucault' in D. Austin-Broos (ed.) *Creating Culture: Profiles in the Study of Culture* Sydney: Allen & Unwin

Pedler, M. Burgoyne, J. & Boydell, T. 1991 *The Learning Company: A Strategy for Sustainable Development* London: McGraw-Hill

Perry, W. 1970 *Forms of Intellectual and Ethical Development in the College Years* New York: Holt, Rinehart & Winston

Peters, M. & Marshall, J. 1996 *Individualism and Community: Education and Social Policy in the Postmodern Condition* London: The Falmer Press.

Peters, J., Jarvis, P. et al. 1991 *Adult Education: Evolution and Achievements in a Developing Field of Study* San Francisco: Jossey-Bass

Peterson, M. 1992 *At Personal Risk: Boundary Violations in Professional–Client Relationships* New York: W.W. Norton

Pettman, J.J. 1991 'Towards a (personal) politics of location' *Studies in Continuing Education* 13(2), pp. 153–66

—— 1996 'Making the difference/teaching the international' in David Boud & Nod Miller (eds) *Working with Experience: Animating Learning* London & New York: Kogan Page

Philp, M. 1985 'Michel Foucuault' in Q. Skinner (ed.) *The Return of Grand Theory in the Human Sciences* Cambridge: Cambridge University Press

Piaget, J. 1972 'Intellectual evolution from adolescence to adulthood' *Human Development* 15, pp. 1–12

Pierce, G. 1987 'Management workshop: towards a new paradigm' in V. Marsick (ed.) *Learning in the Workplace* London: Croom Helm, pp. 31–49

Pollert, A. 1991 'The orthodoxy of flexibility' in A. Pollert (ed.) *Farewell to Flexibilty?* Oxford: Basil Blackwell

Popham, W.J. 1993 *Educational Evaluation, 3rd edn* Boston: Allyn & Bacon

Popper, Karl 1968 *The Logic of Scientific Discovery* London: Hutchinson

Pratt, D.O. 1981 'Teacher effectiveness—future directions for adult education' *Studies in Adult Education* 13(2), pp. 112–19

Price Waterhouse Change Integration Team (1996) *The Paradox Principles: How High Performance Companies Manage Chaos, Complexity and Contradiction to Achieve Superior Results* Chicago: Irwin

Pusey, M. 1991 *Economic Rationalism in Canberra* Cambridge: Cambridge University Press

Queensland Dept of Education 1994 *Cultural Understandings as the Eighth Key Competency* Brisbane: Department of Education

Quinn, J. 1992 *Intelligent Enterprise: A Knowledge and Service-Based Paradigm for Industry* New York: The Free Press

Rachal, J. & Courtney, S. 1986 'Response: focus on adult education research questions' *Adult Education Quarterly* 36, pp. 157–65

Raffe, D. 1996 'F.E. at the interface: a strategic research agenda' in F. Coffield (ed.) *Strategic Research in Further Education* Newcastle: University of Newcastle

Reason, P. (ed.) 1988 *Human Inquiry in Action* London: Sage

Reason, P. & Rowan, J. (eds) 1981 *Human Inquiry: A Sourcebook of New Paradigm Research* Chichester: Wiley

Rees, S., Rodley, G. & Stilwell, F. 1993 *Beyond the Market: Alternatives to Economic Rationalism* Sydney: Pluto Press

Regnier, R. 1991 'Nuclear advocacy and adult education: a case for counter-hegemonic struggle' *Canadian Journal for the Study of Adult Education* 5(2)

Reich, R. 1993 *The Work of Nations: A Blueprint for the Future* London: Simon & Schuster

Resnick, L.B. 1987 *Education and Learning to Think* Washington, DC: National Academy Press

Review of Post-Arrival Programs and Services to Migrants (Galbally report) 1978 *Migrant Services and Programs: Report of the Review of Post-Arrival Programs and Services for Migrants* Canberra: Australian Government Printing Service

Rhodes, C. 1997 'The legitimation of learning in organizational change' *Journal of Organisational Change Management* 10(1), pp. 10–20

Riegel, K.F. 1976 'The dialectics of human development' *American Psychologist* October, pp. 689–99

Rist, R. 1970 'Student social class and teacher expectations' *Harvard Educational Review* 40(3), pp. 411–51

Robbins, D. 1988 *The Rise of Independent Study: The Politics and the Philosophy of an Educational Innovation, 1970–87* SRHE & Open University Press

Robinson, K.R. 1988 *A Handbook of Training Management* London: Kogan Page

Robinson, V.M. 1993 *Problem-based Methodology: Research for the Improvement of Practice* Oxford: Pergamon Press

——1997 'Introducing women's studies' in V. Robinson & D. Richardson (eds) *Introducing Women's Studies: Feminist Theory and Practice, 2nd edn* London: Macmillan

Rogers, A. 1990 *Teaching Adults* Milton Keynes: Open University Press

——1992 *Adults Learning for Development* London: Cassell

Rogers, C. 1969 *Freedom to Learn* Westerville, OH: Merrill

——1973 *Encounter Groups* Harmondsworth: Penguin

——1978 *Carl Rogers on Personal Power* New York: Delta

——1983 *Freedom to Learn for the 80s* New York: Charles E. Merrill

Rogers, J. 1989 *Adults Learning, 3rd edn* Milton Keynes: Open University Press

Rogoff, B. & Lave, J. (eds) 1984 *Everyday Cognition: Its Development in Social Context* Cambridge, MA: Cambridge University Press

314

Romm, C., Pliskin, N. & Rifkin, W.D. (1996) 'Diffusion of e-mail: an organizational learning perspective' *Information Management* 31(1), pp. 37–46

Rosenstock, L. 1991 'The walls come tumbling down: the overdue reunification of vocational and academic education' *Phi Delta Kappa* February

Rossi, P.H. & Freeman, H.E. 1993 *Evaluation: A Systematic Approach, 5th edn* Newbury Park, CA: Sage

Rowan, J. 1976 *Ordinary Ecstasy: Humanistic Psychology in Action* London: Routledge & Kegan Paul

Russell, T. 1987 'Reframing the theory-practice relationship in inservice teacher education' in L. Newton et al. (eds) *Re-thinking Teacher Education* Toronto: Joint Council on Eduation

Russell, T. et al. 1988 'Learning the professional knowledge of teaching: metaphors, puzzles and the theory-practice relationship' in P.P. Grimmet & G.L. Erickson (eds) *Reflection in Teacher Education* Vancouver: Pacific Press

Salzberger-Wittenberg, I. et al. 1983 *The Emotional Experience of Teaching and Learning* London: Routledge & Kegan Paul

Sanguinetti, J. 1994 'The sound of babble and the language of friendship: an exploration of critical and feminist pedagogies and their application in teaching ESL and literacy to women' *Australian Journal of Adult and Community Education* 34(1) April, pp. 18–38

Sargant, N. with J. Field, H. Francis, T. Schuller and A. Tuckett 1997 *The Learning Divide. A Study of Participation in Adult Learning in the United Kingdom* Leicester: NIACE.

Sarup, M. 1978 *Marxism and Education* London: Routledge & Kegan Paul

Schaie, K.W. 1975 'Age changes in adult intellegence' in D. Woodruff & J. Sirren (eds) *Aging: Scientific Perspectives and Social Issues* New York: Van Nostrand

Schaie, K. & Willis, S. 1986 'Can adult intellectual decline be reversed?' *Developmental Psychology* 22, pp. 223–32

Schmidt, H.G., Norman, G.R. & Boshuizen, H.P.A. 1990 'A cognitive perspective on medical expertise: theory and implications' *Academic Medicine* 65(10), pp. 611–21

Schon, D. 1983 *The Reflective Practitioner: How Professionals Think in Action* New York: Basic Books

——1987 *Educating the Reflective Practitioner: Toward a New Design for Teaching and Learning in the Professions* San Francisco: Jossey-Bass

Schwartz, H. (1987) 'Anti-social actions of committed organizational participants: an existential psychoanalytic perspective' *Organizational Studies* 8(4), pp. 327–40

Scott, G. 1985 *Adult Teaching and Learning: A Resource Guide* Sydney: ITATE

——1990 *The Change Process in a Teacher Education Institution,* EdD thesis, Toronto: University of Toronto

——1992 'Challenges facing vocational teachers and trainers in the 1990s' in A. Gonczi (ed.) *Developing a Competent Workforce* Adelaide: National Centre for Vocational Education Research

——1996 'The effective management and evaluation of flexible learning innovations in higher education' *Innovations in Education and Training International* 33(4) November, 154–70

——1999 *Change Matters: Making a Difference in Education and Training* Sydney: Allen & Unwin

Scribner, S. 1984 'Studying working intelligence' in B. Rogoff & J. Lave (eds) *Everyday Cognition: Its Development in Social Context* Cambridge: Cambridge University Press

——1985 'Thinking in action: some characteristics of practical thought' in R.J. Sternberg & R.K. Wagner (eds) *Practical Intelligence: Nature and Origins of Competence* Cambridge: Cambridge University Press

Scriven, M. 1967 'The methodology of evaluation' in R.W. Tyler, R.M. Gagne & M. Scriven (eds) *Perspectives of Curriculum and Evaluation* Chicago: Rand McNally

——1991 *Evaluation Thesaurus, 4th edn* Newbury Park, CA: Sage

Senate Standing Committee on Employment, Education and Training 1991 *Come in Cinderella: The Emergence of Adult and Community Education* Canberra: Australian Government Publishing Service

Shah, S. 1994 'Kaleidoscope people: locating the "subject" of pedagogic discourse' *Journal of Access Studies* 9, pp. 257–70

Sharp, R. & Green, A. 1975 *Education and Social Control: A Study in Progressive Primary Education* London: Routledge & Kegan Paul

Shor, I. 1980 *Critical Teaching and Everyday Life* Boston: South End Press

Shulman, L. 1986 'Paradigms and research programs in the study of teaching: a contemporary perspective' in M. Wittrock (ed.) *Handbook of Research on Teaching, 3rd edn* New York: Macmillan

Sivage, C.R. et al. 1982 'Politics, power and personality: the roles of deans in Deans' Grant Projects' ERIC document no. ED223 588 Washington DC: OSER

Smart, B. 1993 *Postmodernity* London: Routledge

Smith, D.L. (ed.) 1993 *Australian Curriculum Reform: Action and Reaction* Australian Curriculum Studies Association

Smith, E.R. & Tyler, R.W. 1942 *Adventure in American Education, vol. 3: Appraising and Recording Student Progress* New York: Harper & Row

Snell, G.R. 1984 'The Sydney school of arts: 150 years of community service' *Riverina Library Review* 1(1), Autumn, pp. 36–46

Snow, D. 1993 *A New Politics of Colonisation: Recent Aboriginal Education* Auckland: Department of Education, University of Auckland

Spender, D. & Sarah, E. (eds) 1980 *Learning to Lose: Sexism and Education* London: The Women's Press

Spilich, G.J. 1979 'Text processing of domain related information for individuals with high and low domain knowledge' *Journal of Verbal Learning and Verbal Behaviour* 18, pp. 275–90

Stacey, J. 1997 'Feminist theory: capital F, capital T' in V. Robinson & D. Richardson (eds) *Introducing Women's Studies: Feminist Theory and Practice, 2nd edn* London: Macmillan

Stake, R. 1967 'The countenance of educational evaluation' *Teachers College Record* 68, pp. 523–40

State Training Board 1988 *TAFE Student Profile Survey 1987* Melbourne: Office of Technical and Further Education, Victoria

Stecher, B.M. & Davis, W.A. 1987 *How to Focus an Evaluation* Newbury Park, CA: Sage

Steedman, C. 1986 *Landscape for a Good Woman* London: Virago

Sternberg, R.J. 1990a 'Intelligence and adult learning' *Papers from an Institute Sponsored by the Center for Adult Learning Research, Montana State University* pp. 1–16

——1990b 'Wisdom and its relations to intelligence and creativity' in R.J. Sternberg (ed.) *Wisdom: Its Nature, Origins and Development* Cambridge: Cambridge University Press

Sternberg, R.J. & Wagner, R. (eds) 1985 *Practical Intelligence: Nature and Origin of Competence* Cambridge: Cambridge University Press

Stevenson, J. 1986 'Adaptability: theoretical considerations' and 'Adaptability: experimental studies' *Journal of Structural Learning* 9, pp. 107–17, 118–39

——1991 'Cognitive structures for the teaching of adaptability in vocational education' in G. Evans (ed.) *Learning and Teaching Cognitive Skills* Melbourne: Australian Council for Educational Research

——(ed.) 1994 *Cognition at Work* Adelaide: National Centre for Vocational Education Research

Stevenson, J.C. & McKavanagh, C.W. 1992 'Skill formation in the workplace' in M. Poole (ed.) *Education and Work* Melbourne: Australian Council for Educational Research

Storz, M. n.d. *Asia's Business and Cross-Cultural Communication Skills* Unpublished training program

Streiner, D.L. 1984 'Sample size formulae for parameter estimation' *Perceptual and Motor Skills* 78, pp. 275–84

Stufflebeam, D.L. 1971 *Educational Evaluation and Decision Making* Itasca, IL: F.E. Peacock

——1983 'The CIPP model for program evaluation' in G. Madaus, M. Scriven & D.L. Stufflebeam (eds) *Evaluation Models: Viewpoints on Educational and Human Services Evaluation* Boston: Kluwer-Nijhof

Taking Liberties Collective 1989 *Learning the Hard Way: Women's Oppression in Men's Education* Basingstoke: Macmillan

Tannen, D. 1990 *You Just Don't Understand: Women and Men in Conversation* New York: Ballantine

——1993 *Gender and Conversational Interaction* Oxford: Oxford University Press

Taylor, P. 1997 'Creating contexts conducive to flexibility' *Studies in Continuing Education* 19(2), pp. 112–23

Taylor, P.V. 1993 *The Texts of Paulo Freire* Buckingham: Open University Press

Taylor, S., Rizvi F., Lingard, B. & Henry, M. (1997) *Educational Policy and the Politics of Change* London: Routledge

Tennant, M. 1997 *Psychology and Adult Learning, 2nd edn* London: Routledge

——(ed.) 1991 *Adult and Continuing Education in Australia: Issues and Practices* London: Routledge

Tennant, M. & Pogson, P. 1995 *Learning and Change in Adulthood* San Francisco: Jossey-Bass

Thomas, R. (1993) *What Machines Can't Do: Politics and Technology in the Industrial Enterprise* Berkeley: University of California Press

Thompson, E.P. 1968 *The Making of the English Working Class* Harmondsworth: Penguin

Thompson, J. 1983 *Learning Liberation: Women's Response to Men's Education* London: Croom Helm

——1988 'Adult education and the women's movement' in T. Lovett (ed.) *Radical Approaches to Adult Education* London: Routledge

——1997 *Words in Edgeways: Radical Learning for Social Change* Leicester: NIACE

Thurow, L. 1992 *Head to Head: The Coming Economic Battle among Japan, Europe and America* Sydney: Allen & Unwin

Tough, A. 1979 *The Adult's Learning Projects: A Fresh Approach to Theory and Practice in Adult Learning* Toronto: OISE

Trist, E. 1989 'Psychoanalytic issues in organisational research and consultation' in L. Klein (ed.) *Working with Organisations* London: Tavistock Institute of Human Relations

Trow, M.A. 1970 'Methodological problems in the evaluation of innovation' in M.C. Wittrock & D.E. Wiley (eds) *The Evaluation of Instruction* New York: Holt Rinehart & Winston

Tuckman, B. 1965 'Developmental sequence in small groups' *Psychological Bulletin* 63

Tyler, R.W. 1949 *Basic Principles of Curriculum and Instruction* Chicago: University of Chicago Press

UNESCO 1997a 'Discussion guide. Adult learning: empowerment for local and global change in the twenty-first century' *Adult Education and Development* 49: special issue on the UNESCO Fifth International Conference on Adult Education, Hamburg, pp. 231–9

——1997b 'The Hamburg Declaration on Adult Learning' *Adult Education and Development* 49: special issue on the UNESCO Fifth International Conference on Adult Education, Hamburg, pp. 251–9

Usher, R. 1996 A critique of the neglected epistemological assumptions of education research. Ch.2 in D. Scott and R. Usher (eds.) *Understanding Educational Research.* London: Routledge.

Usher, R. 1987 'The place of theory in designing curricula for the continuing education of adult educators' *Studies in the Education of Adults* 19(1), pp. 26–36

——1989 'Locating adult education in the practical' in B. Bright (ed.) *Theory and Practice in the Study of Adult Education* London: Routledge

Usher, R. & Bryant, I. 1989 *The Captive Triangle: Adult Education as Theory, Practice and Research* London: Routledge

Usher, R. & Edwards, R. 1994 *Postmodernism and Education* London: Routledge

Usher, R., Bryant, I. & Johnston, R. 1997 *Adult Education and the Postmodern Challenge* London: Routledge

Van Buskirk, W. & McGrath, D. 1992 'Organisational stories as a window on affect in organisations' *Journal of Organisational Change Management* 5(2), pp. 9–24

Walberg, H.J. & Haertel, G.D. 1990 *The International Encyclopaedia of Educational Evaluation* Oxford: Pergamon Press

Walker, J. 1988 *Louts and Legends: Male Youth Culture in an Inner City School* Sydney: Allen and Unwin.

Walker, J.C. & Evers, C.W. 1988 'The epistemological unity of educational research' in J.P. Keeves (ed.) *Educational Research, Methodology and Measurement: An International Handbook* Oxford: Pergamon Press

Walkerdine, V. 1984 'Developmental psychology and the child centred pedagogy' in J. Henriques, W. Hollway, C. Urwin, C. Venn & V. Walkerdine (eds) *Changing the Subject: Psychology, Social Regulation and Subjectivity* London: Methuen

Waller, W. 1932 *The Sociology of Teaching* (3rd printing, 1967) New York: Wiley

Wallerstein, N. 1983 *Language and Culture in Conflict: Problem Posing in the ESL Classroom* Reading, MA: Addison-Wesley

Wangoola, P. & Youngman, F. (eds) 1996 *Towards a Transformative Political Economy of Adult Education: Theoretical and Practical Challenges* De Kalb, IL: LEPS Press

Warburton, J.W. 1963 'Schools of arts' *Australian Quarterly* 35(4), pp. 72–80

Webster, F. 1995 *Theories of the Information Society* London: Routledge

Weedon, C. 1987 *Feminist Practice and Post-Structuralist Theory* Oxford: Blackwell

Weil, S. & McGill, I. 1989 *Making Sense of Experiential Learning* Buckingham: SRHE & Open University Press

Weiner, G. 1994 *Feminisms in Education* Buckingham: Open University Press

Welton, M. 1987 'Vivisecting the nightingale: reflections on adult education as an object of study' *Studies in the Education of Adults* 19, pp. 46–68

——(ed.) 1995 *In Defense of the Lifeworld: Critical Perspectives on Adult Learning* Albany, NY: State University of New York Press

Wesson, G. (ed.) 1975 *Brian's Wife and Jenny's Mum* Melbourne: Dove Communications

West, R. 1998 *Learning for Life: Final Report. Review of Higher Education Finance and Policy* Canberra: Commonwealth of Australia

Wexler, P. 1987 *Social Analysis of Education: After the New Sociology* London: Routledge

Whyte, A. 1994 *Competence in Practice: Frameworks for Competence in Management in ACE* Canberra: AAACE

Wickert, R. 1989 *No Single Measure: A Survey of Australian Adult Literacy* Sydney: Institute of Technical and Adult Teacher Education, Sydney College of Advanced Education

——1993 'Constructing adult literacy: mythologies and identities' in A. Luke & P. Gilbert (eds) *Literacy in Contexts* Sydney: Allen & Unwin

Wickert, R. & Baynham, M. 1994 'Just like farmland and goldmines: workplace literacies in an era of unemployment' in M. Brown (ed.) *Literacies and the Workplace: A Collection of Original Essays* Geelong: Deakin University Press

Wickham, A. 1986 *Women and Training* Milton Keynes: Open University Press

Wickham-Crowley, T. 1992 'Democratic organisation for social change: Latin American Christian base communities and literacy campaigns' *Social Forces* 71(2)

Williams, R. 1961 *The Long Revolution* Harmondsworth: Penguin

——1976 *Keywords* London: Fontana

——1983 *Towards 2000* Harmondsworth: Penguin

——1989 *Resources of Hope. Culture, Democracy, Socialism* London: Verso

Willing, K. 1985 *Helping Adults Develop Their Learning Strategies: A Practical Guide* Sydney: Adult Migrant English Service

——1992 *Talking it Through: Clarification and Problem-Solving in Professional Work* Sydney: National Centre for English Language Teaching and Research, Macquarie University

Willis, P. & Neville, B. 1997 *Qualitative research practice in adult education.* Melbourne: David Lovell Publishing.

Willis, Paul 1978 *Learning to Labour: How Working-Class Kids Get Working-Class Jobs* London: Saxon House

Willis, Peter 1988 *Patrons and Riders: Conflicting Roles and Hidden Objectives in an Aboriginal Development Program* Adelaide: Centre for Research in Education and Work, University of South Australia

Wilmot, M. & McLean, M. 1994 'Evaluating flexible learning' *Journal of Further and Higher Education* 18(3), pp. 99–108

Wood, E.M. 1986 *The Retreat from Class: A New 'True' Socialism* London: Verso

——1991 *The Pristine Culture of Capitalism: An Historical Essay on Old Regimes and Modern States* London: Verso

——1995 *Democracy against Capitalism: Renewing Historical Materialism* Cambridge: Cambridge University Press

Woodruffe, C. 1990 *Assessment Centres: Identifying and Developing Competence* London: Institute of Personnel Management

Wright, N. 1990 *Assessing Radical Education: A Critical Review of the Radical Movement in English Schooling 1960–80* Milton Keynes: Open University Press

Yeatman, A. 1990 *Bureaucrats, Technocrats, Femocrats* Sydney: Allen & Unwin

——1993 'Corporate managerialism and the shift from the welfare to the competition state' *Discourse* 13, pp. 3–9

——1994 *Postmodern Revisionings of the Political* London: Routledge

Young, M.D.F. (ed.) 1971 *Knowledge and Control: New Directions for the Sociology of Education* London: Collier Macmillan

Youngman, F. 1986 *Adult Education and Socialist Pedagogy* London: Croom Helm

——1999 *The Political Economy of Adult Education in Botswana* London: Zed

Zuboff, S. 1988 *In the Age of the Smart Machine* New York: Basic Books

Subject Index

Name Index